MY LIFE WITH AN ENIGMA

MY LIFE WITH AN ENIGMA

Unscrambling the paradoxes of an iron-willed romantic

Linda Paul

"No matter how hard a writer strives to get the details right, a memoir is always just one of many different true stories that can be told about the same events."
Lad Tobin; *The Permission Slip*, published in "The Sun" Nov. 2015

Yry Press

Copyright © 2019 by Linda Paul

All rights reserved, including the right to reproduce this book or portions thereof in any form whatsoever without express permission of the author except for the use of brief quotations in a review.
    Direct inquiries to lindadpaul@gmail.com

Cover design by Eyespot Creative: eyespotcreative@gmail.com
Editing by Ken Rogers: ken@kennethrodgers.com

ISBN: 978-0-578-60016-1

Yry Press
Boise, Idaho

Dedication

For my mother without whom this story would not exist. And for Erich Korte, a man of patience and wisdom, enhanced by an infinite sense of wonder. My friend, my mentor, and my stability during parts of this story; may you rest in peace.

Introduction

The story that follows is one that I cannot tell without weaving myself into it. The prodding of countless friends—both hers and mine—has produced this, my best effort to tell the story of my mother's life. Yramiris. Iramiris, Yry, Yri, Iri, Eirie (pronounced like the canal). She had as many personas as she had names; being my mother was one persona and, of course, the most important one to me. The pronunciation and the spelling of her name vexed friends and acquaintances throughout her life. Rather than fighting the inevitable, my mother embraced her many identities and even added to her mystique by occasionally writing under *noms de plume* like Ruth and Patricia and perhaps others of which I am yet unaware. She was not just an unusual person, she was elusive. Her flair for the dramatic, paired with a fear of intimacy and exposure, resulted in a wake of similar, but never matching stories of her past. I studied letters, journals, and diaries from her childhood and youth, I coughed up memories of things she'd told me, I milked the stories she had told various friends. Rarely did these stories match in their entirety, but there was always a thread that tied them together. It is that thread of her being that I hope to capture.

Memory itself is ephemeral. And when we doctor our stories to fit predefined mores of society, it is easy to inhabit those stories as our own truths. The lines between truth and fiction are a murky pudding. In trying to make sense of my mother's pudding I'm sure I've gotten some things wrong. But hopefully I have captured the complex nature that drew people to shake their heads in wonder and sometimes in disapproval, but to love her just the same.

Part I: I am the Queen of England!

"A true story, a story based on real life, can never be written completely, anymore than an entire river can be carried in your hand." Ann Patchett

Plastic slats block all but pinholes of yellow spring glow. I perch in a Forest Service-green plastic chair pulled up to the left side of the hospital bed that sprouts a daunting array of wires, cords, tubes, buttons, and geegaws. My Tandy rides the table of my knees.

"Are you sure you don't want me to crack the blinds just a bit?"

"No. Hurts my eyes." The voice is almost unrecognizable—flat and grumpy.

Grasping at something to break the emptiness, my mind rumbles for a question to prime the pump. "So Mom, tell me about the trip to America. What was that like? Was it frightening or exciting?"

After a too-long pause, the diminished form answers with little enthusiasm.

April 1991 was an awkward time for my mother and me. No—it was an awkward time for me; it was an agonizing time for Mother. All her life Mom had relied on self-diagnosis accompanied by the talismans of vitamins, minerals, enzymes, and determination in lieu of doctors and hospitals. Ten days earlier she'd called me in Boise to ask for my help—

a first. Now, sitting beside her hospital bed in Fort Collins, I felt responsible for the heaviness of time. The following day she was scheduled for a surgical procedure that would enable long-term kidney dialysis. She'd been putting this off for several years. As a means of filling long, empty hours of doing nothing, I mined Mother's memories. Through the years, I'd overheard many intriguing family tales, but I'd only listened to the exciting parts and retained none of the important details nor the threads that connected the stories. Perhaps now, with nothing to sidetrack me, I could record them. Balancing the laptop on my knees, I coaxed her. She was tired and lethargic, but grateful to have a distraction. Her voice was hollow and lifeless, devoid of her characteristic flamboyance. At times, some vision would breathe a half-hearted grin into her voice:

"Yah. I wasn't quite eleven yet. It was Oct 25, 1924 ..."

Then silence, again. Such a simple answer seemed to suck all the energy out of her. Had she gone to sleep? Was she breathing? Journalists make interviewing look so easy, I thought, as I stared at the lump under the white bedclothes. Desperate to get the memories flowing, I blurted out another question. "What was the voyage like?" God, what a lame question. Without bothering to open her eyes, Mom sucked in stale, medicinal air and began to describe the events that brought her to America. Little by little the story of Mother's childhood emerged as I sat beside her bed.

~~~

It took ten days for the S.S. "Resolute" to cross the Atlantic from Hamburg to New York City. For a child of eleven, the trip was a grand adventure. It was also an opportunity to distance herself from the hubbub and turmoil of a large extended family of aunts and uncles and cousins. For her mother, Norah, the journey was less adventure and a lot more uncertainty and discomfort. Norah had already paid a dear price for falling in love with a German.

In the beginning

Lenore Dillon met Herman Paul by chance. They were each strolling one evening with their respective dogs in the town of Manchester, England. Norah was from a well-to-do Catholic family. She had been a naïve and sheltered young woman—"well bred" by the standards of the day. At 17 she had married a "good Catholic man." The marriage was bewildering, unsatisfying, and childless. She struggled for ten years to make the best of it, then came the shocking discovery that her husband had syphilis. That outrage, she felt, released her of any obligation to the man. Her parents understood her desertion, and took her in, but they could do little more for her. She was Catholic and Catholic marriages are forever.

One of Norah's few pleasures was going for walks with Jack, her high-stepping terrier, coifed with a silky white mane and a trim little derriere. Captivated by the smart little dog trotting towards him, Herman's eyes follow the leash upward coming to rest on an attractive, fair-skinned young woman with auburn hair piled in ornate swirls. At five-eight, Herman stood only two inches taller than Norah. His intense blue eyes locked onto her gray eyes with interest. While Jack investigated every inch of Herman's dog, Herman greeted the woman in front of him and introduced himself. Norah's heart skipped a beat as she responded to his mellow voice. They continued on their separate trajectories. She looked forward to more encounters with this polite, handsome, dark-haired gentleman with an alluring accent.

Frederick Herman Paul was a German merchant living and working in England along with his brother, Willy, who was a banker. Herman was a thoughtful man, interested in art, literature, and philosophy. Occasionally he took a turn on stage in an amateur theatre group. Herman and Norah's visits expanded in frequency and duration. Light bantering morphed into serious, soul-searching explorations. Affection blossomed into love. Officially, marriage was out of the question, but filled with vigor and optimism, they flouted the rules and Norah moved into the house that Herman shared with his brother.

Their union produced one child. Yramiris was named, she claimed, after an Egyptian mummy that her father had imported to England for his import-export business. And it is here, at the very beginning of her story, that the riddles begin. Upon closer investigation, her given name was Hertha Iramiris Dillon Paul. Hertha, a name my mother detested and refused to acknowledge, is Germanic for the goddess of fertility. But it also implies strength or vigor. The English boy's name, Irim means bright; its feminized version is Iram. The name Iris implies rainbow or colorful. Were her parents mixing her Germanic-British lineage and imbuing their little girl with strength and a bright, colorful life? If so, they succeeded beyond their wildest imaginings.

Yry was born into a Hadean world of international conflict. Her parents' union linked two discordant countries and breached the mores of the era. On the day of her birth, Nov 20, 1913, London was in a vortex of volatility. The Ottoman Empire had all but collapsed. Germany was amassing naval power at an alarming rate, which stimulated a similar buildup in England. Each country feared losing control over their respective colonies. Meanwhile tensions were increasing in the Balkans. The world stood at the brink of a black hole.

As Yry was learning to walk, France, Russia, and Britain were learning to use each other as ballast against Germany and her allies. Yry's mother was English. Her father was German. As she toddled around the house, lurching from chair leg to table leg for stability, she was innocent of the twisted trajectory that lay in store for her and her parents.

Within days of England's declaration of war against Germany, Parliament passed the Aliens Restriction Act, which required men between the ages of 17 and 55, of German or Austrian nationality, to report to internment camps. Brothers Herman and Willy had no recourse but to comply with the edict. By 1919, 600 camps in the Commonwealth housed up to 32,000 civilian prisoners. The media

I am the Queen of England!

portrayed Germans as bloody savages and tricky spies in the same way that America would do for Japanese Americans some 20 years later. The wife of a bloody Kraut, Norah became an outcast. With her daughter, she moved into a one-room basement apartment and hoarded her dwindling resources as best she could, while steeling herself for angry epithets when she ventured outside to shop or for arduous journeys to visit her husband.

The brothers spent four years in a tent village that, thanks to incessant rain, became a cesspool. The prisoners were reasonably well-treated. The residents of the camps organized themselves into social hierarchies to provide entertainment and comfort to each other. But the cold and damp conditions leached Willy's strength. Despite Herman's efforts to hoard extra food and blankets for him, Willy grew so weak that he had to be hospitalized, which inevitably saved his life.

Detainees were allowed monthly, 15-minute visits by no more than two relatives or friends at a time. The visits were monitored by guards and conversation was limited to English. For those precious few minutes with her husband each month, Norah endured the full-day, round-trip journey by bus and by train, often bringing the baby with her.

With his brother isolated, Herman occupied his time by devouring books as a lifeline to sanity. Though he lacked a college education, intense reading and study expanded his knowledge, perhaps beyond what he might have learned in a university. He spruced up his French, Spanish, English, and Italian, and taught himself Greek, Russian, and Chinese. His literary and acting skills made him a popular attraction at the impromptu performances that the internees presented to pass the time.

Meanwhile, from the camp hospital, Willy contacted their father who smuggled money to Norah. Yry and her mother spent nights huddled together during blackouts. First they suffered the devasting new technology of bombs dropped from the belly of a Zeppelin, and later from low-flying airplanes whose angry buzzing vibrated windows and dishes, just before their cargo whistled through the air and thudded to their deadly destinations. War noise was forever etched into Yry's memory, making fireworks an agony in later years.

Germany

The war ended, but the family's struggles continued. After release from the camp, the brothers found that their work visas had been revoked, so they were forced to leave England. They sailed first to Holland. From there, Herman arranged passage for his wife and child. Uncle Willy picked up Norah and Yry in Amsterdam and escorted them into northern Germany where he situated them temporarily with relatives while Herman searched for a place to live in Karlsruhe. Failing that, they ended up farther south in Langen with a new batch of relatives. Herman found work at a shellac factory and was quickly promoted to director of that factory. It was late summer of 1919.

Yry's parents took three weeks to rekindle their romance as they searched the cratered countryside for a place for the three of them to live. Yry, not quite six, remained in Langen with the relatives. Till that time, life had consisted of two extremes: wartime chaos or quiet solitude. She'd spent little time with other children. Like any normal five-year-old, she was proud of her growing communication skills and was a good English conversationalist with adults. But with the speed of a shooting star, she landed in a void of incomprehension. When she spoke, her cousins gawped and giggled.

Are they savages, she wondered? They act like hungry dogs roaming the streets. Their table manners are atrocious!

Initially she shrank into the shadows and refused to acknowledge their silliness. The Dutch and German cousins responded with taunts about her lack of manners and snootiness. She responded by scurrying under the dining room table. Sheltered by the folds of the tablecloth, and in true British fashion, she crossed her arms and proclaimed, "*I am the Queen of England!*"

Over time, the patience and kindness of adult aunts and uncles softened her defiant husk. Curiosity drove her to guess the content of family dinner conversations and she began to pick up bits and pieces of the German language. Whereas her life in London had been one of seclusion and fear, this new life in Germany was full of aunts and uncles and cousins who jabbered, laughed, and pulled pranks on each other. Eventually, Yry learned how to play with her cousins and came to cherish them individually for their unique contributions to the family entertainment.

Herman's brother-in-law was her favorite uncle. Uncle Philip was a child at heart who entertained the kids with walks and sleigh rides and wild stories. His favorite stories involved *der Schwartzmann*, the black man, who comes after bad little children. His teasing never frightened Yry. She recognized him for the clown that he was. Besides, *der Schwartzmann* came for German kids and SHE, after all, was the Queen of England!

Eventually Yry's parents moved to Darmstadt, where they rented two rooms of a large house owned by an elderly bachelor. Their landlord was a scruffy fellow with wild white hair escaping the confines of a well-worn flat cap. Just below the bill of his cap, bristly white eyebrows made a shelf over deep set eyes. His white mustache would have looked dashing if only it had not presided over irregularly-shaved jowls which twitched nervously in tandem with the eyebrows. The old man spent much of his day tramping through the woods behind the house. One day he came home with a canvas pouch filled with mushrooms which he cooked in lard. When he offered Yry a bowl of these morsels from the forest floor, she remembered Uncle Philip's tales about der Schwartzman. There was something about these mushrooms, offered by a strange, lonely, old man, from a forest with which she was unfamiliar, that gave her pause.

An elderly woman also roomed in the Darmstadt house. This woman's maid helped Norah with laundry and scouring the always shabby wooden floors. The maid had worked and saved every penny she earned to buy herself a better life. But Germany's postwar economy plunged, taking the woman's money with it. It was a tragic but common story, and one that Yry remembered and took to heart.

Things were going well for the family now. The next move was to a large, two-story house at Ritterstrasse 6, in Mainz, Germany. It was a beautiful, two-story, masonry house. Three broad steps, flanked by concrete wings, opened onto a porch with a swinging bench and chairs. Huge trees with gnarly trunks shaded an expansive lawn. This house came to host many wonderful family gatherings. By this time, Yry's German skills had improved. Her parents had taught her both English and German, as well as arithmetic, and geography. But she had never gone to school and was shy about interacting with other kids. Herman encouraged her to introduce herself to the neighborhood children, but each time she screwed up her nerve to approach a group of kids, they laughed at her English accent.

Occasionally the family traveled to Bavaria to visit friends who lived in the country just outside of Füssen. The Müllers had a son about Yry's age. Wide-eyed, she shadowed this tow-headed little boy around the barnyard. She loved visits to the Müllers, and she loved this little boy! During one visit, she flew out of the barn to catch up with him. As she careened around the corner, she lost her footing and down she went, landing on hands and knees in a ripe pile of cow manure, ruining her fancy dress and white stockings. Norah and Herman were not pleased about the long stinky trip back to Mainz with their wild child.

The Treaty of Versailles obligated Germany to pay reparations to the Allied countries for war-related damage and loss. These hefty payments decimated the economy and caused rocketing inflation. In urban areas, food supplies were spotty and unreliable. Fresh vegetables and dairy products were dearest of all.

I am the Queen of England!

Though she was a spirited child with a curious and quick mind, Yry was thin and pale. It was difficult to get good, healthy food. A week's worth of earnings barely covered a quart of buttermilk, a rare commodity which Herman hoped would plump up his puny little girl. His sacrifice was met by a long nose and wrinkled lips as she struggled to choke down the detested sour concoction.

Schools were also in disarray. Herman was convinced that no German school could provide an adequate education for his little Girlie, as he'd taken to calling her. He'd hired a few private tutors to supplement the lessons that he and Norah pressed upon her, but it was time for formal education. The French Occupation of Germany had resulted in an influx of French civilians, along with their families. Elite French schools bloomed to educate the children of the occupation. Ever resourceful, Herman finagled to enroll Yry in one of these highly recommended French schools.

During this period, Herman worked for a German businessman. He and his wife, Elise, had no children of their own. They were frequent dinner guests at the Ritterstrasse house. Elise adored Yry and delighted in plopping onto the floor to play games with her. She sensed loneliness in that house filled with preoccupied and stern parents. Norah was mentally and emotionally exhausted. The war had taken its toll, and she felt the ever-present burden of trying to maintain a household as she felt it should be kept. And, like Yry, she dealt with the isolation that comes with immersion in customs and expectations so different from her own—something that can be exciting, until the longing for family and familiar routine sets in. Aside from overseeing her daughter's lessons, Norah spent little time with her child; so when Elise offered to take Yry on outings to the park or for walks in the woods, Norah sighed with relief. Yry returned Elise's admiration with unabashed joy. She loved this beautiful, exuberant woman.

~~~

My Life With an Enigma

Huddled beside Mother's hospital bed with the laptop's cursor blinking, her voice grew momentarily animated as she described the day she learned to ride Elise's beautiful bicycle.

~~~

I was dying to ride that bike. Finally, one sunny afternoon Elise took me out with the bike and coached me. She was patient and calm with me and soon I got the hang of it. I was on top of the world, sailing up and down the street with Elise clapping and cheering. We were having so much fun that we completely lost track of time. When Elise noticed how the late afternoon sun had lengthened the shadows, she was mortified because she hadn't yet done the marketing for supper. How on earth could she explain to her husband that she'd been so busy playing with a child that she had neglected to prepare his meal?

Elise had an ice cellar to keep a few perishables cool. But even so, food was scarce, and marketing was a daily chore. Women queued up at the *Marktplatz* with ever larger fists full of cash and high hopes of purchasing fresh eggs, milk, and meat, if any were to be had. Some women with access to a patch of dirt tended vegetable gardens; others relied on vegetable stalls. Limited amounts of these items could be found and each, only at the appropriate merchant's shop or stall in the *Marktplatz*. Farmers market days were limited to one or two per week. Business hours were strictly limited. Transportation was limited to foot, bicycle, or streetcar. Bread was made at home. Elise had prepared a loaf that morning and left it to rise on the banked oven while she frolicked with Yry. But her cantankerous stove needed careful stoking and plenty of time to coax into the proper temperature to bake the bread. At that late hour of the afternoon it would be difficult to scrounge up anything fresh to prepare for dinner, so Elise's panic was legitimate.

Normally Elise accompanied Yry on the trolley all the way back to Ritterstrasse. But that day she was so distressed by the late hour that she gratefully accepted Yry's assurances that she could ride the trolley home by herself.

After all, I was feeling confident and grown up after mastering that big bike. I knew the way home by heart. What on earth could go wrong? But time seemed to have declared war on me that day. As I arrived at the station, the trolley was just pulling out. The next trolley wouldn't arrive for another 20 minutes. It was growing dark and my father's predictable tongue-lashing echoed in my head. Well, for Pete's sake, I knew the way home! I had two good legs! I would walk!

So off she went, with a bounce in her step, buoyed by her success on the bike and Elise's abundant encouragement and confidence in her.

After about five minutes, a French soldier approached and very politely asked, in German, how to get to the Marktplatz. Naturally, I responded in German. Then he grabbed my hand and pleaded, 'Come, dear, show me, please.' His uniform frightened me. Although I went to a French school and spoke some French, France was the occupying power in Germany. We never knew quite what to expect from them. It was nearly dark, and I couldn't get a good look at his eyes. My stomach lurched and saliva pooled in my mouth as he pulled me back in the direction from which I'd just come. I needed to get home before it was completely dark or Father would hit the roof. But here I was, being pulled in the opposite direction.

Without releasing his grip on my hand, a piece of candy magically appeared in his other hand. He seemed too eager.

Something just felt wrong. Struggling to free my hand, I murmured, in French now, 'Aucuns merci vous. Je ne peux pas. J'ai besoin d'obtenir aller.' No thank you, I can't. I must be going.

Yry was really frightened. Good manners had been drilled in—children must always be polite to adults. He wore the uniform of authority. What to do? She stopped short of physically resisting him. That was just not done.

The man dragged me along till we got to a barracks building where he stopped and jiggled the door, but it was locked. He jerked me further down the street to an apartment building with a courtyard. The next thing I knew he'd pushed me into a really dark corner and his hands began sliding over my clothes, looking for a way in or under. He pressed his rough face down against mine. He reeked of rancid fat and ashtrays. I forced down bile that bubbled up the back of my throat, and began struggling in earnest. I screamed and kicked at him, jerking and pulling to free my hands, as by now he had both of them in one of his hands. I heard the buttons on my blouse hit the cobblestones. Time that a few minutes before had been fleeing like a runaway horse, now stalled like a bicycle on a steep hill. His free hand plunged under my skirt and slithered up the inside of my thigh and his German dissolved into French. 'Fermer! Chienne' Shut up! Bitch! This really infuriated me, and I screamed all the louder and fought like a wild Indian.

One bit of providence prevailed that day; a German man appeared at one of the apartment windows above the courtyard and inquired about the ruckus. The distracted soldier momentarily loosened his grip on the hellion writhing in his hands, allowing her to slip loose and dash back towards the trolley line. Adrenaline-

I am the Queen of England!

powered, she leaped onto a moving trolley headed in the direction of home. The trolley slowed at the base of a hill near her house before heading off in another direction. She jumped off at this point and trudged slowly up the hill in the dark. Her stomach churning and her knees knocking. Her heart had slowed to half of its earlier pace, but it still ticked hard against her chest. She stood at the steps for a minute to settle her nerves, then quietly crept in the back door, hoping to avoid the immediate wrath of her father.

Disappearing into her bedroom, she changed her torn clothes, combed her hair, and vigorously scrubbed her hands and face before she came to the dinner table where she sat, stunned and subdued. Her mother was out that evening. Her father's anger at her tardiness was tempered by the recognition that something wasn't right with his little Girlie. He questioned her throughout the meal. She picked at her food and evaded his questions, but eventually it all spilled out.

Her father's reaction tripled her anxiety. His initial outburst was followed by a spanking, which may have been a first, as his voice and penetrating gaze had always been enough to discipline his daughter.

"What a foolish ninny you are! If you'd spoken English to him, he'd have left you alone!"

While German speaking citizens were bullied and abused by their former war adversaries, the French occupiers treated the British with the respect due their esteemed allies.

After the spanking and the lecture, the maid was ordered to draw a scalding hot bath for Yry, as if this could cleanse her—of what, she was unsure. Was it her evil or the soldier's that her father hoped to expunge? During this time alone with Yry, maid Marie tried to soothe the sobbing child. She quietly explained, as best she could, the implications of the attack. This was Yry's sole birds and bees talk. From then on Yry spoke only English on those rare occasions that speaking to strangers was unavoidable.

Yry's humiliation was not complete. The following day her father hauled her off to the family doctor who assured Herman that there was no permanent damage from the attack. However, he had noted the unmistakable symptoms of acute anemia. Again, Germany's postwar conditions influenced Yry's life. The good, nutritious dairy products so vital to a growing child were unavailable. Even Herman's forced buttermilk regimen was not enough to counteract the poor diet. Herman arranged for her to stay at a children's health sanitarium in Arosa, Switzerland. It was March of 1924.

~~~

After hearing this story, several pieces of my mother's puzzle cha-chinged into place for me. It had infuriated me when she insisted that I enroll in Spanish rather than French in the seventh grade. Her argument—that Spanish would serve me better than French in the western United States—was sound, but not good enough for me. And for a person who abhorred racism, she was blind to her own prejudice against anything French, be it French food, the French language, or French people. I was ashamed for the times I had rolled my eyes at Mother's veiled references to a "nasty French soldier." I had suspected her of über dramatics, as if she'd had to fight off the entire male race single-handedly. Now I understood that this episode with the French soldier was a rightfully defining moment that left my mother with a fear of strangers and a lifetime phobia. And also, I know that women suffered deeply, the penetrating gaze and lewd comments of unleashed males before the enlightenment of the women's movement infiltrated the public conscience of North America and Europe during the later third of the twentieth century. I was too little, too ignorant, and too caught up in my own childhood anguishes to recognize the ugliness that women endured when unaccompanied by a male companion.

I am the Queen of England!

Switzerland

The untrammeled pastoral villages of Switzerland were the best places for western Europeans to physically recover from the ravages of WWI. The crisp, clean, high altitude was thought to be especially good for tubercular patients. Switzerland's neutrality during the war had saved the countryside from bombings that decimated farm country in other parts of Europe. The comparative abundance of fresh dairy products lured wealthy Germans, French, and Austrians seeking to restore vigor and calm nerves. Arosa had served as a leading health resort or sanitarium since the 1880's.

On the heels of the most frightening event in her life, Yry's things were suddenly packed and she was sent away. There was no explanation for her banishment. Not until she was much older did she understand the ramifications of anemia. Instead, this seemed like a steroidal version of standing in the corner. She had been a bad girl. Her father was disappointed in her.

At age ten Yry was completely alone in yet another foreign environment. A stash of letters that she wrote to her parents and to her Granny in Darmstadt reveal a devoted and lonely child. She wrote faithfully to each parent at least once a month in a labored childhood scrawl on lined, baby-blue note paper. Most letters were written in English, but some were written in German and an occasional French word testified to her diligence in learning that language as well. In each letter she asked about her "Birdie" and her "Pussy," as well as maid Marie and her friend Elise. She begged for pictures of her pets or postcards from home. Her letters were signed "Girlie"or infrequently, her given, but detested, name of Hertha.

Vendredi le 11 April 1924
My dear daddy.
I hope you are getting on well.
I am not pleased that you do not visit me.
Many grettings to Lang.
Much much love from your much loving, girlie.

Herman, a self-taught linguist, placed great emphasis on languages. He spent freely for tutors to assist Yry with her language skills. Even in Arosa, he paid extra for a tutor to hone her German. He often inquired about her French lessons. She usually ignored those questions. Fulfilling his role as an authoritarian disciplinarian, his letters stuck to preachy warnings and advice to work and study harder. The only scraps of warmth came from the few letters her mother wrote, but often Norah only penned a few sentences written in the margins of Herman's letters.

The Swiss landscape soothed Yry's soul. Arosa is a tiny village nestled in a valley shadowed by a chain of ancient peaks, the largest thrusting to over 8,000 feet. The region is a mixture of calendar-green alpine pastures, forests, glacial lakes, and foothills that decorate the feet of the icy alps. The nascent ski industry was born here. Yry had traveled around southern Germany with her parents, vacationing in Bavaria and in the Black Forest, but she had never spent extended time in such grandiose mountains as these.

The brilliance of Arosa lifted her spirits. Linen-clean air tickled Yry's nose hairs and planted the seed for a lifelong reverence of nature. Sunshine glinted off dazzling peaks set against a bluer than blue sky. On some days, magnificent clouds thundered up around the peaks, ballooning and shape-shifting, omens of storms that would soon unleash more snow on the valley. The school was administered by nuns. The other children that shared her fate ranged in age from five to fourteen. Two or three kids were assigned to each bedroom. No lit candles were allowed in the rooms at night. The frail children needed plenty of rest. Long, sunny afternoons lying on the sun decks were prescribed, as well as sleigh rides, tobogganing, and ice skating—and with arrival of spring—brisk hikes.

She was unfazed by the incredible cold of Arosa. It was a different flavor of cold than what she'd experienced before. She knew it was very cold because her breath hung in foggy puffs, and ice crystals floated in the air. It was a crisp, dry cold that nipped exposed skin but failed to penetrate deep into the bones like the damp, foggy cold she had known in Germany and England. This cold was fun! It transformed the world into a magical dreamscape dotted with white pillows where rocks had been. Instead of looking barren and naked, the trees and bushes sported diamond-studded coats of frost. Water froze in its tracks; trapped waterfalls formed fanciful ice statues that stood in awkward arabesques, waiting for spring to breathe life into them.

Easter eased in a slow transformation. Frozen brooks began to trickle icy-cold water. Waterfalls danced to life, still decked in fanciful trimmings of glassy rock jewelry and hoar hair. Tiny rivulets of water descended from the peaks above, gathering force as they approached the green pastures below. In protected nooks the sun kissed tender buds of early crocuses; they responded with masses of color to announce spring. The cheerful chirping and twittering of songbirds broke winter's silence, as they preened their feathers in golden rays of sun. In Arosa, children shed layers of protective clothing as their hikes ranged further.

It was good for Yry to be in the company of children. One friend was a little girl called Frieda, who came from the nearby village of Chur. Several years younger than Yry, Frieda shadowed her with the awe that younger children often have of older kids. Frieda begged to wear the chic new sunglasses Norah had sent from Mainz. Imitation being the highest compliment, Yry complied with a smile and then discovered the downside of having small disciples. With the sunglasses perched precariously on her nose, Frieda pirouetted with joyous abandon, sending the glasses sailing off her tiny face. Staring at the stone patio where shattered bits of her prized possession glinted in the sunlight, Yry turned away to shield the disappointed child from her fury and disappointment.

Dressed in her black habit, the school's piano teacher resembled a mortician rather than a musician. Piano would not become one of Yry's best talents. It was difficult to corral her thoughts from the sounds of nature just outside the door. She enjoyed singing in the choir more than practicing the piano.

Every child was expected to eat each nutritious morsel on his or her plate. This was challenging. Yry's first experience with the exotic treat of fresh pineapple left an indelible impression. The fruit's benign color and interesting appearance in the bowl belied its strong pungence and stringy texture. Anticipating juicy sweetness, she wrapped her lips around a big piece and nearly gagged. Puddings were served frequently, often garnished with a generous splash of cinnamon, which she hated. But she stuffed them down to avoid the wrath of the nuns.

Each week the doctor arrived to examine the children and determine who was eating properly and who was being too fussy. Weekly he pronounced small improvements in Yry's blood counts and weight. Impatient to return home, she wrote glowing reports about her progress and the doctor's encouragements. After eight months in Arosa, she finally received word that Daddy would be coming to bring her home to Mainz and Mamma, and Pussy, and Birdie. She was on cloud nine.

Part II: America, here we come!

Yry had gained weight and her cheeks were rosy. Everyone commented on how wonderful she looked. But her elation at being home was dampened when she discovered that the concept of *home* was about to shift again. One week after returning from Switzerland, Yry and her mother were scheduled to leave Germany for the United States! She tried to recall just where, on the big, colorful globe at school, she had seen this country called America. Or was it called the United States? This was as perplexing as the Netherlands, also known as Holland, where the Dutch lived.

The massive task of moving the household across the Atlantic Ocean usurped her homecoming. Norah was in a tizzy over packing and preparations. Many wistful goodbyes loomed. They took a train to Darmstadt to say goodbye to Granny and all the aunts, uncles, and cousins whom Yry had come to love. Surely the full ramifications of this event failed to sink in. How wrenching would her goodbyes have been if she'd known how many years it would be and what they'd each have to endure before they saw each other again? She wrote a letter to her aunt and uncle in Holland because there wasn't time to visit them.

~~~

I have often wondered at my grandfather's prescience in moving his family across the ocean to America in 1924. Tucking WWI into the past, feelings of hope and harmony surfaced in many parts of the world. Germany, however, struggled with the burdens engendered by the Treaty of Versailles. A lack of foreign investment crumpled the German economy and created factory closures and rampant unemployment. I suspect Herman was uneasy about the emergence of dictators like Mussolini and Lenin. Adolph Hitler had been sponging up support for his National Socialist German Worker's Party from which the Nazi Party emerged. Acts of violence were common, often led by Brownshirts, precursors to Storm Troopers or *Sturm Abteilung*, (SA). Social and racial upheaval in the Balkans alarmed Herman because of the mixed ethnicity of his own family. Also, the loss of his British visa after World War I, broke the link to his wife's homeland. Perhaps his entrepreneurial spirit chafed in a mundane factory management position. Whatever the reason, my grandfather made the leap while his brother, Willy, remained in Germany. In doing so, Herman may have saved more than his immediate family.

Herman's transition from employee to private businessman is also a mystery. Mother never filled in details about her father's activities. Her parents probably refrained from discussing business in front of her and, as a child, she probably had little interest. When I probed for details late in her life, she commented quite simply, "My fatheh was frequently away from home. His business trips took him to many exotic places. I rarely knew where he was, but letters would arrive from India, Egypt, Italy, and Africa." This casual acceptance of a father's absence may be normal for a period during which unpleasantness went unacknowledged. An old photo album from 1923 and '24 contains images of a dapper looking man called Fred (or Oscar) Lang in India. In some photos he wears a uniform, and in others he's dressed as a civilian. I suspect he was a business associate. A man called Walter Weiss also showed up in India and in New York.

And forever in the background of her memory lurks the image of Adolph Levi. In photo albums he is sometimes identified as Levi Paul or Levi Kracoph. Much to Yry's disdain, she was expected to address this man as "Uncle" Adolph. Herman's friendship with Adolph Levi is documented in a formal studio photograph taken in 1903 with Adolph posed between brothers Herman, 21, and Willy, 18. Mother muttered that Adolph and her father had sworn a blood oath to each other. Was she serious? Isn't that something ten-year-old Boy Scouts do when they run out of explosives to play with? I struggle to imagine my stern grandfather swearing a blood oath to anyone. Why would he do that? What on earth could compel him to such an agreement? He treated family with the utmost responsibility. I would consider such an oath superfluous in the larger context of my grandfather's character. It was "Uncle" Adolph who accompanied my grandmother and Mother across the ocean in 1924. Why wasn't Herman with them?

If Mother had qualms about leaving family, friends, and home, she kept them to herself. Instead, she capitalized on the adventure at hand. From her hospital bed some 67 years later, she recalled the excitement.

> *I loved the adventure. I explored all the nooks and crannies of the ship. I spent as much time on deck as possible. There were a bunch of games I had never played before. And a wonderful swimming pool which fascinated me. I asked the crew all sorts of questions. They responded kindly. Occasionally I'd get a special tour. Below deck, everyone was sick. It smelled bad down there. It was dark and nasty. I tried to get Mother to join me in games upstairs but usually she just lay on her bunk feeling and looking green.*

Mother paused, gathering the past ... and her breath.

> *Thank God I had my cat. Poor Pussy. She was sentenced to her tiny cage. But I lugged it around with me. I wanted to show her the sights. Poor thing almost missed the boat.*

Another pause. Her sentences were truncated and uncharacteristically flat, with long pauses between them, as if the simple task of talking zapped all her strength.

We were in Hamburg. Waiting for our departure. I opened her cage to show her the fancy cars. And the people all dressed to the nines. Pussy wasn't impressed. The bedlam scared the bejeezus out of her.

Now that's a bit more like the mother I know, I thought as my fingers raced across the keys to record her memories.

When she saw that door open, she dashed for freedom. She disappeared under the nearby trolley. There were some warehouses on the other side of the trolley. I pulled mother with me and ran over there. We started knocking on doors. Mother was beside herself. She chastised me for my stupidity. WE WILL NOT MISS OUR BOAT for the sake of your cat! Finally, time was up. Mother insisted that we return to the dock. I begged her to try just one more door. There, unbelievably, we found poor Pussy huddled into a tiny ball in a dark corner of the attic.

New York City, 1924

On October 14, a formal dinner awaited first-class passengers of the S.S. "Resolute" to commemorate the next morning's arrival in New York Harbor. The embossed invitation with Yry's name on it made her feel important and grown up. The weather was good and the ocean calm. Norah looked beautiful in her fancy dress. With Uncle Adolph escorting them, they appeared to be a normal family. Yry was surprised to realize just how many people had been hiding out below deck. Now, with the lengthy trip nearly over, many new faces ventured forward and even mustered smiles and hearty appetites. The menu included delicacies like caviar, turtle soup, salmon cutlets, filet mignon, and artichokes. Remembering the awful soups in Arosa, Yry declined the turtle soup. She'd had few encounters with fish, so she felt quite adventuresome when she ordered the salmon. She found the artichokes rather strange, but bathed in butter they were quite bearable.

Due to Norah's English citizenship, Yry's visitor's pass, and Adolph's well-worn American visa, they avoided the chaos of Ellis Island. Uncle Adolph's previous visits to the states made him the perfect escort. As soon as they debarked the ship he hustled them through throngs of people and ushered them down narrow corridors that ran between enormous buildings. Yry's neck twisted this way and that, gaping at the buildings that blocked out the sun. It wasn't that she'd never been in a big city before, but this was New York! This was America! Excitement thrummed around her, as horns honked impatiently, streetcars screeched, and elbows flailed. Disentangled from the crowd, Adolph flagged down a taxi that whisked them to their first residence, Hotel Majestic, near Riverside Drive. They carried light satchels with overnight necessities. The remainder of their luggage was delivered the following day.

They ate their first American Thanksgiving meal at the hotel and Yry celebrated her eleventh birthday there. Pussy once again dashed for freedom by jumping out the open hotel window. She landed feet first on the canvass awning jutting over the window below them. Yry and Norah had to introduce themselves to the occupants of the rooms on that floor and beseech them to allow Yry to enter their room with a tin of tuna to entice the cat back to civilization.

Just before Christmas in 1924, the three, Norah, Yry, and Adolph moved to a newly constructed house in New Rochelle, an upper-class suburb of New York City, located on the northern shore of Long Island Sound. Meanwhile, Herman was still traveling, probably in India.

Photo albums from October 1924 through early summer of 1925 document a family threesome of Norah, Uncle Adolph, and Yry. With a bow that resembled a coronet sprouting from her hair, Yry was neatly dressed and looked happy, although her diaries during that time indicate that she hated Uncle Adolph's constant presence. Norah camouflaged a no longer girlish figure with lovely flowing gowns and dropped-waist dresses.

Herman entrusted to Uncle Adolph the care of not only his wife and child, but also of funds to purchase land, build a house, and establish a business partnership. It was Uncle Adolph who selected the lot, the builders, and the plans for the home in New Rochelle. The house that Adolph built with Herman's nest-egg, was an immense two-and-a-half story stucco with a magnificent garden, a fishpond, a gazebo, and private tennis court. The house at 819 North Avenue was a Cape Code minus the clapboard siding. It was one of the first homes built in a new subdivision called Wykagyl Park. Initially miles of undeveloped woodland surrounded their property.

Though Yry resented Uncle Adolph, she had no complaints about the house. She roamed the woods and dreamed of the Wild West. She was astonished to be given choices about her room decor. Unlike her quarters in Germany, where she'd had to make do with whatever was available during post-war scrounging, Yry got everything she asked for in her new bedroom.

~~~

Was this, perhaps, an attempt by Norah to soften my mother's dislike for Adolph? I think back to how my mother prepared me for the disruption in our lives when I was 14. I was blindsided when she announced her engagement to Mr. Tracy. Within months, we left our house in town and moved with Mr. Tracy and his 19-year-old daughter into the house on Mom's ranch. For the first time in my life, I had carte blanche for the décor of my own bedroom. Mirror images?

~~~

Yry's new bedroom cocooned her for the next eight years and she loved every aspect of it. Positioned on the top floor, her room

America, here we come!

was large, but the space was cut by the canted eves of the roof. At the far end of the room, the chimney bisected the wall. The chimney was flanked by two little fan-shaped windows on either side of it. Below each window, a built-in storage bench, covered with pillows, provided a cozy perch from which Yry surveyed the entire valley and noted changes as the neighborhood filled in. She devoured books by authors like Zane Grey and Owen Wister. Those bucolic forested hills behind the house shape-shifted into rugged Rocky Mountains populated by cowboys and Indians and horses.

After years of chaos and scrounging Norah was happy. This was the style of life she had been raised to expect. A butler, Cyril, doubled as a chauffeur for their Rickenbacker. They had a full-time maid and a Chinese cook whom Yry never forgave for her awful soups and spinach that tasted like it had gone directly from the ground to the plate.

Meanwhile, Uncle Adolph was working to launch the New York City base of an import/export business partnership. The details of how this came to be are once again unavailable. But future business partners, brothers Fred and Joe Stein, begin to show up in family photos in the winter of 1925. During that same time, photos of Uncle Adolph appear on nearly every page of the album. He was a pudgy man with a mustache, pipe, and fedora. He proudly escorted Norah and Yry to nearby landmarks. One Saturday, Cyril drove them north to Kensico Reservoir for a picnic outing. They motored across the dam, stopping along the way for photos. Construction on the dam had begun in 1911 and had lasted for nearly four years. Yry was amused that she and the dam were the same age.

Yry was eager to start school in America, but was blindsided by what the public school system had in store for her in January of 1925. With a cursory glance at her penmanship on the school entrance form, The Roosevelt School principal harrumphed.

"This child's handwriting is illegible. Why, she can't even write a proper w!" What might this illustrious principal have said about the Queen Mum's British handwriting?! Twelve-year-old Yry, already showing signs of puberty, was placed in the third grade. She matched this indignity by getting into her first and only school fight.

Classes had been in session for two weeks when the teacher stepped out of the classroom momentarily. During her absence, Yry began arguing with another girl over the meaning of a word in their reading exercise. Yry had already developed a scalding low opinion of this girl, with her fiery red hair, fur coat, and outspoken opinions and had dubbed her Miss Prissy. The altercation heated up and, goaded by their classmates, a shoving match ensued. When the teacher returned, the two girls were out of their seats and Miss Prissy was whining and sniffling. Yry stood firm, with her head up, her hands stiffly at her sides, the next, the teacher assumed the bigger, stony-faced girl to be the aggressor in the situation and sent Yry to the principal's office for a dressing down.

~~~

"I've hated redheads ever since that day," she remarked when she related this story from her hospital bed so many years later. I laughed. First of all, in my very dim memory, Grandma Noni had bright, red hair; and secondly, in the fourth grade, I got into a similar battle with the only redhead in my class. I, too, have fought the urge to summarily dislike redheads.

~~~

Four months later, Yry had mastered her w's and proved to the school administrators that, lack of formal education aside, she knew a lot more than they thought she did. She was promoted to the fourth grade. For the remaining two months of that school year she was dumped into a new class with another set of unfamiliar classmates. To her complete bewilderment, her former classmates from the third grade would no longer have anything to do with her. Again, she was the newcomer, the odd one out. The social hierarchy puzzled a child who had spent so much time alone, or with relatives, or at the health sanitarium where children of all ages had no choice but to mingle. The following term she entered the fifth grade. She persevered despite, or maybe because of, social ostracism. The school newspaper, *The Roosevelt Bugle*, showcased several of her poems and short stories.

Snowstorms pounded the east coast during their second and third winters in New Rochelle. Photos show piles of snow cleared off the driveway and piled as high as the first story of the house. Yry was enchanted, once again, by the mystical transformation that snow worked on the landscape.

In the summer of 1925, Herman reappears in the photo album, looking pleased with the house and garden. He and Adolph pose together under the gazebo, looking comfortable and relaxed. It confounds that a man would travel the world while delegating the care of his family and finances to another man. Wouldn't building a new home in a new country have been his primary concern? Why didn't Adolph travel the world to make business connections? What was going on?

Although socially isolated, Yry loved the freedom of the large house and beautiful garden. She spent solitary hours observing the Teutonic diligence of ants. These weren't your wimpy little table ants. These were big and they were strong! They tugged objects a hundred times the size of their own bodies towards some mysterious destination. She'd try to divert their attention by blocking their path with a rock or some other object, but they stubbornly returned to their invisible highway. Sometimes she'd toss an ant into the fishpond to see if it could swim and if it could, would it resume its line of travel even in the water? Lucky for the ants, the fish were zoned out in their bleak la-la-land. She took pity on the ants, though, and used twigs to flip their sogginess out of the water just before they sank.

No longer relegated to a quick ride on a borrowed bike, now she had her own beautiful bicycle to ride through the elm- and maple-shaded streets of New Rochelle. It was a pretty town with many ponds and lakes, rolling fairways, flowered lawns, and gentle hills. This new freedom was enchanting, and she thrilled at top-speed flights down the hills.

For her thirteenth birthday, in 1926, Yry received a shiny new scooter, an early version of today's Razor. A photo of her standing before the front door in a fur-collared coat and patent leather shoes with her new scooter reveals how much she had matured. The ubiquitous bow overshadowing her head was gone. She posed rather demurely with a sleek, chin-length pageboy.

Leisurely trips to the mountains to escape the blistering summer heat of the city became routine. Rather than whizzing down razor-straight freeways with carefully engineered curves that invite maximum speed, and dashing off the road for quick pit stops spaced to conveniently sate the appetites of both the car and its occupants, 1920s road trips were leisurely and refined. The roads were often dusty and rutted and required cautious negotiation.

Yry described one such trip in her diary. The first stop for tea and fuel was at a little place called "The Oakes" in Fishkill, New York. It was a small house with a large veranda and comfortable tables and chairs for *al fresco* dining. An hour later they drove onto the ferry at Newburgh and crossed the Hudson River to Highland. In the village of Kingston they stopped again for tea and toast and filled the tank. The first day's journey ended at a small inn outside of Selkirk, not even 150 miles from home. In the morning they settled around a large pedestal oak table in the dining room and nibbled at toast with creamery butter and homemade blackberry jam, accompanied by eggs, scrambled with fresh shallots and herbs. Norah nursed a cup of English tea while the men downed strong black coffee. Herman and Adolph shared a morning paper while Norah and Yry visited with a pair of lovebirds celebrating their first married holiday.

After breakfast and a casual stroll around the grounds, they loaded up again and headed for Albany, where they stopped to gawk at the Gothic architecture of the Hudson Terminal building as well as the State House, the Capitol, and the Governor's residence. Then, on to Schenectady and Saratoga Springs. Rolling hills and freshwater springs dotted the landscape. Occasionally they'd detour from the main road, lured by the vista promised by a mountaintop. One of these side trips took them to a place called Grant's Cottage. Yry was disappointed to find a plain old house instead of what she pictured as a quaint little stone cottage.

They traveled at this pace for several days, stopping at unadvertised but inviting little places along the way. Yry never failed to gawp at the occasional stable that advertised horseback rides. Her pleas to stop, though, passed through the car as if she were in a parallel universe. At St Hubert, Adolph at last consented to hire a horse and buggy to carry them to Upper Ausable Lakes, which lay nestled in a dense private forest. There, Adolph proudly rowed them out into the lake while Norah worried. They picnicked and swam in the lakes and rested in the shade of the magnificent hardwood trees. Later they explored Hurricane Lodge in the Hurricane Mountains. They marveled at the 450-year-old elm called Caesar, famous for being the oldest tree in New York State. Then, on through Lake Placid and to a place in Blue Ridge called The White House. Mrs. May, the proprietor, was friendly and kind, but not the best cook. Her whole wheat griddle cakes hit the belly like sack of flour dropped from the top of old Caesar.

Blue Ridge was quiet and peaceful. Few tourists came to this spot; it felt like their own private resort. They swam and rowed on the pristine lakes nearby and played badminton on the lawn. After spending two or three nights at the White House they packed up once more and headed home, vowing to return the next year. Their tour took fifteen days.

Family road trips, both near and far, provided entertainment as well as a foundation for understanding their new country and the history of its people. In the large cities of the Northeast, Herman and Norah investigated museums, art galleries, and historic monuments. Yry loved these explorations. Their trips were punctuated with geographic, geological, and historical lessons. They visited Niagara Falls, and often went to New Hampshire, staying at Lake Sunapee or their favorite retreat at Crawford Notch.

~~~

When I found references to Crawford's Notch among my mother's papers and photo albums, I thought of my drive through New Hampshire's autumn colors. I knew that my mother had loved the countryside of upstate New York, Vermont, and New Hampshire, and I tried to visualize it as she might have seen it. The "Notch" nomenclature fascinated me. A notch is what I have always called a pass, or a saddle, between two mountains. I remember passing by Crawford Notch and Franconia Notch near Mount Washington. Viewed from US Highway 302, Mount Washington looked positively tame the day I drove by. With typical western conceit, I hardly considered those gentle looking old hills of the east coast capable of producing the hardships that my Rocky Mountains are known for. I was shocked to discover Mount Washington's reputation for erratic and downright deadly weather supersedes that of any of my favorite western mountain ranges. At 231 miles per hour, Mount Washington holds the record for the highest wind speed measured on the earth's surface. Weather patterns from the Atlantic, the Gulf, and the Pacific Northwest converge above this modest 6,288-foot peak to produce winds of over 100 mph for nearly a third of the year. My mother's wilderness wasn't as bucolic as I'd always imagined it.

~~~

At home, Yry developed a few new friendships. Ellen, with her eager and puckish smile, was the dearest. Ellen and Yry tramped through the woods and climbed trees together, egging each other on to new heights. They walked their dogs through rain, snow, or sunshine and spent hours combing each other's hair and trying new styles. Together they dreamed of their futures. How grand life would be! What adventures lay before them! The friendship endured through junior high school and well beyond.

Yry's dog, Jeff, was the object of great entertainment. He was a handsome fellow who endured her attempts to teach him circus tricks, bi-monthly baths, and her momentary lapses in patience when he didn't understand what she expected of him.

Younger neighbor kids were drawn to Yry and her pets. Sometimes she organized neighborhood "dress up parties." Rather than the kids dressing up, it was the pets that had to put up with looking foolish. Jeff's alert ears, sprouting from under bows and hats, gave him a perplexed look in the posed photos. Through the years she added cats, kittens, birds, and more dogs to her menagerie.

~ ~ ~

My mother spent hours on the bench below the fan-shaped window, reading, daydreaming, and writing volumes of poetry. Her neat and well-spaced fountain pen script is entirely unlike the erratic scrawl that I came to know. She experimented with numerous *nom de plumes*. Throughout her life, she played liberally with these identities, making it a challenge to piece together the threads of her life. A saying she coined at 13, reveals a kernel of her character:

> We all grow up to be what we make of ourselves when we are young, not what other people may try to make us. That is why we should start to make ourselves early in life. If we start too late we won't get finished.

Under one of her favorite pen names, a poem book from 1926 records carefully printed couplets about animals, the holidays, the seasons, and finally, a boy! Enter Phil Cochrane.

My Life With an Enigma

> **My Sweetheart,** by Ruth Paul 13 years old
> *Blue his eyes, like summer skies,*
> *Lips like cherries red;*
> *Cheeks of rose, tip-tilted nose,*
> *Pretty dark-blond head.*
> *Do I love this boy, so sweet and fair?*
> *Yes, truly, dearly I declare.*
> *He's my sweetheart, don't you see?*
> *What's his age? Just ten is he.*

What a surprise to realize that at this tender age my mother's gaze went toward a younger man. Is this what comes of being held back in school? She would reverse that trend later. From this point forward, her poetry is consumed with Phil for several years. She collected photos of Phil as if they were precious marbles. Her passion for Philip was a recurring theme that traced her throughout life. I would find a lock of Philip's hair stashed in a secret hiding place. I would find allusions to her first love in future writings. These relics followed her for all those years, all those moves, all those miles of her life! She was really caught.

Her love was not in vain. Going through memorabilia she had clung to through many moves and upheavals, I found a *Nestor Gianaclis* cigarette tin. Tucked inside were folded and age-browned scraps of paper that document a torrid, youthful affair. Heavy pencil scrawl screams worship and a proposal of marriage. Mixed into the beloved scraps of paper are photos of a handsome, dark-haired boy in short pants.

> *My Darling Iramiris,*
> *Have you ever stopped to think how important love is. Iramiris, my Darling, I worship you. I adore you, I love you Iramiris. My Sweetheart, I can't explain how much I adore you ... my Dearest, will you marry me Please. I love you. Your loving Shatz, Phil Cochrane*

America, here we come!

In 1927 she had promised, in writing, on a plain, cream-colored sheet of paper, to marry Philip in 15 years, to love him and be with him forever, signing it with her pet name, Nawitta. Even as I sat beside her in the hospital 64 years later, Philip crept into her world with a tender smile.

> *Whatever has become of Shatzy (dear or darling in German) with his thick dark hair and serious hazel eyes? I didn't lie to him. I do still love Philip, and he is still with me in my heart.*

And what, I wonder, does it say of me, that as I read these scraps of her life, coveted and hidden away, that I snicker at the tawdriness of her emotion? Why can't I take her feelings seriously? Who among us can forget our first love? World-weary adults patronize the perceived innocence and shallowness of young love. Yet each of us carries a sharp memory of that very first love. It is the awakening of our utmost possibilities. In love, we see ourselves from a refreshingly new perspective. We leave behind, at least for a while, parental authority and sibling disapproval. No matter how long or how short the first love is, or how passionately acknowledged or secretly hidden away, we remember it forever like the first taste of an exquisite candy.

I remember my first beloved with a warm smile. I think of our dark, cramped hideaway where we both screwed up the nerve to share our first *I love yous* and I remember the thumping of my heart at that moment—the exhilarating feeling of discovering that some other human being found value in my existence. It was cute, it was fun, we went steady, his chewing gum prize, the key to my fidelity. But even in the sixth grade, a warning bell went off in my head, reminding me that this was only practice. Unlike my mother, I was not one to be hijacked by drama.

~~~

Yry and Philip spent every possible moment together, sometimes alone and sometimes with neighborhood friends. The heat of new passion burned through her fog of isolation. She was fulfilled. Her life had purpose. She guarded Philip like a bulldog, defending him from physical or verbal assaults. Her lofty age offered an excuse to display worldly wisdom. She advised him on his schoolwork and chastised him for being naughty to his grandmother. Philip was as much a younger sibling figure for her as he was a romantic interest. She reveled in the role of older, more mature partner. Philip accepted her rebukes with humility and promises to try to be a better person.

Shortly before Uncle Adolph had the car packed for their summer tour, Yry received an anguished letter from Philip who was distraught that she was abandoning him for England! Perhaps young Philip's geography was a bit off. Maybe she said New England and he only heard England. Or, did Yry lead him to believe that she'd be traveling to Europe? Was this her way of managing young Philip?

Yry enjoyed this trip through Pennsylvania, upstate New York, Vermont, and New Hampshire. They crossed from New York into Vermont on a steamship over Lake Champlain. Ubiquitous covered bridges were picturesque, and the family enjoyed swimming and canoeing at every opportunity along the way. One photo shows Yry perched somewhat seductively on a tree trunk beside Clear Pond. The rather impish grin on her face contrasts sharply with the womanly body revealed by her one-piece swimsuit. She tomboyed with friends who were still mere kids, but her body was on its own timetable.

In between adventures, Yry and Philip continued their gushing romance. She loved pointing her camera at him in different poses around the garden. They shared a love of reading and poetry. Philip's worship nourished her self-confidence.

Eventually though, Philip's mother grew concerned about Yry's constant presence in the boy's life. She devised ways to intervene; there were summer schools, day camps, visits with distant relatives, and tennis and golf lessons. The absences took their toll. After a few years, Philip began to grow up and grow apart from Yry. His time was filled with other people and other excitements. That anything more important than her could enter his life shocked and devastated Yry. She had come to rely upon his presence and his idolatry. Spilling her misery in gloomy ink, she wallowed in loss for years after the two friends parted in 1929.

Fixated on the West

During the summer of 1927, Yry's father traveled by train to San Francisco for business. He wrote her a letter on embossed stationery from the Hotel St. Francis.

. . . Leaving Denver one passes through the Royal Gorge which is of singular beauty and of the very wildest character. One admires the full hearted men who fifty years ago came this way into unknown country harassed by wild beast and Indian tribes. Scarcely out of Colorado, one enters a wilderness, a most arid country, partly sand deserts, and this continues through Utah and Nevada. There are a few fertile, green oases, but on the whole these two provinces are sterile and scarcely populated. This whole region wants exploitation by geologists.

With insightful clarity, he postulated how ripe the arid land was for geologists, engineers, and miners. His commentary fit the prevailing paradigm of Manifest Destiny. Gazing from the windows of the observation car, he considered the vast, unused prairie that stretched like an ocean of gold around the dark ship hurtling down the rails. A brief stop in Salt Lake City filled him with admiration for Brigham Young's "work of untold labor and hardship." His perspective contrasts starkly with Yry's opinions about religion, its religious leaders, and the principles of the LDS faith, in particular. Herman signed off, "heartily, your Daddy."

My Life With an Enigma

~~~

Aside from the signature, his prose is more suitable for an annual report than a personal letter to his teenage daughter. His third person narrative is distant and formal. He screens his humanity behind the pronoun "one." His perspectives, though common for the day, surprise me in the discordant note of today's socio-political standards. I somehow envisioned my grandfather as a man who was above shallow judgments about heathen natives. However, he was indeed keenly observant. He described the land as looking like the bottom of a dry ocean. I'm not sure if he had read about the geological history of the region or if this was his own analogy. His concept is, of course, correct. It is difficult for me to keep harsh judgments of him at bay. I have not read many personal letters from the 1920s. He may have been using common vernacular. Times were more formal. He had an analytical mind. I wish I could divine more about his feelings.

Herman's lyrical description of the western landscape fueled Mother's growing obsession with the West. She was already studying and imitating Indian lore. Patiently she strung colorful beads, imitating Indian bracelets, rings, and necklaces that she saw at the museum. Perched on her bench below the fan-shaped window with a view of the forested hills surrounding the house, she devoured books about the west. For a school project she researched the Louisiana Purchase and the resulting westward migration across the United States, laboriously clipping maps and copies of engravings from magazines and newspapers to paste into her reports—1920s' clipart. She read about the Indian wars, precipitated by the influx of rude and ignorant white families. She read about the great Indian chiefs, Sitting Bull and Chief Joseph. She also studied the history of the Union Pacific and Santa Fe railroads, all the while wishing she could be on one of those locomotives. As she read more history of the American West, she came to the conclusion—unusual for that time—that the American

America, here we come!

Indian had gotten a bum deal. She longed to see the wildness that her father described. She could feel the wind against her face and her hair flying as she imagined herself a young Indian scout galloping bareback across the prairie in search of buffalo for his tribe. Squaw, my mother? Not hardly. She identified with the males who had all the fun and adventure, not the women, who as far as she could tell, were little more than indentured servants.

The December 1927 issue of *The Roosevelt Bugle* headlined Mother's fiction story about camping. Her work covered the entire three-column front page. The story illustrates her enchantment with the woods. She spins a tale about a group of boys on a camping trip gone awry. This piece is one of the few creative efforts I found among her papers that was absolutely free of romanticized passion. An excerpt of the dialogue she created for the boys displays great promise:

> Rob woke up in the middle of a nice thunderstorm and saw something white go by. He felt his bones stiffening.
> "Boys," he called. "Boys, wake up," he called again with a trembling voice.
> "What's up?" demanded a sleepy voice.
> "Are you afraid of the storm?" asked Will.
> "No, I saw something white go by."
> "Oh! Ooooo!" Splash!
> "Oh, what was that!" cried Will, rushing outside. "Get your torches, boys, something seems wrong."
> After searching around for a few minutes, Rob flashed his torch on the lake. "Oh, look, Will, is there not something moving there?" he said, pointing his finger towards the lake.
> "Yes, something is moving. Come on and fish it out." announced Will.
> Everybody was at the lake in a few seconds. Rob splashed into the lake and a minute later, he cried to those on shore, "It's Harry."

My mother viewed the adolescence of the United States through a lens of romanticism, which was, and still is, a common perspective. However, unlike her father, she recognized the taking of American soil from those who were here before for the European invasion. She grieved for the underdog. Long before the social unrest of the 1960s, which in turn lead to the 1973 uprising at Pine Ridge, South Dakota—an event that ultimately rewrote American history—my mother recognized America's injustice to Native Americans.

Also my mother, I think, worried that the west would be tamed before she could experience its rich mystery. The pull of the west was as visceral for her as the universal drive for reproduction.

Adolph, Yry, Herman & Norah - 1929

Part III: An ill wind in the air

As novelist, Colum McCann, says: *"Who owns history? Who has a right to tell it? What about the smaller, more anonymous moments? Aren't they the glue of history? What about the little guy?"* My mother will always own her own history. As all of us do, she played a role in the larger history of the events of her time.

~~~

My mother and grandmother both looked forward to the daily mail. Picking through the stack of paper that landed on the floor in front of the door twice a day, they weeded out the bills and advertisements, searching for the pale blue onion-skin envelopes with dark blue and red flags marching around the edges. These had flown across the ocean from relatives scattered about Germany, England, and South America. Norah's parents and sisters were living in Rio de Janeiro. Like Herman, Grandfather Dillon's business was also international. What business? That is another mystery. I remember only shadows of the grisly tales Mother told about atrocities the Dillon family endured in Brazil. But that would be another story for another time.

It is enough to recognize that Grandfather Alfred Dillon was a positive, though distant, mentor as my mother negotiated puberty. He encouraged Mother's writing with the kindness and eagerness of a man hungry for family ties. Besides piano and voice lessons, Mom practiced drawing, painting, and photography. She tried to enclose some small personal creation or at least a photograph with each letter to her grandfather. He reciprocated with stamps for her philatelic collection. As his wife grew increasingly frail, Alfred took on all the correspondence, careful to include his wife's good wishes at the end of each missive. Mother described her grandfather as having "a thin face and wild red hair. His Irish temper matched his hair, but if left alone after an outburst, he always calmed down." In sepia photos I found of him in his later years, he looks like a thin Colonel Sanders.

None of the Dillon clan settled in one place for long. Some deep circannual rhythm kept them all tracing elusive dreams or looking for excitement in new places. Norah's brother traveled frequently and, while they were capable, both Alfred and his wife frequently crossed the ocean between Europe and South America. Alfred's loneliness increased after his wife's death in 1928. He was quick to chastise Mother if her replies were too slow. Each letter from him contained some word of advice about how she must be diligent in her studies. He preached the importance of language fluency and asked repeatedly if she was practicing her French and the little Portuguese he'd tried to teach her—and of course, she was not.

In searching through the correspondence between my mother and her grandfather, I find an alarming harbinger. In October of 1928, Alfred wrote:

> *Tell your dear mother & father & Mr. Levi not to sell the house you live in without letting me know at least one month before hand. My reasons are powerful ones and I can't bear the idea of your poor mother having to give up her home again, it is a sad thing to have to leave your home after spending a fortune on it...*

An ill wind in the air

Please ask your Uncle Levi to let me know what he knows about Messrs. Pain, Webber & Co. 25 Broad Street, New York. Are they capable of putting a loan of 5,000.000 Franks on the N. Y. market successfully?

Mr. Levi is a reference to the dreaded Uncle Adolph. I am as surprised by his reference to "giving up the house" as I am that he would discuss such issues with a financially innocent fifteen-year-old. Then oddly, in a letter written to his daughter Norah in 1929, there is no reference to an impending move. He did, however, complain of the deteriorating political situation in Brazil that was disrupting his business. The lapses in information, I realize, may be due to missing letters. But what was going on?

After a rocky start in the American school system, Mother made electrifying progress. In the fall of 1929 she performed the role of executioner in the Latin play, "Atlanta and the Golden Appás," launching a dramatic inclination that would follow her through life. Since the theatre had played a role in their courtship, her parents supported her endeavor. Countless photos document the importance of this event. Apparently it was filmed. Who did the filming? Probably some well-meaning parent, eager to show off an acquisition and mastery of the latest technology.

In the spring of 1930, at the age of 16, Mother graduated from Central Junior High School of New Rochelle. She was listed in the graduation ceremonies as Iramiris Phyllis Paul. She'd earned good grades, but lacked enthusiasm. The only schoolwork that appealed was, as always, writing. Her short story about a young man undergoing a crisis in faith appeared in the final edition of the class literary journal.

In August, she received a congratulatory letter from Grandpa Dillon. His letter was full of warmth and encouragement—something perhaps lacking in her home life. It is clear from this letter that he was enormously proud of his granddaughter. He included a magazine clipping of a beautiful, elegantly dressed woman, donning a big-brimmed hat, and wrote, "this is how I expect you look now, my dear

Yramiris." Several years later she photographed herself in a similar hat—the resemblance was remarkable.

Norah still appeared stylish and well-coifed, but her body betrayed her. First there had been the thickening mid-section and then came miserable aching joints. She was often indisposed—a common phrase of the day that hinted at anything from psychoses to migraines and hormonal imbalances. Grandfather Dillon complained in nearly all his letters about rheumatism and often questioned Norah about her own sufferings. Clearly she inherited his physical misery. Though only in her 40's, she often appears in photos with a cane, which I do not believe was an affectation.

As Norah's health deteriorated, she and her daughter began knocking heads. Mother grew more headstrong and stubborn with each year. Norah expected her to behave like a "young lady." This, of course, did not include climbing trees and racing through the woods perched on a bicycle. As tall as her mother and well endowed, she looked older than her years. Her classmates were excited about balls and coming out parties. Even Cousin Verena, whom she so adored, reported in letters from Germany how much she loved her dance lessons. But Mom scorned dancing. Hiking through the woods was more her style. Some days she'd tramp through the forest for five miles, dreaming of horses, mountains, and cowboys. Her dreaminess distanced her from classmates, and she found school tedious. Secretly she harbored a suspicion that she was brighter and a deeper thinker than some of her teachers.

Sitting at her small green desk with the drop-down writing leaf, Yry ruminated about the merry-go-round of high school romance. "The little ninnies slobber all over some boy one day, only to find his best friend more attractive the next day." These shallow, mean-spirited girls had no idea what real love was. She, on the other hand, was a survivor. She knew real heartbreak. She had no interest in joining the snotty, conniving little prima donnas.

Instead, she struggled with iambic pentameter and rhyme, catharting her anguish on paper. Theater provided an outlet to lose herself onstage, backstage, and even in script writing. She journaled prolifically and established a life-long habit of scribbling thoughts and quotes on any available scrap of paper which she saved for future reference, providing acerbic commentary to her experiences and a disjointed path through her life.

The American West still consumed her. She developed elaborate fantasies about her future life in the west. When she voiced a desire to live in some isolated place and scratch a living from the empty landscape, her parents chuckled and assured her that such a life would soon grow tiresome. She dreamed on, despite ridicule. Yry played the gypsy one day, the elegant horse rider another day, and when called upon, she posed as the stoic young lady.

In 1931 both Herman and Norah became naturalized citizens of the United States. A storm was brewing around the world and Herman wanted to secure their rights and voices in the democratic process. Citizenship also provided a measure of protection for overseas travel, which was crucial for his work. Yry had entered the country on a US visa which was valid as long as she was in school. With high school graduation looming, she applied for an adjustment of immigration status. The adjustment had to be arranged from outside of the country, so the following year the family vacationed in Montreal. The paperwork took about two weeks, during which time they practiced speaking French while seeing the sites and visiting museums.

Letters continued to arrive from Rio de Janeiro. Alfred's letters to Norah were warm and thoughtful. Despite his own failing health, he never missed an opportunity to inquire about hers. Her doctor had advised her to lose weight. Her father commiserated, "When we've had to sacrifice so much, it is just too cruel to also have to sacrifice good food." He was also interested in Herman's business. Father and son-in-law, both merchants, worried about stormy global politics. The Brazilian government had ceded power to the military in a struggle between the landed-gentry and the growing industrial complex. The military purged high ranking officers who might have held allegiances to the ousted gentry. The country was in turmoil and trade was tenuous. Herman and Norah often slipped $30 into their letters to Grandfather Dillon. Alfred had mused about returning to Germany, but his wife's illness had prevented the journey, and now his health was too frail and his pocketbook too thin. He was stuck in Brazil's turbulence.

Adolph

Yry's fantasy world exploded sometime after 1931. She and her parents were gathered at the breakfast table waiting for Adolph to join them. From behind his newspaper, Papa asked, "Where is Adolph?"

"I have no idea, I haven't seen or heard from him this morning," Norah replied as she tipped the silver teapot toward her empty china cup.

Herman, dropped his right hand to peer around the paper at Yry, "Why don't you run upstairs and knock on Adolph's door. Tell him breakfast is on the table. We're waiting."

Sighing, she reluctantly pushed back her chair and took the stairs two at a time, feeling her mother's pursed-lips and gaze focused on her back. She raised her hand to knock on Adolph's door but hesitated. What was that feeling? It was barely perceptible, unidentifiable, but lodged darkly between her stomach and her heart. Shaking herself out of a stupor, she gently rapped on the door. "Dolphi? We're waiting for you to join us." No answer. Another gentle knock. "Uncle Adolph, Papa's getting grouchy. You know how he is when he gets hungry." Still no answer. "Adolph...? Dolphi? Are you there?"

Cautiously she tested the door. It swung open to reveal a chaotic sitting room with an empty liquor bottle akimbo on the floor, papers scattered as if blown by a fan. Her eyes skimmed the

An ill wind in the air

open bedroom. Soft morning sunlight filtered through sheer curtains to reveal a bed made, but disheveled. The bathroom door was closed. With a knot tightening in her abdomen she tapped gently on the bathroom door. Silence. She knocked again and ever so gently jiggled the doorknob. "Uncle Adolph? Are you in there? Are you okay?" The bathroom door was locked.

With a hasty about-face, she raced to the dining room and breathlessly reported what she had not found.

"Cyril, would you come here?" Norah commanded.

The butler strode into the dining room as Herman rose from the table and said, "Something's wrong upstairs." The two men hurried up the stairs while Norah and Yry stared at each other over the everyday china place settings. Their eyes widened at a crashing noise coming from upstairs, followed by a duet of gasps.

Adolph was fully submerged in the claw-footed tub filled with once-steaming, now tepid, water. Pandemonium ensued: phone calls, strangers in and out of the house, ambulance, police officers, depositions, reporters. The drowning was ruled accidental. Lulled by the hot water, Adolph lost consciousness and slid under water. But Yry never bought that. With the settling of his "estate" came a revelation about Adolph Levi. The man her father had trusted as a brother was an almost-clever charlatan.

After Adolph's death, Herman learned the truth about his partner's financial plan. Adolph had never discussed his financial strategy with Herman, even though their money had been intertwined for many years. Now it came out that Adolph had invested in the rapid growth of the Stock Exchange. He had been so bullish on America's corporate future that he borrowed against company assets to purchase stock. Black Tuesday had wiped out his assets, as well as a huge chunk of Herman's.

The beautiful home in New Rochelle was sacrificed. I wonder what Grandfather Dillon knew of these goings on. The Paul family retreated to a nice flat overlooking the Hudson river in the upper West Side. By all rights, they still lived a comfortable, upper-class life, but the social demotion devastated Norah. Gone were the butler, the gardener, the maid, and the cook. Now the full force of physically managing a household was in her hands. Stress exacerbated her bouts of depression and increased the pain of arthritis that had been creeping into her joints. Shopping and cooking were demeaning activities that wore her out physically and emotionally.

The Big Apple

A concrete jungle replaced Yry's forested knolls and grottos. Skyscrapers hugged the marine fog tighter to the earth, painting the entire cityscape in a depressing monochrome for days on end and coveting the stench of diesel, industry, and garbage. Her father tried to soften the blow by providing riding lessons at a stable in Central Park. Horses symbolized freedom and independence. As she rode the bridle paths of Central Park, she dreamed that she was high in the mountains of the Rockies where the air was pure and the sun always bright. The back of a horse promised safety and protection from all the French soldiers, depraved "gentlemen," or drunken idiots of the world. But she had more to learn about men.

The move coincided with Yry's journey out of adolescence and into adulthood. Having graduated from New Rochelle High, she rarely saw her circle of friends. She was adrift. If she couldn't live in the natural world, she would write about it. Cocooned in her room, she plotted stories and poems. During the summer, she collected her best works—stories that varied from 460 to over 2,000 words and that employed animals as protagonists. These she typed and submitted to the Newspaper Institute of America, Inc., an organization that claimed to launch writing careers for "People Who Want to Write, but can't get started."

Early in August an envelope arrived from the editorial department of the Institute. Breathless, she tore it open to find a two-page, typed critique of her efforts. Editor R.M.S. cut her no slack. First he (or was it a she in disguise?) chastised Yry for not following the submission requirements of "one story of not more than eight thousand words."

> ... Each short story regardless of length presents the same problems of construction and requires the same amount of analysis ... Frankly none of the stories you submit strike me as real commercial possibilities .... They are all too slight to appeal to any magazines I know of that use this sort of story.

The letter goes on to cite several specific stories, claiming that they might get by, "if they did not dwell on such sombre matters as bllod and death. (sic)"

> Most editors of children's magazines avoid these subjects as they would the plague ... the real fault is that the stories are just anecdotes. They are too baldly instructive. They lack simple, strong, plots. What you need is some normal problems of young people that require actual solutions through their own actions. These stories you've submitted have been done over and over.

After that whipping, Yry deserves credit for not laying her pen aside forever. She was indignant at the shallow mentality of the editors and publishers. She believed she was addressing far more real concerns than these ivory-towered executives could conceive of. *The world is a dark and gloomy place*, she thought. *How are kids ever going to make their way through to adulthood if they are presented with only "pretty" stories about good and evil, where good always wins and everyone knows right up front what is evil and what is not?*

~~~

Throughout all subsequent moves, Mother carried a folder containing these stories, with "first serial rights" and word counts marked on the top page, and signed by author, Phyllis Dillon (Nom de plume). And really, the copy editor was cruel, but correct. The stories about animals and little boys are preachy and dark. The moral comes at you like a pile driver. That folder corroborated some of the stories she told me on one of our vacations together.

In 1984, after a day of hiking to the vanishing glaciers at Glacier National Park, we were celebrating our adventure over dinner at Many Glaciers Hotel. I asked Mother what she did after high school.

"I tried a bunch of things," Mom admitted. "First there was journalism. I'd always done well in writing and had been editor of the newspaper in high school, so this seemed like a shoo-in. But that Lindbergh affair did it for me." She took a sip from her martini.

"What do you mean, Mom?"

"Ach, that spoiled little rich boy was nothing but a racist. He painted himself to be a grand hero and wanted the government's help in finding his son, then his son's abductor. There was something fishy about that whole abduction thing. Bruno Hauptmann was convicted by the press, not by the evidence."

"Who was Bruno Hauptmann?"

"He's the poor sucker who was executed based on circumstantial evidence. He was an uneducated guy who'd fled a miserably poor life in Germany. He'd snuck into the states illegally after being convicted in Germany of thefts and burglaries, but lots of people had to steal to survive in Germany in those days."

The mop-haired young waiter with the proud beginnings of a whispy mustache and goatee stepped up to the table with a pair of spinach salads. His name tag said he was from North Carolina, and I wondered what he thought of those massive granite peaks that guarded the lake below the hotel.

Mom, smiling at the thick chunks of blue cheese on her salad, continued, "Hauptmann found work as a carpenter in the States,

An ill wind in the air

got married and was living a quiet life in the Bronx." She massaged the dressing into the spinach as she spoke. "Someone reported him to the police and the jig was up. An illegal alien—a German at that—he was an easy target for the fear and pandemonium the press had been stirring up for months. The headlines kept the fire hot—ransom notes and instructions copied word-for-word right there in the paper. Maybe even the kidnappers were being scammed." She stabbed another forkful of lettuce.

"Yabutt, who turned him in?"

"Somehow his car was associated with the ransom money. Then a couple of dubious witnesses said they saw him on Lindbergh property. I think he was framed. The police found a bunch of money in his garage. He said it belonged to a friend whose stuff he was storing. He didn't even know there was money in there."

"So what did all this have to do with journalism? What do you mean the press convicted him?"

"The papers were filled with sensationalized reports. Those papers became a tool for whoever abducted the kid. Now, when that happens, how in the world can you report impartially? It was yellow journalism at its worst, all fanned by a man with too much money and a Texas-sized ego." She shoved a forkful of greens into her mouth, munched a bit, then continued.

"Then that man had the audacity to declare that Jewish Americans were war agitators! His anti-Semitism and anti-communism were the seeds of the McCarthy era persecutions that followed."

"So, ah, what other careers did you try?" I asked, recognizing a rant brewing and eager to move the story forward.

"I'd always loved the theatre, so I enrolled in drama classes. But it didn't take long to recognize that a requisite roll in the sheets had to precede the best roles. That was not for me."

Children's books were selling like hotcakes, so I thought maybe I could sell some stories to youth magazines and children's book publishers."

Finished with my salad, I absent-mindedly traced designs in the remnants of dressing in the bottom of my plate. This sounded so *Mother*. That last comment reminded me of the times as a kid I'd been downtown with her and she'd hustle around a street corner, grumbling about the lecherous old men ogling her bust or her legs. Always so dramatic, so certain she was the center of the world. At this time I'd heard only vague allusions to her experience with the French soldier. Even as a young woman accompanying my mother on a sightseeing adventure, I considered her reactions overly dramatic.

She continued the narrative. "Then I went back to writing. Her eyebrows greeted each other like a pair of caterpillars as she rumbled about writing literature when all the publishers wanted were heroic fantasies. This revelation predated my discovery of her packet of failed submissions.

Our young waiter cleared our salad plates and a slightly older waitress, hailing from Michigan, arrived with the bottle of wine we'd ordered. Dinner was on its way, she assured us, as she filled our wine glasses.

I looked at Mom quizzically, afraid to interrupt this unusual information dump by debating the merits of children's literary needs.

"My fatheh wanted me to come work for him at the office. I kept putting him off. I really had no interest in his business."

The conversation was interrupted when dinner arrived. After which plans for the next day's adventures took over.

~~~

Yry was rootless in the city. Her strolls through Central Park and visits to the zoo were no replacement for woods she'd so enjoyed in New Rochelle. Her tomboy tendencies gave way to new adventures: museums, galleries, off Broadway theatre, concerts, clubs. With her camera and notebook as companions, she walked about the city looking for interesting angles. Her friend Ellen sometimes came to the city to join her for a little shopping spree. They'd race home with their purchases and experiment with new hair styles and makeup tricks. Black and white portraits show them practicing both serious and sensuous gazes. Ellen resembled actress Helen Bonham Carter. The girls frequented night clubs and nice restaurants in the city. Yry looks stunning in a photo snapped atop the Barbizon on the Upper East Side—a hotel with strict dress codes for young professional women. They were two lovely girls looking for fun, excitement, and a future amidst the beat of the big city. On weekends they sometimes escaped with several male friends to the countryside in a beautiful Chrysler. These were interesting diversions, but Yry found the young men vacuous and transparent. She longed for a relationship with more substance.

Even as she crafted a new existence in the city, depression lurked around the edges. Each time she stepped into the hell pot of summer heat or dirt encrusted snow and smog of winter, Yry cursed Adolph anew.

Hoping to ground his rebellious daughter in a useful occupation, Herman set her up with her own desk at the office. Here, he was convinced, she could put her literary skills to work proofing and typing letters, and she could file documents and make ledger entries. Yry, however, stared into the dark tunnel of a future, locked into the tarry minutia of clerical work. Even if she pushed her way up in the firm, business was cold work, lacking humanity. While her father spent hours lost in professional journals and trade magazines, she couldn't get past the drab covers, much less study the numbers and strategies. It was reassuring to have some sort of employment to fall back on, but her hatred for the business grew along with feelings of suffocation in the city.

"You're trying to turn me into the son you never had!" she screeched one particularly trying afternoon in the hot, stuffy office.

Her father was hurt and angered by her immaturity. Perhaps her mother's Dillon genes imprinted her with an itchy foot and dissatisfaction. Or maybe Herman's colorful tales of frequent and exotic travels created the boiling magma that compelled her mind to drift outdoors, to mountains, trees, birds, flowers, and places she'd heard of and read about but never seen. The state of Montana took on epic visions in her imagination: Montana, the state with the fewest people per square mile. She craved the state's stupendous open sky, the wild mountains, and vast emptiness. And horses. Those mystical beings whose dark, bottomless eyes could look right into a young woman's heart.

Norah convinced Herman to fund more riding lessons at the Central Park stable. She thought perhaps more time with horses would pull Yry out from under the blanket of depression. Yry rode the bridle paths of Central Park and dreamed that she was high in the mountains of the Rockies where the air was pure and the sun always bright.

The riding instructor

At the stables, Heinrich, the riding instructor, looked forward to Yry's visits. He fussed over her and helped her saddle and mount her horse. Heinrich was in his 40's—tall, lean, with dark, wavy hair, peppered with gray at the edges. His blue eyes danced when he spoke to Yry with his thick Austrian accent. Soon she was anticipating Heinrich as much as she was looking forward to her rides. The story of his life dribbled out a bit at a time. His parents had been poor and so, at an early age, full of enthusiasm and patriotism he had enlisted in the Army. He alluded to the trenches of WWI without really talking about them. She sensed a familiar deep misery. He didn't need to spell it out, she understood his pain; they were kindred spirits. After four years of mud, hunger, blood, gore, and loss, his ideals about life, love, religion, and patriotism had been sucked out and replaced by callous pragmatism.

An ill wind in the air

Yry, her heart still smarting from that long-ago first love of Philip, and the disappointment of failing to establish her place in the world, was drawn to Heinrich's mystique. He was interested in all she had to offer, especially her stunning figure and dramatic looks. The more attention he paid her, the more appealing he seemed. His worldly experience and hardened view of politics swept her off her boot heels. An aura of elusiveness and danger lured Yry like the scent of warm horseflesh lures young girls. After several months of skillful courting, he invited her to dinner at his apartment on 77th Street.

She strode onto this stage with passion and confidence. Danger and rebellion boiled beneath the surface. Here, at last, was a man who loved her unconditionally. In his arms, she was all woman. The impulsive child was replaced by a wise and capable adult. No longer did she worry about where she was headed in life. She was in love! He became her everything. She showered him with attention, understanding, and sexual gratification. Her love would pierce his sore heart and heal the wounds in it. She would rebuild his lost faith and restore everything that was fine and noble about him. The whole world would be a better place for their divine love.

Herman was increasingly concerned about his impetuous and vulnerable daughter. He wasn't completely aware of her liaisons with Heinrich, but he was growing impatient about her lack of direction. She spent more and more time away from home, and that time was unaccounted for. Her work at the office was passable, but her attitude was aloof and disinterested. And there were no fine eligible young men on the horizon. Herman and Yry danced around each other. Arguments about her future erupted with the least provocation. In a fit of frustration she moved out of the house and rented a room on 70th street, conveniently close to Heinrich's place. Herman exploded—and disinherited her.

Fine, she thought, *I don't need or want his damned money anyway!* She earned rent money by caring for a wealthy elderly woman to whom

Heinrich had introduced her. She shopped, cooked, and cleaned for this woman and walked her dog.

She and Heinrich slipped into a routine: He bought the fixings for dinner and she cooked at his flat. At first it seemed new and wonderful and grown up. But cracks emerged in utopia. She considered herself Heinrich's equal, but he merely humored her long enough to get his meals cooked and his back rubbed. His cauterized heart was not softening.

One evening she tuned his radio to her favorite station so she could listen to the next segment of a serialized story while she prepared the meal. He promptly switched the station to the evening news without consulting her. Her jaw clamped around adrenaline. She served dinner with trembling hands.

He ignored her attempts to create a romantic atmosphere for their evening meals. He spurned her romantic advances. Sex had to be on his terms only. If she approached him, he turned his back and accused her of being a slut. So much for being a grown-up woman in control of her sexuality. She had disobeyed her father and struck out on her own, yet she was being patronized and treated like a child, or worse—a servant, by the man who supposedly loved her.

This was not going as she had envisioned, but she reminded herself that life needed its downs along with its ups and she was determined to ride out the difficulties. Then one day the sky fell in. Heinrich characteristically tuned the radio to world news. She stomped over to the radio and tuned it back to her Sherlock Homes mystery. "I was listening to that program! Why don't you just read your old newspaper?"

"Vell, little lady, you may az vell find yourself some udder damnt place to lizen to your trash. You've vorn out your velcome heea!" The argument spun out of control until Heinrich revealed that he was engaged to be married and the wedding date was fast approaching.

Yry stumbled out of the apartment, gasping for air. For hours she marched through the city streets and into Central Park, trying to absorb a new reality. During the following days her mind ground on her soap opera life. She belched the bile of ravaged pride. Her appetite waned. Nights were a torment of twisted sheets. She purged her pain onto pages and pages of poems and laments.

She couldn't give up horse therapy despite the ever present worry of seeing him at the stables. She avoided Heinrich for two months. Then, one afternoon several weeks after the wedding, he cornered her in the tack room. He pleaded with her to hear him out. The marriage was awful, he avowed. He really hadn't married for love, but only to legitimize his residency in America. Could he see her again just to talk?

What? She wondered bitterly, *was the new bride failing to put out?* Wriggling free of his clutching arms, she retorted, "Never!" and escaped the stables, blood thudding in her ears.

Back at her apartment, she contemplated this new twist. Again, she walked to settle her nerves. Long after the sun set, arguments raged in her head. *If Heinrich didn't love his wife, what rights did the wife have, after all? If the wife was incapable of satisfying him, Yry most certainly could. Did that fact not absolve the wife's claim to him? His predicament before the marriage had probably been the cause of his harsh treatment of her earlier. There was still hope for saving his tortured soul!*

Even after her vigorous walk, she paced the floor long into the night. The following day she returned to the stables, light-headed from lack of sleep. When she spotted Heinrich engaged in his daily routine she felt like she'd returned home. Nothing mattered really, except this poor man's tortured soul. And so began the secret meetings.

Heinrich's selfishness resumed. They carefully planned secret liaisons. He stood her up frequently. Generally, there was some semi-plausible excuse, but often he seemed to simply have forgotten. Sequestered in an affair, most of her friendships had lapsed. Even Ellen spent most of her time with her own fiancé or his family. But one night, in desperation, Yry reached out to her best friend with a late night phone call.

"Yry, it's so good to hear from you! It's been ages since we've talked."

"Oh Ellen. What a mess. I don't know what I'm going to do."

"What's wrong, Yry? I thought you were so much happier now, living on your own and all."

"You'd think, wouldn't you? But, well ..." she sniffled.

"What? What's going on?" Tears from Yry were alarming.

"It's Heinrich again. Damn him!"

"Heinrich?! Oh Yry, I thought you'd kissed him off for good. What did he do now? You're not ... ah ... no, you couldn't be ... ?"

"He's gone! He left for Europe without even saying goodbye!" she wailed. "I am so lonely, Ellen. I've been so foolish."

"Wait a minute, Yry. Didn't he marry some other woman?"

Yry sobbed now. "YES! He did." She hiccupped, then more tumbled out. "But he just kept coming around at the stable and being helpful and trying to apologize."

She could hear Ellen lighting up a cigarette on the other end. "Then about two months ago, he cornered me in the tack room. He was so contrite. He was all choked up and his eyes were wet. There was some problem with his visa, he said, and he thought this marriage would prevent being deported. He was deathly worried about having to go back to Austria and being conscripted back into the army again."

"Doesn't that sound kind of fishy?" Ellen ventured, exhaling a lungful of smoke.

"Oh, I don't know. Maybe? But maybe not. Everything is so messed up these days, and ... anyway, he said the marriage was a huge mistake. He's miserable. I felt so bad for him, Ellen. He's so lonely, just like I am." She paused as a siren wailed outside. "And when he put his arms around me, it just felt so ... so right."

"But?" Ellen coaxed gently.

"Well, he came over here a couple of times ... and, well ... and now he's gone! Dammit. He just left, without a boo, hi, or howdy. How could he *do* that to me?" She blew her nose.

"Did he get deported or something?" Ellen asked almost hopefully.

"No, I doubt that. The bitch went with him. I think he was planning it all along. I guess all he ever wanted from me was sex. I can't believe I *fell* for that."

"Oh Yry, I'm so sorry," Ellen whispered. "Don't be so hard on yourself. Sometimes our hearts overrule our minds. And you believed in him because you're such an honest person that you can't even conceive of how conniving some people are. I'm just so sorry you've had to go through all this."

Throughout the upheavals between Yry and her father, Norah maintained contact with her daughter. Norah's health wavered between bouts of depression and increasing pain. Sometimes she'd call Yry and plead with her to come home, but Yry resisted. Occasionally, however, she stopped by her parents' flat with a few bags of groceries when she knew her father was away. While doing loads of laundry, she and her mother chatted, cautiously skirting the topic of Herman.

Yry took up sewing, thinking perhaps of breaking into dressmaking and fashion design. Most of her clothes were hand sewn, even her coats and hats. And she continued to fill notebooks with poems and stories in which she was the protagonist with a made-up name. She read books from a broad assortment of topics and authors, copying noteworthy quotations into her notebooks.

The years crawled by. She had a handful of new friends now, but most were married with husbands and children. Playing with her friends' kids and sewing charming outfits for them stirred a soup of desire for a family of her own.

Animosity between her and her father gradually dissipated. She began arriving in the afternoon and staying into the evening, cooking dinner for her parents. Herman's frequent travel gave the women time to comfort each other.

Meanwhile, letters from both English and German cousins spoke of difficult times: political unrest, long lines to buy essentials, exponential inflation, and rhetoric about Aryan superiority. Yry spent Independence Day in 1935 seeing her father off on a ship that would take him to Amsterdam for a visit with his brother. Herman hoped to convince Willy to immigrate to America.

Several months later Herman returned from Europe with a heavy heart. Staring vacantly out the window at the Hudson River as it pushed toward the Atlantic bearing the wealth of a nation, he spoke of the poverty, the turmoil, the broken spirits of his countrymen. Two years into his Chancellorship, Hitler was replacing the fledgling German Democracy with his vision of the *Deutsches Reich* which centralized power not just with his party, the National Socialist German Workers' Party, but with Hitler himself as the grand leader of the "new power in the world." Stirring up nationalism by casting liberals, revolutionaries, and Jews as the reason for the country's woes, anti-Semitism had swept the country into a maelstrom of hate crimes and sanctioned gangs that terrorized Jews and outsiders. In violation of the Treaty of Versailles, Hitler was rebuilding a military force and stripping wide swaths of people, mostly Jews, of their citizenship. Germans were turning on one another like cocks in a pen, looking for any chance to rat out a neighbor, or even sometimes a family member, for suspicious activity—and the most mundane behavior could look suspicious given the right spin. The press delivered Hitler's message inside and outside of the country. Journalists and jurists alike lost their jobs and their livelihoods if they failed to follow the party line.

Despite all that was happening, Herman's brother was still firmly attached to German soil. Willy was adamant that he and Nelly could not and would not leave her aging parents to weather the chaos alone.

A shocking revelation

On that April day in 1991 when I sat beside my mother's bed, scratching the walls inside my empty head to keep the conversation going, I asked that dreadfully trite question, "Mom, is there anything you wish you could do over again, but differently?"

At that time, I considered myself unflappable. There was nothing my mother could say that would shock me. Till she responded.

"Well, not really, I don't think. You know I loved having you kids." (I'd heard this before and disbelieved it then as I did now.) "But I guess if I could do anything I wanted, I'd have six or seven children... each with a different man ... each with a different nationality."

It's a miracle my jaw didn't crack the linoleum. Then we laughed. What else could we do?

But I would ponder that nugget in the years to come. And when I found, in her stacks of hand-written stories, one in which the narrator falls in love with a Chinese man, I remembered her surprisingly studious attempt to learn Chinese after the death of my stepfather. At the time, she explained this away as something she'd always wanted to do. And since her nemesis, President Nixon, had thawed Chinese-American ice in 1972 in his historic meeting with Chairman Mao Zedong, which opened the door for American tourism in China, she thought it possible that finally she'd be able to swing a long overdue visit to that fascinating country.

She'd realized two of her six or seven children with different fathers. Maybe she'd come closer than I ever realized to the other four or five. The browned pages of her story take on a breath of reality forming the next wild chapter in her life.

~~~

In 1939 New York City city buzzed in anticipation of the World's Fair which was scheduled to open at the end of April. Begun in 1936, a massive construction project at Flushing Meadow transformed a former dump into a park and fairground with exhibitions, pavilions, statues, fountains, and public art. A new bridge and a subway line, the IND World's Fair Line, were installed to serve the fair. The project produced precious employment to a city still reeling from the Stock Market crash ten years earlier. Against the backdrop of growing unease about the Nazi threat overseas, the World's Fair was a distraction from war talk. Boasting participation from over 60 countries, the New York World's Fair presented an optimistic vision of "The World of Tomorrow." Countries like Poland and Czechoslovakia, who were under the thumb of the Axis powers, ran their pavilions with a special nationalistic pride. The only major world power that did not participate was Germany, citing budget pressures. The USSR Pavilion, featuring the wildly controversial statue, Joe the Worker, was dismantled after the first season when the USSR signed the non-aggression pact with Hitler and went on to invade Poland, and then Finland.

Yry was again working at F.H. Paul & Stein Bros, where she was always warmly welcomed, even if she did find the work unbearably boring.

Still smarting from Heinrich's infidelity, Yry strengthened her mask of unapproachability. Yet, she kept crossing the path of a young accountant called Yuan Chang. He never failed to compliment her in some small way. She was used to ignoring male attention.

"That hair style is very becoming, Yry," he would half whisper with a winning smile. Or "What a beautiful dress!" Often it was a dress she'd designed and sewn for herself, which doubled the compliment. She began to look forward to his gaze from across the room. He seemed like such a decent man, so serious, so different from Heinrich. She found his sincere attentions soothing.

Yuan asked her to join him for dinner. She demurred several times, but one warm spring morning she arrived at work flushed and enervated from a brisk walk to the office. The air was particularly fragrant, full of the portentous richness of blossoms on the threshold of bursting open. She felt so peaceful and at ease that she shocked herself and Yuan by finally accepting his dinner invitation. The rest of the day jerked by slowly. She argued with herself repeatedly about the fine mess she'd gotten herself into. With trepidation she watched the clock ticking nearer to what she knew would be an uncomfortable evening.

To her surprise the evening sped by. Yuan dazzled the dinner conversation with tales of his family, his life, the countries he'd seen, his work. He spoke about life in China and about his parents who had saved up their money so that he could go to school and have a solid profession. Dinner was followed by shared lunches and more dinners out. He was so easy to talk to, so kind, so interested in *her!* In his quiet, non-threatening manner he drew Yry out of herself in a way no one had before. He had studied poetry and religion, history and politics. They talked about philosophy, about love and loyalty and war and peace. No topic was too large or too deep to discuss. He took her to Chinese restaurants and explained how the food differed from his mother's delicious home-cooked meals. On weekends they visited the World's Fair. She fell madly and passionately in love with Yuan.

Yry had met her soul mate, she was sure of it. One enormous problem lay in their path. As proud and deliriously happy as she was in this new relationship, she could not share her joy with her parents. Yuan had two strikes against him. He was employed by the company and he was Chinese. There was another wrinkle. They both wanted children. But neither of them was willing to bring children into a world that would be filled with ostracism and loneliness.

Yuan knew intimately how the world treated mixed marriages and the children born thereof. His older sister had made the fatal mistake of falling in love with a wealthy French businessman. Against her parents' wishes she had married him. She was cast out of the family. In France, her husband and later even her child were ostracized for their relationship to a "chink." Eventually the marriage fell apart, leaving his sister Mai Ling dependent upon meager support checks from the

French father of her child. But the father's situation was grim also. His reputation among piers and business colleagues had been ruined. He lost his job and began living in the bottle. He died, dirty and alone on a deserted street in Paris. The support checks ended, leaving Mai Ling and her child destitute. Yry learned that Yuan was doing everything he could to help his sister, but her life and the life of her child would forever be a struggle.

What an ironic and bitter twist. To Yry it seemed that there was no loftier goal than to be the wife of the man you loved and to bear and raise his children and stand at his side throughout life. That could never happen with Yuan.

Yry buried herself in Chinese lore and history. Yuan tried to teach her to speak Chinese, which she found more difficult than Portuguese and French put together. She found much to admire in his peaceful religion. It answered many of the questions that had troubled her about Christianity.

So the romance continued. Again, Yry was involved with a man her father would disapprove of. Again, she was keeping her whereabouts secret. Again, the great joy of her life had to be kept locked away from the prying eyes of the world.

And again, reality burst Yry's dreamy bubble. Many years earlier Yuan's parents had arranged for his marriage to a Chinese girl as was the Chinese custom. Now they called him home to fulfill the family pledge. His education in the states was complete, he'd gained valuable experience in American commerce. It was time for his return and time for his marriage.

Despite mutual heartbreak, there was no escaping this fate. If Yuan disobeyed his father, the entire family, generations past, and generations into the future, would lose face. Through her study of the culture even rebellious Yry understood why he must go. But that did not make the parting any less difficult. They both wept in despair.

~~~

An ill wind in the air

From my perspective, though, I wonder about this Yuan. He had to know about his marital destiny. It seems rather loutish for him to lure an American woman into romance if he knew he could never formalize a relationship with her. Ah, well, love rarely follows a reasonable path.

A world in turmoil

All that happy international peace and prosperity bugled from the New York World's Fair was a sham. Hidden behind the curtain of global camaraderie, Hitler and his merry pranksters were fully committed to world dominance. The budget issues that prevented Germany from participating in the World's Fair were real and devastating to Germany's neighbors. Peace was not the objective of a Nazi regime that glorified war and blamed all German social ills upon conniving Jews, or power hungry Brits and French. The very pacifism promoted by western powers leading up to and during the World's Fair served Hitler well by allowing him to roll over, either by tanks or cunning manipulation, parts of Poland, Hungary, Austria, Czechoslovakia. He had aligned himself with Spain and Italy, whose rulers he easily outmaneuvered. It even appeared that the diametrically opposed regimes of Nazi and Communist would join forces with the signing of the Nazi-Soviet Pact. Less than six months after the New York World's Fair opened, the second European war had commenced when Great Britain and France declared war on Germany.

America still kept her head down, though. This was a European war, far away, concerning borders and philosophies that meant little to the average American on the street. The gory realities of WWI were still fresh. There was no reason to send America's boys into another hell.

However, another war between Great Britain and Germany spelled catastrophe for the Paul family. By 1940, Germany had unleashed The Blitz on prominent British cities. School children were evacuated from high-target cities. Thousands of civilians died, and air raids destroyed hundreds of homes. Food was rationed. It was hard times for Norah's relatives who still lived in Britain.

My Life With an Enigma

Worse was the communication blackout from Germany. The letter trail dries up between 1939 and late 1945. Brilliantly, sadistically, Hitler profited from his imprisoned labor force of Jews and displaced Poles and Czechs. By 1940, Hitler had gobbled up France. Britain was alone in its war against the *Herrenvolk*, the master race. The Blitz on England reached a frenzy in 1941, but the British Royal Air Force fought with heroic bravery and technological advances. Relenting on the eastern front, Hitler turned his attention backwards and with vicious disregard for the previously signed pact, he turned on his reluctant ally, the Soviet Union. All hell broke loose when, on December 7, 1941, Japan, trying to finagle its own turf in the Pacific, turned on the United States in the fateful bombing of Pearl Harbor, which propelled the US full-bore into the war.

His letters and cables to family in Germany unanswered, Herman agonized over the grim news that blackened the front pages of the papers and blared from stentorian radio broadcasts. On the home front, Herman and Norah were further vexed by an intransigent daughter who seemed always to leap to the left when a right turn made sense, a daughter who had again descended into depression, locking herself in her room and mooning over another lost love.

~~~

It seems that all I touch goes awry
All I desire to do fades with the setting sun.
Realization of my dreams passes me by
Deeds I start to do are left undone."
Patricia Dillon, 1942

As I consider my mother from this side of a new century, I am plagued by doubts. Her writings reveal a headstrong, analytic, young woman with above average intelligence and an ability to adapt to changing circumstances. So why did she flounder so miserably in her early to mid-twenties? Sure, the western world did not nurture women to be strong, independent, and capable beings, able to manage themselves, a company, or a country. My mother was raised in a sheltered environment that presupposed her union with a fitting male who would cement her place in society and provide all her creature comforts. But she was not that woman. She was opinionated, argumentative, and unwilling or unable to compromise.

There are countless examples of other women of her generation who straddled continents, who overcame prejudice, hardship, and ostracism, and who rose above negative prospects to become respected leaders in their fields. Take Bella Kaufman, for example, whose youth mimicked Yry's in many ways. She emigrated from Russia to America at the age of twelve, learned English, became a high school teacher and later, a New York Times bestselling author.

Austrian born Hedy Lamarr was, besides being a talented actress, a self-educated inventor who helped develop a secret communications system that is credited with foiling the Nazi war machine.

Rachel Carson was nearly the same age as Yry, yet she found it within herself to buck sexism in the scientific community and to become an aquatic biologist for the US Bureau of Fisheries, later becoming a renowned and prize-winning author.

Is it possible that my mother shared with me an inherently debilitating flaw? Did she lack an imagination? So she wrote poems and stories—but none of what remain appear to contain much originality. They are blatant coppings of her own story, told and retold with different character names and plots that tread the same well-worn path. Was she, like I was as a young woman, incapable of imagining that she could successfully compete in that wide world of male dominance? Was she paralyzed by her father's apparent wealth and wisdom? I can't account for my mother's rudderless position at the age of 27 in any other way. She was not a lazy woman. But she was stubborn as all hell and impetuous to boot—traits she constantly warned me to overcome.

~~~

Herman suggested college, work at some other office, work at a bookstore. His suggestions failed to move her. Worse, his prodding infuriated her and devolved into painful arguments. Norah tried to interest her in trips to the art museum or social clubs where she could meet new friends and get out of the house more. But stubbornly she hibernated in her room, hemorrhaging on paper. It was time for a complete change of scenery. Norah wrote to a friend whose husband had invested in a cattle ranch in Wyoming. With America fully involved in the war, able bodied young men were sucked out of the workforce and into the armed services. Claire agreed to take Yry in and give her a taste of Wyoming. There was plenty of work waiting for her.

Yry's demeanor transformed the instant she heard about the proposal. At last she was to have a real adventure! At last she could see for herself the wonders she'd read about in so many books, the landscapes her father had written about on his trips across the country.

The tandem celebration of Herman's birthday and Yry's great adventure called for an exquisite meal at the Gotham Restaurant. As usual, the Maître d' greeted them warmly, addressing each by name and seating them at a special table. Nick was an institution; a Gotham evening was incomplete without Nick's merry greeting. He ushered them to a table and suggested the perfect celebratory Champagne.

Part IV: Wyoming, August 1942

Eyes focused forward, she scrambled up the narrow iron stairs, eager to stake out a seat by the window. Squeezing down the aisle with her purse and several canvas bags sprouting from her arms like pigeons on a power line, a pair of vacant seats in the middle of the car beckoned. She released her burden on the aisle seat—a hopeful foil to company—and slid quickly into the window seat. Her parents, standing side by side on the platform, not quite touching, her mother's body tilting slightly toward her cane, looked already lonely and bewildered. Dropping the window, Yry stuck her head out.

"...boooord!" bellowed the conductor, a final warning an instant before the door slammed shut and a violent hiss announced brakes releasing. The train jolted to life. She waved and blew kisses out the window.

"Write as soon as you get there, Yry!" Her father's shout was barely audible over the clanking of metal.

"I will! I promise. Bye Mother, bye Papa!" Her parents began to shrink as the horizon widened to embrace New York City's skyline. When they were too small to discern, she settled into her seat and began to pick through her flock of parcels, arranging and rearranging them. Satisfied that she hadn't forgotten anything, she sat back and let her head rest on the seat back. A deep breath, eyes closed briefly, and a smile playing at the corners of her mouth—*Free! I'm free at last!*

The dizzying pace of preparations had been exhausting. Papa's suggestion that she live on a ranch in Wyoming for the summer had so shocked Yry that she had reined in her excitement, afraid some last-minute detail or change of heart by her father or by her hosts would upend the fantasy. She'd tossed and turned throughout the night, repacking every item in her mind and occasionally dashing out of bed to double-check that she had, in fact, tucked some little necessity into her suitcase.

The train gathered speed, carooming through soot-blackened brick tenements and industrial buildings. Smoothing her skirt across her knees, she pulled a magazine from one of her tote bags. Beginning on page one, she read every headline and every article in *The Western Horseman*, hoping to imprint every detail of the exotic land into her being. She stared at the western tack, so different from the flat saddle and elegant bridles she knew. She whispered the truncated grammar of the articles and letters to the editor, trying to hone a dialect that would always hover slightly out of reach. She stalled over the advertisements, gathering in details about western fashion.

The farther from home the train took her, the more often her eyes glanced up to inspect the passing scenery. For a while the train kept company with a river. Between the Catskills and Albany, the countryside was wild and lonely; the mists of dusk rose to shroud savage vegetation, painting it with a dreamlike unreality. With a thumb holding her place in the magazine and the gathering darkness obscuring the view, she blinked at a Mohican chief with shaved head and topknot of hair and feathers, naked to his loins, and hands gripping a bow and arrow. Her heart jolted, then she grinned at the tricks a tired brain plays.

Her mind went still. Looking across the aisle to the windows on the other side, the sun was a lava-hot glow on the black line

Wyoming, August 1942

between land and twilight. When she turned back to her own window just seconds later, the train had entered the surreal blackness of a storm. Lightening fractured the sky. Mist solidified into sheets slapping the windows. Darkness swallowed all shape and form outside the window. Yry's head relaxed into the seat cushion, her eyelids drooped, and she succumbed to intermittent dozing like the other tired and bored passengers in the car.

After a surprisingly tasty meal served in the dining car by a starched, black-as-the-night waiter with a tight round face and impossibly white eyes and teeth, Yry tipsied to the cubbyhole marked WC, then rocked back to her seat, hoping not to land in some stranger's lap as the train tossed her about. Back in the safety of her window seat she rearranged the canvas totes around herself like wagons circled up for the night. Again her head fell back and her eyes closed. In a half-dream-half-wake cycle, images of the past reeled.

She smiled and her heart bumped at the vision of Philip Cochrane, her first beloved. Oh the passionate love letters they wrote back and forth to each other. But time had diminished Philip's power. Yry's romantic life was not bound by the love of one boy. At 18, she had begun compiling her little black *Book of Lovers* by Iramiris Paul. And indeed, she had filled it with her broken heart. Memory drifted to Heinrich—that scoundrel sure played her for the fool! The clickety clackety rail racket lulled her until the memory she'd worked so hard to banish popped up like an over-wound jack-in-the-box. The memory of that awful breakfast...

I didn't ask enough questions as a child. When we emigrated, why did Papa insist on staying in Germany? Why had he entrusted so much to Adolph? To send his wife and only child across the Atlantic Ocean, along with access to his bank account! I'm not the only gullible person in the family. It was ludicrous, really. Okay, Adolph had connections in New York. He helped us get established. But that man! And I had to call that creep "Uncle" Adolph! Why, he was nothing like dear Uncle Willy or Uncle Philip. They had been so kind and gentle with her during that bewildering time when she first came to Germany. She remembered the doll's bed Uncle Philip had made from scrap wood that he sanded and painted. She would treasure that gift forever.

She woke abruptly at 5:30 to watch the first streaks of light brighten the landscape as it flew by. The land was flat now. In Chicago she changed trains. Miles of flat, open land stretched out like an ocean. A huge bridge spanned the Mississippi River, the signal that she was now officially in the *West*. Iowa was a corn field. The train chugged steadily through miles and miles of open prairie headed ever onward toward the Rockies. While other passengers snoozed through the unending drabness of the scenery, Yry was enraptured by the vastness of it all. As far as the eye could see, endless prairie reached toward an endless blue sky, broken only by the occasional farm or by sporadic puffs of clouds in the sky. She recalled the history of Indians hunting buffalo. Now that she saw the immensity of the land firsthand, she marveled at the courage and resourcefulness of the pioneers in their wagon trains. Little seizures of grief pierced her heart if she allowed her thoughts to drift toward the lost loves of her life, but overall she was buoyed by the realization of a dream coming true.

She recognized her parents' blatant maneuvering, and to be honest, she loved them for it. What better way to get over Yuan than by a new adventure? With her life teetering on the edge of a dark abyss, the unexpected opportunity to live in Wyoming was the door to a new and better life, a lifeline to recover her broken heart and shattered pride.

The train pulled into Lincoln, Nebraska late at night. Yry killed time and stretched her legs by strolling about the station as she waited for her next connection. The eastern horizon was beginning to take shape in the dawn sky when she boarded the next train and located an empty seat by the window. As the train pulled out, she kept her nose pressed to the glass like a dog drinking in the sights from an open car window.

Wyoming, August 1942

Eventually she had to acknowledge the young soldier parked on the seat across the aisle. The sight of his uniform jumbled her feelings. On the one hand, she violently opposed the war. But on the other hand, she recognized that this young man, like so many just like him, probably grasped at the glorious possibilities advertised by clever recruiters. *My God, that sweet baby face barely needs a razor!* She wondered how much he understood about the politics of war. He probably bought into the "duty and honor to country" bit hook, line, and sinker. He smiled shyly at her and fumbled with the ridiculous little cloth cap in his hand.

"Howdy, ma'am."

"Hello," she replied, determined to ignore his loneliness. For self-defense she pulled a copy of *My Life on the Range* from her satchel. Her eyes danced between the text and the window, with quick furtive glances at the fellow beside her.

After about an hour, the young man cleared his throat and leaned her way. "Excuse me, Ma'am, but I'm headed for the dining car for breakfast. Could I bring ya somthing?"

"Oh noooo, thanks ... I have an apple here in my bag, ... but thank you for offering."

He tipped his head and rose to leave, "No problem, ya sure now? How about some juice or coffee?"

"Well, yes, coffee sounds nice. If it wouldn't be any trouble. Thank you."

He smiled broadly and strode off in the direction of the dining car and observation deck.

Half an hour later the young soldier returned, seriously concentrating on not spilling the two sloshing cups of hot coffee. She freed him of one cup and thanked him.

"Where ya headed?" he asked.

She sighed, partly exasperated by his persistence and partly proud of her destination. "Oh, I'm going to Sheridan, Wyoming. I'll be spending the summer cowpunching." Each word clearly enunciated, with the slightest emphasis on the last word. She read the hint of a smile that played over his soft lips as admiration for her worthy mission. "And what about you? Where are you going?"

"I'm headed home to Moorcroft. It's not far from Sherid'n," he pointed out, knowing instinctively that the tiny town of Moorcroft would mean nothing to her. "I get a two-week furlough to visit my famly. Then I ship out for Africa. That'll be pretty different, I reckon."

"Hmm. Ya." She really didn't know what to say. She remembered reading something about the hottest American fighting occurring in the African theater. She was certain that she knew better than he what horrors awaited him. His uniform brought visions of Cousin Hermann to mind. It had been so long since any news had come from Germany. Was it possible that he, too, wore a uniform? Was it possible that one day he might come rifle-to-rifle with this naïve young American?

Yry tried to redirect her thoughts. "What is Moorcroft like?" she asked.

"There's nothin' much there," he admitted. "Lots a cattle, lots a sagebrush, an lots a dust. But my folks got a spread there. I can't wait to taste Ma's bread and some fresh, sweet cream butter. Lord, what we gotta eat at mess is miserable."

The miles slipped by. When dinner was announced, the two shuffled down the narrow, rocking aisle to the dining car where they shared a white-linened table. After dinner Yry excused herself to visit the observation car. The afternoon sun scalded deep shadows into the landscape. The young soldier accompanied her to the observation car. She stifled a sigh.

The train was traveling through his big back yard now. He directed her attention to herds of antelope and a coyote and a few foxes that loped through the dry sage. Occasional farms and ranches blurred by.

"My dad won't have no Herefords on his place." he said, nodding toward a herd of brown and white cattle that huddled in the corner of a fence near the tracks.

"Why is that?"

"Well, they got all that white skin round their eyes an ... uh ... their udders. They're prone to getting sun scald and then ya got all kinds a problems. They get sore eyes an can't nurse their babies. It's a nuisance."

"So what kind of cattle does your fatheh raise?"

"Angus. They're the best. They're strong an healthy an fatten up real nice an you don't have to do any dehorning or anything like at."

"Well, why then, would anyone mess around with the Herefords?" she inquired.

"Some folks think Herefords winter over better and some say they're easier to handle. Pound for pound they're near 'bout the same."

"Hmm. That's interesting. But what about those over there? They look awful scrawny." She was pointing to a string of Guernseys that were ambling nose to tail toward a large well-lit barn.

He lifted an eyebrow and explained that those weren't for eating, those were for milking.

"Oh, I know that," she retorted, "but they still look pretty scrawny." The little smile tugged at the corners of his mouth again.

"Oh, look," he crooned.

"What, where?"

"Oh, shucks, ya missed im. It was a jackalope."

"A WHAT?"

"A jackalope. Haven't ya ever seen one? Why, when a jack rabbit and a antelope, er, get together, they produce a jackalope."

"Nooo! "You're pulling my leg."

"Soldier's honor ... really. They're kinda rare, but they're real neat. They look like a real tall, leggy, jack rabbit with horns on their heads."

Later, he pointed to some rounded hills that rolled by and explained how the lateral ledges decorating the side of the hill had been made by a side-hill gouger. He launched into a serious description of a critter a little larger than a skunk whose legs are longer on one side than the other. The poor critter has no choice but to keep going round and round the mountain ... hence the name, side-hill gouger. He waited expectantly for her reaction.

She briefly considered the young man and decided that the story was so well told, and his enthusiasm was so great, that he deserved the expected response, so she gratified him with a marvelous look of astonishment. Emboldened, he grew animated as he filled the time with stories about wild Indians and warned her to be very careful around the evil redskins. After all, they had absolutely no respect for the delicacy of such a fine lady as she—and they were still prone to hacking off a prized scalp to adorn their belts now and then!

The more she humored him the more avidly he launched into the next story. She decided he was competition for Zane Grey. She peered through the darkening windows till there was nothing left but imagination. In the dark, she was a captive audience. They made their way back to their seats. The soldier then spoke about his family and his boyhood on the family ranch. As they drew closer to his home, he described nearby Devil's Tower and related the legend about some little Indian girls who encountered a bear while playing. They ran away as fast as they could, but the bear was catching up so they leaped onto a rock and prayed to the Great Spirit to save them. The rock began to grow, lifting them to the sky. The angry bear clawed at the stone but couldn't get the little girls who reached the sky and became stars. The soldier's company helped pass the time and his teasing was good experience for her, as she'd soon find herself the object of a great deal more joviality.

In the small hours of morning, the train slowed to a stop at a one-room shack that served as a train station in Moorcoft. A small group of people clustered under a single gas lamp. Her companion stepped off the train and into the embrace of a heavy-set older

Wyoming, August 1942

woman, while a pigtailed child bounced between a tall, thin cowboy and her brother—the soldier. The train had barely stopped before it slowly began to pick up speed again. Alone with her thoughts and her excitement, she was disappointed to find only her face reflected back in the window. The train rocked her back into a dreamy-dozy sleep.

Sheridan

She awoke when the train lurched to yet another stop. There was some commotion but no one in her car paid any attention. Eventually the train chugged back to life and crawled out of the nondescript wide spot along the tracks. A faint glow of blue edged the horizon and a few minutes later, wisps of tangerine streamed across the sky. The landscape had changed again. The train was steadily gaining elevation and the flat lands were punctuated by occasional rim rocks and high plateaus. The closer she got to her destination, the slower the train seemed to move. She was in a fever of anticipation. Oddly it felt like she was coming home.

The train arrived in Sheridan half an hour late. George and Claire Cormack were waiting on the platform outside a tidy, two-story red brick building, early morning light casting a warm glow over the scene. After hearty introductions and greetings, George gathered her bags and led the way to the car. The "CX RANCH" brand tastefully emblazoned on the door of the Ford station wagon sparked a thrill of excitement.

The first stop was for breakfast at the many-gabled Sheridan Inn. Along with a musty smell of age, the hotel was filled with history of the west. A thin layer of dust covered roughly hewn wooden beams in the lobby. Indian woven-wool blankets adorned the walls and lay like throws on large, leather-covered furniture in the lobby. Several large oil paintings of western scenes depicting cowboys and Indians hung on the walls, as well as black-and-white photographs of Buffalo Bill Cody and his Wild West Show, below which was a typed note bragging that the company used to lodge at the Inn when they passed through Sheridan.

Without prompting, the waitress filled three large mugs with black coffee. Yry was startled to discover pork chops and steak on the breakfast menu. Claire ordered a short stack with one egg over easy. Yry asked for toast and jam and a soft-boiled egg. The waitress looked over her notepad and fixed Yry with a hard stare. "We don't do boiled eggs. Scrambled, over easy, over medium, or over hard."

"Over easy will do," stammered Yry.

"That's not enough to keep a bird alive," George boomed before he ordered biscuits and gravy, ham and three eggs over hard for himself. "Yry, you better have some bacon or ham with that measly little ol' egg. We're gonna be putting you to work right off the bat!"

Wide-eyed, she glanced at the waitress who was still staring at her like she came from Mars. "Okay, please add bacon to my order. Thank you."

She sipped the coffee and wondered if the waitress had forgotten something; it tasted like dirty hot water. She gaped as another waitress waddled out of the kitchen; a mound of huge platters of food crawled up her left arm. On one of the plates towered a three-high stack of pancakes the size of flattened basketballs. Clutched in the woman's right hand was a large carafe of syrup. Yry was beginning to feel unsettled.

After breakfast they climbed back into the station wagon and bumped down 25 miles of dirt corduroy to the ranch. Gulping the first of many breaths of dusty Wyoming air, the load of greasy bacon churned in Yry's stomach. Throughout the drive Claire pumped Yry for the latest news from the city. "How was Norah's health? How was Herman's business doing? What was the latest talk about the war? What did they hear from her relatives in Germany? What shows had she seen recently?" Yry fielded the questions as best she could while bile crept upwards with each pothole.

Wyoming, August 1942

At the ranch, Claire ushered her into the house via the backdoor, which was, in fact, the main entrance. They walked through a small washroom with worn linoleum, nearly buried under assorted boots, overshoes, and the ubiquitous boot horn. Coats and hats hung from hooks along the walls, and a deep, metal washbasin stood near the door that opened into a galley kitchen. A bank of windows brightened the north wall of the kitchen. In the living room Yry met Claire's mother, Netti, who rose slowly from a wing backed chair to greet her. The two Cormack children bounced in from somewhere outside and ceremoniously shook her hand. The tour of the house ended when they reached Yry's bedroom at the end of the upstairs hallway.

"You go ahead and freshen up. George will bring your bags up and you can unpack and change into something more comfortable. There are towels on the bed."

Yry gratefully closed the door behind her and collapsed on the bed, holding her rumbling stomach and breathing deeply to control waves of nausea. She was startled out of a deep sleep ten minutes later when George knocked on the door and boomed that she must have brought a small pony in her luggage.

The catnap had settled her stomach and her nerves. She quickly organized her things in the closet and bureau drawers then drifted to the window to gaze at the huge, red-roofed barn and network of empty wood-railed corrals just across the road. South of the corrals lay undulating terrain of tall yellow grass, bushy green shrubs, and cottonwoods through which a thin stream trickled. Directly behind the corrals stood a barren looking mound, covered in sagebrush and dry yellow grass that glinted gold in the morning light. It seemed too quiet. Where were the horses, the cattle, the chickens, the hired hands ... the cars, the traffic?

After a quick sponge bath in the bathroom down the hall, she threw on a shirt-waist dress with red bands of polka-dotted trim and a pair of white sox under sandals. She found Claire in the kitchen. "My, don't you look nice and refreshed," Claire commented. "I think George is outside waiting to show you around."

She ventured into the bright sun and found George in the shade of the house, where a vine of morning glories climbed up trellises of baling wire to the eaves over the kitchen windows. He was roughhousing with his red Chow dog, Chickie. The top button of his long-sleeved khaki shirt was open, revealing a cotton t-shirt and a few sprouts of hair inching out of the neckline. His dusty-kneed, brown canvas pants were belted with a one-inch wide belt and a simple silver buckle. His shirt and pants stretched firmly over an ample waist, and plain, brown boots peeked from under his pant legs. Notably, his tall-crowned, broad-brimmed felt hat bathed his face and ears in shade and added inches to his stature. He had a quick, quirky smile and kind eyes nestled in a web of crow's feet. He showed her the vegetable garden, the barns and corrals and explained that Dallas, Claire's brother, was out bringing in the horses. There were dogs and cats, horses, chickens, pigs all of whom Yry would learn more about in the future. Most of the cattle, of course, were out on summer pasture. The big roundup at the end of next month was when they'd most need her help.

Meanwhile, there were chores to do. George fired up a rickety old pickup with wooden fence slats sprouting from the bed. "Jump in," he commanded. "I'll show you the lay of the land." Now she saw the bunk houses and a guest house nestled in the cottonwoods by the creek. The guest house was closed up for the season and the bunk houses were empty, thanks to the wartime man-drain. He showed her where the milk cows pastured, pointed out the hay meadow and the well. She saw large, black birds clustered in the air and pointed them out. "Ya," George muttered. "We probably lost another damned heifer over there. Dal will tell us when he gets back."

Wyoming, August 1942

Dumbfounded, Yry discovered that George and Claire owned and leased more land than could be traveled in a day! Not all spreads in Johnson County were as elaborate and well maintained as the CX Ranch. George had retired from a lucrative sales position, which was, of course, how Yry's parents had been acquainted with the Cormacks. He was a sharp, well-educated, and curious man whose expertise and diplomacy were recognized by the community. She would learn that he was also involved in politics and was running for county sheriff in the November elections.

Back at the house again, he told her to go to the chicken coop and grab as many eggs as she could and bring them up to the kitchen. "Claire will have lunch about ready, I reckon. Then we'll get you up on a horse and see what you can do. Ah, you have some other clothes, I hope."

"Oh, yes," she gushed. "I brought my riding clothes. That's probably why my trunk was so heavy. The boots, you know ..."

She struggled with the latch on the chicken coop and nearly gagged when she stepped in. The hens quackled at her intrusion and flapped a tornado of fine dust in the dim light. As she reached for an exposed egg, a hen startled her with an indignant peck to her hand. Timidly, she prized away four eggs, one of which was slick with poop.

She tumbled into the kitchen and exuberantly reported, "I brought the eggs, Claire," as she plunked down the coffee can with four lonely eggs rolling around the bottom of it. Claire glanced dismissively at the bounty and exchanged a glance with Netti who sat on a tall stool at the counter, shucking peas.

"I think those ol' biddies are holding out on you, Yry. I'll go with you next time and show you a few of their little tricks."

The kitchen table was piled with food: thick slabs of homemade bread, a crock of butter, preserves, thick slabs of bacon, sliced tomatoes and onions, a bowl of potato salad, and a plate of oatmeal cookies, and of course, a big pot of perked coffee. She wondered how anyone could be hungry so soon after that big breakfast. But George thundered in, followed by Dallas and two teenaged neighbor boys. The men washed up and crowded around the table. Bedlam ensued as food traveled every which way and they kidded one another.

After lunch Yry helped clear the table, but Claire encouraged her to run along and change her clothes. "You need some riding clothes, dear. I think they want to fit you up with a horse or two and some tack."

She bounded upstairs, intent on not missing a thing. A few minutes later she emerged, wearing woolen riding breeches that flapped loosely around her thighs, narrowed at the knee and disappeared into tall, shiny, low-heeled boots. She wore a long-sleeved white blouse and a pair of black, kid-skin leather gloves.

"Whoeee! Look at you!" exclaimed Netti, once again exchanging a look with Claire whose lips seemed intent on restraining a smile.

"Hurry up now," Claire murmured. "The men hate waiting on women, you know."

Yry hustled out the door and down the stairs, strutting toward the corral that had come alive with milling saddle horses. Dallas was first to catch a glimpse of the new ranch hand. He swiveled on his heel to face the corral and stifle a guffaw. Looking around him in curiosity, the two boys howled. George nodded his head and smiled gently at the approaching figure. "Well, Yry, you look like you're ready for the parade next week." Her expectant eyes dropped to the ground uncertainly.

"We're thinkin' maybe this little saddle will fit you nicely. Dal caught this little mare for you. We call her Silver. You go ahead and saddle up while we get ready."

"Where are the brushes and hoof picks?" she inquired.

"Glad to hear you askin' that question, little lady. The brushes are in the tack room, there to the right in the barn. You won't be needin' a pick for these ponies. They ain't shod, so they don't pick up much in their hooves." Dallas responded.

Wyoming, August 1942

The weight of the saddle surprised her and made her grateful that the horse wasn't as tall as the ones she'd ridden at home. Collecting a riddle of heavy stirrup, mysterious strings, straps, and heavy, cotton latigo on the broad seat of the saddle, she approached Silver's left side and with a grunt, hoisted the saddle onto the woolen Navajo saddle blanket. Once in place, that odd latigo vexed her. It had no buckles like the girths she was accustomed to. Dallas came up behind her surreptitiously and demonstrated how to loop the leather three times through the two rings, and loop it like a necktie knot at the top.

The men were all saddled and ready to head out. But George wanted to test his new hand's horsemanship. She had not demonstrated attributes to recommend confidence. He ordered her to mount, then he adjusted her stirrups and told her to ride a couple of circles in the corral.

"The stirrups are too long." She complained.

"Get used to 'em. They're just about perfect for you."

She began circling to the right at a walk, her spine ruler-straight, her ears, shoulders, and ankles plumb. Her hands, with a rein in each hand, stretched to either side of the horse's withers. She pressed the horse into a trot and began posting on the inside beat, as she'd been taught. The men's eyebrows lifted, and they exchanged glances. She reversed directions and repeated the drill, then gaining confidence, she pushed the horse into a canter. The animal chaffed at the bit and danced, unable to find the proper rhythm.

"Give her some head," barked George. "Loosen those reins!"

The relieved animal extended into a gentle lope. Yry still sat ramrod straight, rocking her hips back and forth to the horse's motion, her arms reaching uncomfortably beyond the tall horn.

"Yeah. Okay, Yry. That's fine for now."

She slowed the animal and guided it toward the fence. "These horses out here neck rein. You need to hold your reins looser and in one hand. And for God's sake, relax. You're gonna be up there all dang day long. Use the back of that saddle. Let the horse to do work."

"But which hand should I use for the reins?"

"It doesn't matter much, unless you're ropin.' In that case, you're going to want to rein with the left and aim with the right."

At last they were all saddled and ready to pull out. The men's saddlebags bulged with pliers, cutters, staples, and a wire stretcher. A roll of wire hung from the front straps of Dallas's saddle. They spent the afternoon appraising Yry's horsemanship and teaching her how to fix fence. After a couple hours of work she ruefully stripped off the tattered remains of her beautiful kid gloves.

When they returned late in the afternoon, the milk cows were already bunched and complaining at the entrance to the milk shed. After caring for the tack and the horses, Dallas ushered Yry to the milk shed. By now, each of the men had ridden off into an arroyo or behind a bush, but Yry hadn't urinated since lunch. Her bladder was an overfilled balloon on the verge of popping. But she was determined, so she held a bit longer while Dallas explained how to stanchion the cows, grain them, and wash their teats before milking them. When the stream of milk squirted against the metal pail between Dallas's knees, Yry could stand it no longer. She excused herself and dashed for the bathroom in the house.

At dinner that evening, George complimented Yry. "You've got some learnin' ahead of you, but I can see you've got grit. You'll be fine. Tomorrow, though, I want Claire to drive you into town and get you properly outfitted."

That night Yry slept sounder than she thought possible. She was completely drained from the excitement of the journey, the lack of sleep on the train, and the long, active day. The house was unbelievably quiet. In the morning her eyes popped open and she was instantly awake, refreshed, and exhilarated. She rushed to the window, which revealed the last wispy bits of blush in the morning sky. Chagrined, she realized that she was the last person up. The birds were well into the third movement of their morning symphony. Dallas was walking toward the house with two buckets of warm milk, and the horses were munching hay in the corral. She heard voices and kitchen noises downstairs.

It wasn't even 6 AM yet. The table was burdened again with food: a pile of thick-cut French toast, a platter of fried eggs, and another platter loaded with sausage patties, plus butter, preserves, maple syrup, coffee, and fresh milk with thick cream floating at the top of the pitcher. This morning she was hungry and dove into the French toast with gusto. The butter was the best she'd ever tasted. The coffee was just as bad as the restaurant coffee, but a good dousing of fresh cream compensated.

After breakfast Yry helped Nettie and Claire clear the table and began washing dishes while the two older women bent their heads over an extensive shopping list. A few minutes later she and Claire were bumping down the corduroy road for a shopping trip in Sheridan. First they stopped at the feed store for some inoculations and supplements for the cows and a bag of chicken feed. Then Claire walked her into the clothing store where she purchased two pairs of denim Levi's, two long-sleeved pearl-button shirts, and two short-sleeved shirts. They spent considerable time in the boot department. Yry was fussy about her shoes. She insisted that she needed very high arches. At last the right combination of boot design plus an arch insert fit the bill, then it was on to a hat that would keep the punishing sun off her noggin and her nose. Before heading back to the ranch, they stopped at the grocery store to restock staples.

Life on the CX ranch was not always serious. The Sheridan-Wyo-Rodeo had been cancelled because of the war. In compensation all attention was focused on the Sheridan horse races in September. Dallas rode George's prize filly to victory in the Futurity, providing good cause for celebration with drinks and dinner at the Sheridan Inn.

A few mornings later, Dallas tossed Silver's reins to Yry and said, "Here's a horse, go bring the rest of 'em in." Eagerly, she galloped across the horse pasture. With her best cowboy whooping and hollering, she expected the horses to gather into a nice little group and race gleefully ahead of her toward the corral. No self-respecting horse is going to comply with such helter-skelter treatment. They split, circled around, and stopped to stare at her in two pods of amazement. She tried again to circle around and spoon them together like peas, but they splintered off in several directions like sparks from a hot fire. Meanwhile, back at the corrals, her performance was the entertainment *du jour*.

Yry craved to blend into her surroundings the way a lizard becomes the ground. But her striking looks and serious demeanor flashed like parrot feathers. As always, her speech set her apart. Cowboy vernacular is punctuated by shrugs, tics, and nods of the head that impart subtle meaning to the incomplete sentences that slide past juicy hanks of chaw, stashed in cheeks or behind lips. Yry's proper grammar and tinges of British, German, and New York accent branded her a foreigner and brought subtle grins to the faces of the cowpokes she met. Even as she picked up and mimicked the slang, she missed the cadence of western speech. Her background once again held her apart from other people. Her naïve enthusiasm provided endless entertainment at the CX Ranch. She was the dramatic lead in a cowboy movie. The drama of her role took the sting out of what might otherwise have been painful ridicule.

You can't live in Wyoming without being able to drive. She knew her way around street cars, trolleys, buses, and subways. But at the age of 29, she had yet to drive a car. One morning she went with Dallas in an old beat up truck to return some plumbing supplies that had been borrowed from a neighbor. Dallas stopped in the middle of the deserted dirt road and got out of the truck. Walking to her side, he opened the door and nodded for her to slide over. She gaped in surprise. He nodded again and commanded, "Git on over there behind the wheel."

The steering wheel was huge. She could barely reach the foot pedals. After a few fumbles with the clutch they lurched into motion and crept down the road. Steering was practically unnecessary on this straight road but up ahead was a gradual descent down a long hill. The truck's momentum increased like a marble rolling down three flights of stairs. She stretched to jam her foot on the brake, but in this old beater the brakes were more decoration than reality. Her panic rose in direct proportion to the descent of the truck. Miraculously they made it to the bottom without disaster. From that day forth she became the world's most ardent brake tester.

Yry was put to work doing anything that needed to be done. She mucked out the horse barns, cleaned the chicken coop, fed the pigs, helped doctor sick animals, and even drove a tractor and an old hay wagon—terribly exciting events for a young woman who had never been behind the wheel of a car. Her horseback riding experiences from New York had given her the rudimentary skills she needed, but western riding was different from the stiff, posture-perfect riding she'd been taught. No task was too dirty or too menial for her. The freedom, the fresh air, and the vast open space was intoxicating.

One of her favorite chores was riding fence; she was usually alone and relished the solitude. The endless tan prairie stretched in all directions. Initially she thought it all looked the same, but in time she recognized landmarks as reliably as a mare recognizes her foal. A gentle rise here; an abrupt hill with a smooth, flat top and steep, jagged red sides there; patches of prickly pear cacti; rocky outcroppings—the road signs by which the locals negotiated the land. And everything encapsulated by the intense blue sky. To a city dweller the sight of that blue sky sliding down to greet the horizon that was visible in all directions was astonishing. Alone in the infinity of landscape, Yry was free to revel in the utter silence of the prairie. There was nothing to interrupt her meditations but the steady shuffle of the horse's hooves across dry grass, or clip-clopping over a sheet of rock; the occasional warble of a meadowlark; the weets of a startled sandpiper skittering helter-skelter and dragging a faux broken wing; the mournful call of a dove; or the distant downward whistle of an airborne raptor. Her mind roved for hours, wrestling with ideas about life, love, religion, and philosophy. Every plant and every rock held a story of its own. In the afternoons, puffy clouds built up, multiplied, shape-shifted, and dissipated in the big blue bowl overhead. Best of all, for a change she felt genuinely independent. She was doing something with her life. No one was looking over her shoulder in disapproval. She was FREE!

Yry was beginning to feel like she knew what she was doing. She'd been at the CX for three weeks when a young friend of Claire's arrived from back east for a visit. This woman was even greener than Yry and a good deal less adventuresome. Claire assumed that both young women would share much in common, so she assigned Yry to show Mrs. Greer the ropes. Perhaps had Claire been more aware of Yry's rebellious tomboy streak, she'd have thought twice about this arrangement.

Yry delighted in repeating the pranks that had been pulled on her and then watching Mrs. Greer's stricken reactions. When it came to horseback riding Mrs. Greer was an easy mark. The sight of her pale face as they raced up and down the hills surrounding the ranch reinforced Yry's devilment. Mrs. Greer had absolutely no sense of direction. She was convinced they'd get lost in the vast landscape and endless blue sky that made her feel like a bubble in an ocean. Repeatedly Mrs. Greer inquired if Yry was sure she knew the way back home. Undoubtedly she had visions of beady-eyed wolves circling with their tongues drooling. Yry relished the illusion that she was master of her universe and knew every gully and hill in the county. She never let on that the ace up her sleeve was the knowledge that horses *always* know the way back to the grain.

At the close of Mrs. Greer's two-week stay Yry offered to drive her into town to catch the bus. This was Yry's third week of driving. It would be her first time out on paved roads, and she was quite excited by the idea of it. Predictably, Mrs. Greer was late

Wyoming, August 1942

getting ready so Yry took it upon herself to make up time on the road. They bounced down the road over Mrs. Greer's protests that she could delay her departure by one day. But oh no, Yry was having the time of her life as she sped toward town. Of course, she nearly had a heart attack when another vehicle came into view headed towards them on the narrow road. This was something she'd not yet encountered on the deserted ranch roads. With her heart in her throat she slowed enough for the cars to pass safely. Then she sped ever more confidently down the road with Mrs. Greer three shades paler but unaware of Yry's moment of doubt. At the station, ashen faced Mrs. Greer stumbled out of the car on weak knees, her breath coming in short gasps. She was on the verge of hyperventilating. Yry grinned in anticipation of her glorious solo drive back to the ranch. Several weeks later, after Mrs. Greer had filled Claire in on her memorable trip to town, Claire quizzed Yry as they were washing dishes together.

"So, did you enjoy driving Mrs. Greer to town?"

Yry replied quickly, "Oh yes! It was marvelous. We had a lovely time."

"You don't think, perhaps, you might have been driving a little too fast?"

"Well, ah, we were a little late. I was trying to make up time so she wouldn't miss her bus."

"Did Mrs. Greer ask you to drive fast?"

Smelling a rat, Yry replied softly, "Well, no. She seemed a little, ah, spooked by the speed." A smile crept across her face as Yry remembered Mrs. Greer's peaked face.

"You were given job to do. We expect you to behave responsibly with our vehicles, our animals, and our friends, Yry. I have it from a reliable source that you were driving as if a fire was chasing you. *And*, I am quite aware that you were thoughtless about some of the rides you took Mrs. Greer on, although she's a lovely sport who would never complain."

Mollified, Yry replied, "I'm sorry. Maybe I did push the pedal to the metal a little too conscientiously ..."

"If I *ever* hear of such shenanigans again, I will not hesitate to send you right back to New York!"

A great privilege was bestowed upon Yry when George offered his own horse for her to ride. Because of an old back injury, George didn't ride much. He said the horse needed exercise. Before long she figured out why George seldom rode. His horse, Golden Fleece, was a beautiful, showy, four-year-old palomino gelding with flowing cream-colored mane and tail. He was calm and gentle, but riding him was akin to managing a hobby horse attached to a pogo-stick—better for parades than for work. Golden Fleece's stiff-ankled lope jarred her right out of the saddle. Horrified, she resorted to grabbing leather to stay anchored. Eventually she worked out a swap with Dallas. He gave her Allegra, a pretty bay mare with a heart of gold and a quiet, easy going, obedient nature. Yry and Allegra spent many hours together and developed a fine friendship.

Branding was a shock of violence. But this was an important aspect of successful ranching. Yry had found her niche at last; she would become a rancher and spend the rest of her life living off the land and raising beef cattle. Branding was something she'd just have to work out in her mind. She cringed at the first, shocking bawl of a small calf when the hot iron seared its flesh, painting the air with an acrid, burned-wool odor. Her own skin prickled in vicarious agony. In quick succession several more calves were run through the chute and the procedure was repeated, along with the castration of the males and earmarking—accomplished by punching a hole in the right ear. The calves stumbled out of the chute on wobbly legs, bleating miserably for their mammies. The air thickened with the warm, iron scent of blood, shit, and scorched hair. When she placed these 60 seconds of painful drama beside the heartache and misery she had suffered throughout her life, it made sense in an odd way. *We must all endure pain and suffering. These animals have the good fortune to live in contentment, safety, and abundance. The price they pay for their kept status is this momentary pain—surely no worse than childbirth—and life when their time is up. Life is a circle.* Yry reckoned that as long as man continued to eat meat for subsistence then the gruesome tasks of ranching had to be accomplished right along with the pleasant ones. She reconciled herself to the fact that branding was necessary, therefore, squeamishness made no sense.

She steeled herself against the plaintive sounds and nauseating smells and pitched in, eager to prove herself and to learn everything she'd need in her future life as a rancher. At times she was to deliver the hot irons from the fire to the man applying the brands. Sometimes she had to help with the smaller calves who were too little to run through the chute. These had to be roped from horseback. Then from the ground, two people held the calf down, one at the head and one on the back legs to keep it still while a third person applied the searing irons. She became adept at straddling a calf's neck and holding on for dear life to prevent it from squirming and ruining the brand.

A few days after branding, all the cows and calves were gathered from the brush and small ravines on the range and driven into a tight cluster. Yry and Dallas trailed the herd 25 long, dusty miles to the rail yards in Sheridan from where they'd be shipped out for sale and slaughter.

The journey began at sunup. She was grateful to be paired up with Dallas. They got along well. He teased her mercilessly, but his teasing was kind and it warmed her heart to recognize that he was paying attention to her and remembered little things she'd mentioned about her life. Between robust horselaughs, his patient tutorage about horses and cattle and the land that supported them filled her head with the possibilities and necessities of her new life. Claire had shared that Dallas was married, but it was a difficult relationship. His wife was often absent. Exactly why or where she went was never mentioned.

At noon a truck from the ranch caught up with them to deliver lunch and two fresh horses. It was a slow and tedious process. The cattle could not be pushed too fast, for fear of burning off precious weight. As the sun rose higher in the sky, so did the temperature. Smells of sweaty horses, warm leather, and green, bovine pungence mingled with the dull rumble of kibitzing cattle. It was lulling. After lunch Yry was surprised to find herself nodding off in the saddle. Just before the sun set they pulled into the ranch of a friend of George's. The cattle squirmed into an enclosure where hay was pitched over the fence to them. Early the next morning they would make the final push to the rail yards a few miles away.

Yry tagged along with the ranchers as they met in town for dinner, drinks, and ranch talk. George bought drinks and dinner for his host who would also be putting all of them up for the night. When Yry was finally shown her little cot for the night, she fell into it and went to sleep immediately, a truly unusual event for her.

The next day they drove the herd to the railroad yards where they were separated into three groups: cows, calves, and steers. The brand inspector weighed and inspected each animal, recording the results on lading sheets before loading them into cattle cars headed for Sioux City Stockyards in Iowa.

Yry's next big adventure was provision of the main course for the Thanksgiving meal. Yry and Dallas drove off early on November 25 in search of pheasants. They bounced across the fields headed for the tall grasses beside the creek. His first shot arrested a magnificent rooster from the sky, mid-stroke. They clambered through the tall grass to the spot where she had watched the inert body drop. It lay in a heap of beautiful, iridescent feathers. Dallas triumphantly jerked it off the ground by its feet, pleased with his marksmanship. How fleeting life is, she thought; how easily snuffed out; someday her time would come, and life

Wyoming, August 1942

would flutter out of her own body just as it had from this poor bird. They crisscrossed the field together, flushing birds as they went. By mid-morning they had bagged ten birds, Yry serving as retriever.

A slow time on the ranch, it was a lovely, fall day—not too cold, but with a nip of winter in the air. Under the shade of a Russian Olive tree growing near the creek, they shared a picnic lunch that Yry had stashed in the back of the truck. Dallas prodded her to share her vision of the ranch she would own someday, and he teased her about who she'd hire to wrangle her cattle.

Later, they took the birds behind the barn to prepare them for the cook. The wings came off first, then the head, the feathers, and the claws. Finally the crop and intestines were pulled free. Chickie waited nearby to claim his pick of the prizes left behind. They handed ten field-dressed pheasants to the cook, who harrumphed at the sight of so many pheasants to hang in the galley.

November 27, 1942

Much of the story so far has been linear and easy to corroborate with letters and diaries. Letters and diaries still abound, but now gaps in dates and abrupt changes in address appear. What happened in the years that followed has morphed into a maze of similar, but slightly different tales, as Mother confidentially shared bits of her life with friends, each of whom hung onto each word as if it were a sacred text. Sacred perhaps. But reliable? The world never agrees on the reliability of sacred texts—with good reason.

I found among my mother's papers, a sheet torn from a page-a-day calendar—November 27, 1942. Half a dozen words written in her hand scrawled across the top: "Starting out for a grand experience." It was the day after Thanksgiving.

At some point between Yry's arrival at the CX on August 20, 1942 and her rather abrupt departure three months later, her world mysteriously shifted. A kind and gracious letter from Claire, coincidentally dated November 27, 1942, counseled Yry to enjoy her new experience, noting that it would surely bring her satisfaction and independence. Claire shared a tidbit of advice that had been given to her at the age of 27. "Try not to take yourself too seriously." Claire continued by addressing her former "tough counseling," but fell short of apologizing for anything she'd said. She stood by her advice—boy would I love to know what that tough counseling was—and wished Yry well. "You leave the CX with much love and hope from everyone."

One thing is clear. Yry's dream was set. One day she would own her own ranch. Among her papers is another letter dated November 27, 1942. This one, from her father, expressed regret at having annoyed her and at their strained communication during the past years. It is clear from this letter that Herman was feeling his 60 years, and not lightly. He acknowledged her love of the west, the wide open spaces, the ruggedness, and her desire to make a life there. Though he admitted that life in the country is more intimate and healthy, he conceded his love of urban life with its driving force and energy. (Hence, I fathom a subtle gulf between Herman and Norah, who adored the bucolic village life realized by the New Rochelle house.) Herman encouraged Yry to consult with her good friends at the CX.

"George is a wise man with brusque exterior but a sensitive and fine soul. Claire is a kind and generous woman. They will both be helpful if you confide in them."

Confide? Confide what?

Continuing his advice, Herman wished he could buy her a ranch, but lamented the narrow financial constraints necessary to reorganize the firm. (Of course, the firm would still be recovering from the double devastation wreaked by the stock market crash and Uncle Adolph.) His final wisdom was that she must learn the business of ranching before diving in.

Meanwhile, ranch or no ranch, Herman was still funding Mother's pinball trajectory through life.

Wyoming, August 1942

Though it is unclear why Mom left the CX when she did, one obvious explanation might be that during the winter months, she'd be hard pressed to earn her keep at the ranch. Life does not come to a complete halt during the winter months on a cattle ranch, but until the cows begin dropping their calves in the spring, things slow down. It would make sense for her to be looking for a more worthwhile winter occupation. But there is also that rift hanging in the balance. Claire's letter hints at some upheaval, some argument. Something was not quite right at the ranch.

~~~

Yry enrolled in a ten-week short course at University of Wyoming in Laramie starting in January. It was an Agriculture program designed for ranchers and farmers. There was time to see a bit more of Wyoming in the weeks before classes began. Rumors spoke of jobs galore in Casper, a town in the center of the state, so she hopped on the bus with high hopes. Watching from her seat by the window, flat sage country flew by. The primordial prairie, now mostly snow-covered, was endless. Mile upon mile passed between towns. Occasionally a clot of shabby buildings and corrals flashed by, testimony to hard scrabble lives eked out on the edge of civilization. *Who lived such an existence?* She wondered. *What accounted for the vast difference between these solemn little hovels and the comfortable accommodations at the CX Ranch? What made some people prosper out here and others fail? Could she be setting herself up for more heartache and failure by pursuing this dream of independence? How could she have spared herself some of the pain she felt? But she was sure she would not have altered a thing. Life was a series of experiences that are thrown at us to deal with as best we can.*

Jobs in Casper turned out to be more rumor and less galore. She got part-time work helping a young woman who had fallen and broken her hip. Mary had a small child and her husband was in the service. Yry cared for Mary and the child and cooked, cleaned, and ran errands. She also did some part-time waitressing. In between jobs she indulged in long walks around town, honing the art of leaning into the very worst of Wyoming's iconic wind.

It was a lonely month in Casper, but perhaps good for healing whatever rift had torpedoed her relationships in Sheridan. She cooked and shared a joyless and hollow Christmas dinner with Mary. On New Year's Eve she endured the evening shift at the restaurant. Customers were festive and inebriated. Moved by too many holiday spirits, men felt justified in mauling a beautiful, young, single woman who was obviously in need of male attention. After slapping off pawing hands for hours, she fell into bed and cried herself to sleep, feeling homesick and sentimental.

On January 5, 1943, Yry again boarded a bus, this one destined for Laramie. As the bus digested distance, she noted "an endless land that seems to have existed forever—miles upon miles between towns and even between ranches." The bus passed through tiny Wheatland, and just past midnight pulled into Cheyenne for an hour layover. Yry left the bus station to explore the state Capitol by twilight. In the dark, she clutched her coat tightly around herself and strolled along Capitol Avenue from 15th to 17th streets, taking in the stores, cafes, the Elks Club building, movie houses, and bars, all of which looked bleak and deserted.

Back inside the station she sat in a secluded corner and observed her fellow travelers. One man served up funny stories to a clot of people who erupted in frequent outbursts, guffaws, and applause. There were a few dark-skinned people—either Mexican or Indian, or both. (None in leathers and feathers though, she noted with some disappointment.) A Chinese or Filipino soldier was wearing dark glasses, and Yry imagined him as a Japanese spy in disguise. Most travelers were dressed in jeans, boots, and leather coats. One lady wore a red velvet turban perched upon a head of tightly curled gray hair, black veil, fur coat, high heels, and of all things, slacks—still celebrating a New Year's Eve masquerade ball?

The bus arrived in Laramie at 4:30 in the morning, too late to waste money on a motel, so she hung around the depot till the sun began to uncloak the empty streets. After a light breakfast at the Connor Hotel she walked a mile to the campus for an 8 o'clock appointment with the Dean of Agriculture.

The dean was friendly and helpful. He summoned Professor Johnston to give her a tour of Laramie and help her find a place to stay, which she found downtown near the hotel she'd just come from.

Yry plunged into Wyoming academia like a bear into a berry patch. She took her assignments far more seriously than her classmates, nearly all of whom were raised on ranches. Counting Yry, there were three women enrolled in the course; the oldest, a woman of about 50, befriended Yry on the first day. Mrs. Miller was the daughter of an esteemed professor of botany. Her husband was a banker who had purchased a ranch south of town. The other woman Yry disdained because of her fancy clothes and fastidious avoidance of dirt. This woman claimed to own a sheep operation, but Yry decided she must be running it by remote control. Yry's studious discipline must have been a source of irritation to her classmates. But she kept them entertained with frequent and unexpected questions.

The classes were divided into three-week sessions and included topics such as sheep production, animal husbandry, feeds and feeding, crop plants and soils, wool production, dairying, beef production, agricultural economics, seed analysis and weed control. War-time shortages restricted much of the equipment they needed for the farm repairs and tools class, so she used her time to outfit herself with handmade halters, spurs, a bridle, and chaps, all of which she was very proud of and which she prized for the rest of her life.

An annoying seepage of soft coal dust from the trains crept through cracks and gaps in the windows and door of her apartment, prompting a move to the Lazy U Motel, which was closer to campus and had a small fridge and hotplate. Her letters home bragged about everything she was learning. She nattered about how "You easterners don't know what a real steak is." Ditto "real butter and real cream." However, in practically the same breath, she berated the locals. "You westerners need to just get acclimatized to your own climate!" Of course, she was never bothered by the cold spells that prompted water-cooler complaints. Always the outsider, this woman.

Yry's letters home bubbled with optimism and excitement; however, her private notes during this time reveal something interesting. Although self-righteously clinging to the notion that she was a fiercely independent loner, these weeks in Laramie proved something different.

> *Sunday is the hardest day of the week—the day when endless silence settles over me like a waterproof mantle shutting out the world and imprisoning me in my own thoughts and feelings until I think I'm ready to burst. No school, no library, not even a good movie to sink into.*

But things were going on.

~~~

As memoirist Mary Karr concedes, time fades and fuzzes memory. I've learned to not trust my memory. But some events shock the brain into indelible recall. Looping replays of an extraordinary incident sear words and scenes deeply into the crevices of the mind. So it happened one night over dinner and a bottle of wine with my mother.

I had been on my own for several years. I took care planning for Mother's yearly visits. Knowing that she craved culture and international cuisine, I scoured my adopted town for the newest, most avant-garde or ethnic restaurants. I blew my budget on tickets to fine arts performances or exhibitions that coincided with Mother's visits. I showed off my cadre of friends with a picnic or party at my house.

Wyoming, August 1942

During this time, I was involved in a tempestuous affair with a married man, which presented the inevitable problem of how to explain my continued singlehood at a time when other people my age were pairing up and starting families.

In retrospect, I suppose Mom had suspicions. We had never talked frankly about personal matters. Perhaps being a single woman in a small western town during the 1950s and 60s molded her to caution and discretion. If she could be taciturn, I could match her tight lips. So here she was, at the end of another extended stay at my house, perhaps suspecting that I was hiding something and hoping to coax it out of me.

During her last night in town, she treated us to a fancy meal at Misty's, a swank establishment that hugged the banks of the Boise river. We started with cocktails. Then she ordered a bottle of wine with the meal. The alcohol loosened our frigid tongues—at least it loosened hers. Sadly, I don't think I ever came clean about my own situation. But the story she told was a nine on the Richter scale.

The Secret

Mom launched her story by describing how distraught she was as she approached her 30th birthday. Since graduating from high school she'd enjoyed some great adventures, but she remained an unmarried, rootless woman, living off the largesse of her parents. She spoke of her father's disappointment in her lack of direction and disinterest in his business.

"Yeah ... Faatheh was always off on a buying trip. That's where our unusual baubles came from: the Hindu prayer wheel, the Japanese tapestries, the silver figurines. He knew seven languages, you know ... all self-taught."

And I can't even get my mouth around German, I thought, as I swigged another swallow from the wine glass.

"He was a driven man. And he expected everyone around him to be just as driven. Yeah, the travel would have been appealing, but not the dickering and wheeling and dealing. And besides, I knew he had no intention of sending me out to do the buying. He wanted me in the office to type letters and answer the phone and keep the books. Plghhh."

"A bit sexist, was he?" The waiter had removed my salad plate, and chin propped on hands, elbows on the table, I watched her eat. Mom was so involved in her memories and her salad that she didn't even comment on my egregious etiquette.

"Well, to be fair," she continued, "that's just the way things were. It was a man's world. No one expected a woman to travel alone to India or China—though I'd have dearly loved to go to China. I even studied Chinese for a while. Actually, I'm enrolled in a Chinese course at the university this fall. You never know, I may get there yet." She grinned around her last mouthful of salad.

Then she mentioned the straw that broke her father's back.

"Heinrich?" This was the first I'd heard about him. The waiter returned with steaming, elegantly dressed plates: a slab of prime rib swimming in bloody juice for Mom and garlic-bathed scampi for me.

"Heinrich ... oh, I fell for him." By now she could chuckle about her youthful passion. She sampled the grilled Brussels sprouts artfully stacked beside the beef on her plate and launched into a description of handsome Heinrich and her scandalous affair with him.

"You didn't get married? Wow. That must have been pretty rad in those days!"

"My poor Faatheh. I put him through some hell in those days," she agreed somewhat wistfully. "But I was so infatuated with Heinrich. He had this dark corner in his soul that just reached out to me. I was sure something terrible had happened to him during the war and I thought with enough love and patience, I could heal that wound." She paused, her eyes focused on the window as she savored her meal.

Wyoming, August 1942

"You've never talked about any of this. What happened?" I prodded.

"Well, some things aren't meant for little ears, you know!" Her eyes danced with a hint of suppressed mirth. "Actually, Faatheh was right in this case. Heinrich was rather a fraud. He had a dark spot of melancholy all right, but I don't think it had much to do with the war. I think ... I think he just tried to mask a selfish, dictatorial nature. I thought he really believed in me as a human—as an equal. But all he wanted was someone to ... wash his clothes, cook his meals, and warm his sheets. It didn't take me too long to wise up."

"But Mom, you were almost 30? I thought you were in Wyoming by then. How'd you get from Central Park to Wyoming?"

"Well, Faatheh, poor man ... he recognized how heartbroken I was. He had this business associate who ran a cattle operation in Wyoming. So he contacted his friend and arranged for me to hire on as a ranch hand."

"You must have loved that! Did you get to stay until the war ended, or what?"

She commenced to talk about her first impressions of the west and about Cody, Wyoming, and the Rhoads family. Interestingly, she never mentioned Sheridan or the Cormack part of the story. Was she trying to head off snooping?

We had finished the last of the wine and ordered dessert and nightcaps when she leaned into the table, and whispered, "You must not ever breathe a word of this to your sister. It would kill Joan to hear it from you."

Shocked, I nodded solemnly. She had my full attention. She went on to explain the details of her affair with a married man. I've wondered how much of the story was real, embellished, or simply concocted as a means of loosening my tongue. But later, as I examined her papers, the evidence of her willful behavior bore out much of what she told me that night.

"I fell in love with more than Wyoming. You know, much of the business of tutoring me in cowboying fell to Elaine's brother." (But here she is, talking about *Elaine* and *Cody*, while I know she broke in her boots in Sheridan before going to Cody. Have I misremembered, or did she obfuscate?) "We spent a lot of time together. I was high on life and my enthusiasm intrigued him. He told me about his horrible relationship with his wife. He was quite depressed about it. She wanted children so badly, but in 15 years that hadn't come to pass. And she was lonely living on the ranch. Honestly, I don't know when that was, because during the entire time I was there, I never met the woman. Besides, I couldn't imagine feeling lonely in that astounding country!"

Our Brandy Alexanders arrived, and I reached for mine as if it were the ripcord on my parachute.

She continued, "I fell madly in love with him. The sun rose on his cheeks in the morning, and set on his ass in the evening."

Thick slabs of chocolate torte arrived, providing me with the break I needed to resume breathing.

"It didn't take long for the whispers to start. Not just in town, but at the ranch, too. Willard and Elaine would exchange looks whenever he and I were in the same room. I'm not stupid, I knew what they were thinking," she growled around a mouthful of chocolate. (*Willard* and *Elaine*? Really? What about George and Claire? I am confused to this day about how these details fail to line up.)

I couldn't understand why he stayed with a woman who was so cruel to him. But he was not one to walk out on a commitment. He just couldn't bring himself to leave her. She had no one else. Her siblings had died as children and both her parents were gone. She needed him. We really did try to hide our feelings for each other, but it was next to impossible. Elaine was angry with me. I can understand that, really I can. But I couldn't help myself."

Wyoming, August 1942

Looking at photos of my mother, I can commiserate with a hearty cowboy's desire. But he should never have told her he was sterile. And she should never have believed that he was sterile, no matter whose brother he was.

After she finished the story and her dessert, it was my turn to talk. "But Mother, why on earth didn't you tell Joan the truth?"

"Well, I tried. God, I tried. But ... you know ... things were different then. Women didn't just have babies out of wedlock. It simply wasn't done. I had to invent a story for the three of us."

"Ya ..." I said, "but at some point, you could surely have taken her aside and explained things."

"You'd think so ... but when she was small and we lived with my parents," a heavy sigh, "things were difficult. Mother was in such pain with her arthritis. She demanded quiet and expected Joan to behave like a 'young lady.' She really expected way more of such a young child than is realistic. And oh, my faatheh!" she exclaimed in her peculiar mix of accents. "Good God. He was totally smitten by Joan. She could do no wrong. If I told her 'no,' he'd wait till my back was turned, wink at her and say 'yes!' He adored her, which of course, made things difficult for me. I couldn't discipline my own child. And she was bright. She knew how to work me against him. She and I were always at odds with each other. There was never a time when she was little that I could have broached the subject. Besides, between taking care of the house and her and nursing my poor motheh, I was ragged."

"But later, when we were in Laramie ..." I exclaimed. "Joan was so interested in the family tree. I remember that school project she worked on so hard—it traced the Dillons and the Pauls way back to the 1800s or something. Surely she asked questions about her father's ancestry?"

"Strangely enough, she mostly focused on my side of the family," Mother replied.

Perhaps she knew there was something lurking and wasn't ready to uncover it yet. I could relate. When I was four or five years old I asked about my own father. I don't remember Mother's words, but I remember the electric warning in her voice. I never broached the subject again.

"Yabutt, Joan is no dummy. Surely she's worked this all out by now!"

"If she has ... she hasn't heard it from me. I can't tell you how many times I've tried to take her aside when I visit. But ... the timing is just never right. The household is always in an uproar. She's always juggling a million different obligations between Jim, the boys, the horses, work, civic projects. I never get a quiet evening like this—with just her and me."

"Well, I'm quite sure she must know by now. It's not that hard to track down things like this, especially for someone with her research skills."

Mother fixed me with a hard stare. "Whatever she knows, she's learned on her own. She does not need to know that I told you but not her."

Which of course, begs the question, *why tell me?* Things had always been difficult between my sister and me, and it had been well over ten years since we'd communicated. I spent the next decade wondering why my mother armed me with such a sharp weapon and then told me to keep the sword sheathed.

Lovesick again

Mother revealed many eye-opening facts to me that evening, but after a life of fabricating history, details were grayed out. From the timeline of her photos and journal entries, it is clear that she was not pregnant when she left the CX ranch in November, nor during her time in Laramie. Journal entries from January reveal her mental state.

> *Dallas, I'm so lonely for you. I wonder why I haven't heard from you in two weeks and what surprise was it Claire spoke of in her letter? She mentioned it but never explained. How long shall I have to wait yet for you. I*

Wyoming, August 1942

miss you more each day. The more I flee from (illegible) the farther I go, the busier I keep myself the more I feel the emptiness of not being near you. I'm no longer whole—a part of me is missing—my love—my 'lover.'

Does this explain the loneliness she described, and why Sundays were such difficult days for her despite her friendship with two other young women who were also staying at the Lazy U Motel?

She was deeply grateful for Mrs. Miller's generous offers to spend weekends at the ranch. The best part was being able to ride, although she was indignant that the Millers worried about her being out on the prairie all by herself. They thought she might get lost, for Pete's sake! *Of course* she knew how to handle herself on the range! She'd been a "westerner" now for five months! On the slim chance that she might get turned around out there, she knew Babe would bring her back to the oats lickety-split. She keenly observed the different routines of another ranch and began to see the land and the plants with her budding rancher's eye. But there was an invisible companion riding beside her through the southeastern Wyoming foothills. *Love, love, why must I be alone?*

Finally, on January 30th, a letter arrived from Dallas. She flew to her room, locked the door and flung herself on the bed to examine the envelope, to gaze at his boyish scrawl, peer at the stamp and the postmark, before carefully unsealing the missive.

Dear Yry,
I have intended writing you for some time. Guess you will think I am rather slow in doing it.
I had to come to the disagreeable thing of getting my teeth out so I am rather smooth mouthed now, but will soon have a pair of store teeth that will work just like hoof nippers so they say.
I read your letters and am very happy to hear you are getting along fine and enjoy the work.

> *I have not gathered the horses yet nor weaned the colts. Weather has been fine here and lots of grass and they are growing fine. You should see Listening Ears. She is growing a lot.*
>
> *Golden Flash and Flash are way up in the far end of the Big Pasture and doing fine. His hair is so long, he looks like a Billy goat.*
>
> *We are all well and living a very quiet life.*
>
> *I went up yesterday and brought that sorrel mare and colt in that were with Frazer's horses and branded them. I had several horse races to get them.*
>
> *Bill is just the same. He is getting fat. Says he's gained 30 lbs. Joe and Mary Ross are fine and want to be remembered to you. Hope you have a good time and meet some good friends as I guess that is the most important thing.*
>
> *Claire said she would write a few lines so will close for now.*
>
> *Dallas*

This innocent little letter is the only one I found from Dallas among the two trunks of correspondence that came home with me after my mother's death. At least he addressed it *Dear Yry*. But given her besotted condition, I wonder how she dealt with the lack of ardor.

Mother pressed on through the month of February, alternately mooning over the tragedy of love and throwing herself into her studies. Her farm materials and tools projects drug along as she waited for supplies for her spurs and chaps to arrive. "Because of the war, one needs to be prepared," she wrote in *Yry Press*, a newsletter she copied and sent to her friends. "I bought 2 pair wool pants, 2 pair cotton gabardine, 1 pair boots." The plan was to be fully stocked with cowgirling necessities by the time her classes were finished. She spent hours in the library reading about

Wyoming, August 1942

horses and horse training, and she stockpiled fistfuls of pamphlets and government bulletins on horse and cattle range, feeds, vegetation, etc. Her friend Mrs. Miller warned that she would have to buck many prejudices along her path to cowgirling and ranching. But Mom was optimistic. She was excelling in school, and her professors seemed impressed with her spunk, some rather grudgingly so. Her dairy professor gave her a lead for a ranch position in Cody.

> *April 2, 1943: Well, I'm off again. I expect to land in Cody, Wyo to get some more experience at ranching, practical this time. But first I'm going to Sheridan for a few days, mainly to see the Dentist as I've a silver filling coming out. I hope I'll get to see Claire and family.*

Ya, I bet she wanted to see Claire *and family!* She wrote copiously in an undated section of *Yry Press* about the bus ride through Cheyenne, Torrington, Lusk, Newcastle, Gillette, Sheridan, Billings to Cody. In her notes she described the sights and the people she encountered.

> *From Gillette to Sheridan was a very long ride. Saw 2 dead cows on the way. Road bad as a result of snows. The Bighorns were in sight long before we got there. Sheridan to Cody! The wait in Billings was 7 hours—very long. Waiting room not comfy ...*

She mentioned Sheridan in one sentence and without a pause, she was on to Cody. Even in her own diaries, she obfuscates. But she spent several unaccounted for days in Sheridan before resuming the bus trip to Cody.

Comments about "two Japs riding the bus on their way to the Jap camp near Cody" are utterly surprising and disturbing. This terminology assaults the very principles this woman drilled into me. But that was written in a journal and it was the common vernacular of the time; she made laborious copies of the Yry Press and mailed them to her friends back east, so perhaps she amended the ethnic slur—or perhaps the slur never occurred to her at that time. When I was a child,

My Life With an Enigma

she corrected my friends when they recited, "eeny meeny, miny moe, catch a nigger by the toe!"

"That's catch a *tiger* by the toe!" she would reprimand with a penetrating stare.

I assume "Japs" was an abbreviation to save her pen hand. But I'm also surprised to find no diatribe about the Heart Mountain detention camp in her papers. I wonder—was she so eager to assume a cowboy identity that she turned her back on her previous convictions? Is it possible she did not know that America was dumping Japanese Americans into concentration camps? But she knew about the "Jap Camp." She's not here to defend herself, but it is difficult to accept her apparent racism.

The first entry from her new location in Cody doesn't occur until April 22nd, 1943. From *Yry Press*, it seems safe to presume that between approximately April 3 – till April 8 (or later), Mother was in Sheridan.

On April 8th, she writes:

My Honey, Now I have to go on without you again and I'd rather just stop breathing—hibernate—till I could be with you again. Why do you do things to me that I never felt before? ... Don't worry, I don't blame you, I'm a little afraid myself sometimes but I'll never take you or anything about us for granted. Never hold you to anything. I only hope and pray that we should both continue caring and understanding each other as at present and that maybe someday these partings may cease. I want you always near darling, you're all I have—the only one who really loves me and understands me or ever did understand and agree with my thoughts. Dallas, I know it must be this way and that I must make the best of it but I don't have to like it. ... I don't want to go anywhere but to be near you. I love you dear so very deeply. Please do write, it means so very much to me. ...

Blah, blah, it rambles for several more tortured lines. Did she ever mail this? She was in the habit of writing a rough draft of her

Wyoming, August 1942

letters, so perhaps she sent a copy. Or perhaps this was simply venting. She goes on:

> *They say that a man wants to be a woman's first love, but I cannot see the point for a first love has no reason behind it, no understanding of what love should be, what it entails, its responsibilities its great power and influence. I would not want to be married to my first or even my second, third, or fourth love for it took me all that and 15 years of experience at loving and disappointment and heartbreak and disillusionment to realize that a real & true & enduring love is not based on physical love alone and some sort of glamorous idealism that for the moment overlooks all undesirable characteristics. ...*

The essay goes on in this manner for several more pages. Surely she didn't copy and mail this. Maybe she sent the first few paragraphs, but I can't imagine that she would bore the poor fellow with prolix philosophy.

The Dudine

In Cody, Yry lived "as one of the family" with her employers, Willard and Elaine Rhoads and their children. She arrived the week before Easter during spring branding. The calves were smaller than the ones branded in the fall at the CX. Willard roped each calf, whereupon, with the rope still taut, her job was to "bust the calf" tying three legs, then straddle the prone body and hold it still till the branding, blackleg injection, castration, dehorning, and earmarking were completed.

> *My clothes and me too are all covered with blood when we have been at it a little while. Tho it does not effect [sic] me at all. I suppose it is one of those things that many women cannot stand.*

She rhapsodized about ranch life, bragging that she rose around six and was riding by nine. Her chores varied: riding fence, circling the cows and calves to make sure everyone was suckling as they should, pitching hay and manure, helping Willard dig ditches and build an earthen dam.

"Willard always tries to spare me. He must think I'm weak and it just burns me up."

She was learning to drive a team and to ride bareback. Willard, concerned about increased rustling due to wartime meat rationing, frequently sent her to check the cattle. After supper, she and Willard sometimes played checkers. The Rhoads turned in around nine or ten. Not Yry. She stayed up until near midnight, writing notes and letters or reading. With an air bordering on defiance, she declared she needed less sleep here than when she lived a tired, nervous life in the city. Everything she was learning about herself and life in the west supported her conviction that she belonged in the west. And what didn't fit she was determined to force.

They (the Rhoads) introduce me to people as their dudine and that takes the wind out of my sails as I've always hated what that word, "dude" stands for.

During quiet moments, Yry ruminated about the ranch of her dreams. There would be only enough chickens to supply eggs, since she wasn't fond of chicken meat—especially now that she knew how filthy they are, pooping every which way into their food and water. She apparently overlooked the same habits in beef cattle. She would have only one or two milk cows so she could milk them by hand rather than using expensive and finicky DeLaval milking machines.

She helped Elaine with shopping in Cody and was fascinated by the Indian women on the streets hawking beautiful, handmade silver jewelry. She referred to them as squaws. Shocked at the price

Wyoming, August 1942

of produce, she was suddenly aware that her requests for more raw fruits and vegetables were an imposition. At least at the ranch they had plenty of fresh dairy products and wonderful meats, including elk and deer meat, which suited her dietary needs very well.

In June, the *Yry Press* reports breathlessly:

> *Hello Folks,*
>
> *You'll never guess what I'm up to now! Well, I'm up at cow camp. I'm living in a 6x9 foot cabin with a bunk, a coal stove, 2 benches, a table, a pail for water, and a washbasin. There are 2 little round corrals and a small overnight pasture for the horse. It is primitive here, with a gas lamp, the spring 100 yards away, and not even an outhouse, or an Eleanor, as they call them out here. In one of the corrals I have a milk cow nursing an orphan calf to supply me with what little milk I need and I have a dog for company. It's a two-hour ride from the ranch.*
>
> *My job is to keep the cattle out of the larkspur that is in high bloom. The blooming plants are highly poisonous to cattle and the cows are too stupid to stay away from it, even though there's plenty of fine grass for them to eat. The draws are really laden with larkspur so I must be up at sunrise to keep the cattle out of the draws. They forage heavily in the mornings.*
>
> *It's a half hour ride to the top of the 8 or 9,000 foot mountain and the terrain is very rocky. There's a herd of horses running in the same area, but they aren't as likely to eat the larkspur. When they come to drink at the spring, I can lure the horses into the corral with oats and pick out which one to ride for the next couple of days. I'm 10 miles north of Shoshone Lake.*
>
> *I'm doing some grand cooking here. Cooked a chow of soya beans and ham. I'd had them sent from NY. They are the first I've had since last July and they sure tasted good.*

> *Lost a fine fat cow to larkspur yesterday. Must be pretty potent stuff. She came down just as W said she would. They pant then fall down and as the poison affects the heart, the point is to get them lying head uphill to prevent the lower organs from crowding the heart. There is medicine one can give if one catches them before it's too late, but W doesn't have much faith in it because giving it causes excitement and stimulates the heart too much. I've been feeling disgusted about it all day and ineffectual. A cow like her is worth over $100!*
>
> *Sure wish I'd had a shooting iron with me today to shoot the coyotes who keep pestering my dog. There's a bounty on coyotes. (A practice she would spurn vociferously in later years.)*

~~~

Reading through Mother's journals, her strident generalizations and labels jump out at me. Interestingly, it was her strident opinions that provoked our clashes, even when I mostly agreed with her. To my horror, I recognize that same tone in my own unbidden opinions.

Her vocabulary is full of "westerners, easterners, New Yorkers." "Bears are generally not dangerous to man, the average city man does not know this." Why *man* instead of people? Was she blind to her own sexism? Yes, it was a different time. But other writers of the times knew better, Rachel Carson and Eudora Welty to name just two. Then there's the city/country prejudice. Perhaps that validated her resolution to live in the west. I can't help but snort over her cravings for urban food like soybeans, which didn't become an edible item in western states till the following century.

And there are the dates. Or the lack of dates. Or the lack of connection between dates. She arrived in Cody in late April. Then, sometime between April and May, she conceived. I have found no

Wyoming, August 1942

written proof, no letters gushing of a momentous meeting, no excitement about impending changes, no mention of queasiness or worry. But the facts are there. Did it happen during that brief visit to "the dentist" in Sheridan before she arrived at the Rhoads' ranch?

~~~

Yry's love of the high country remained true. Her heart thumped in tune with the weather when sharp peaks pricked the clouds cruising overhead and goaded the sky into clashing, gashing thunder and lightning that shattered the sky like broken glass, cracking and rumbling against granite and dumping quick, drenching rains over the dusty land below.

She marveled at dazzling sunrises and sunsets and observed how the landscape morphed beneath the sun as it marched westward each afternoon. She reveled in solitude, just her, the weather, the animals, and the mountains. Even returning, hot and thirsty, to her cabin to discover a dead mouse in her third dipper full of water couldn't dim her enthusiasm. She was amused by the riotous yip yapping of coyotes. She gulped at the thrill of surprising a bear in a clearing and watching its undulating buttocks disappear into the bushes.

In early July the larkspur bloom faded, and she returned from cow camp to resume more mundane ranch chores. Whenever possible, she broke away for a ride into the breaks just to be out there, alone, with the sky for a hat. Her mind floated as her horse picked its way through rocks, cacti, and sage.

~~~

Surely by now, she had to know what lurked in her belly. My gut lurches empathetically as I consider the questions and fears that had to be tumbling over each other. What would she do? What *could* she do? What answers could the ropes of clouds stretching over the distant horizon offer?

A letter from her father bemoaned that he had not yet managed to secure household help for Norah. They were talking about perhaps moving to a smaller flat in the future.

It seems, as if you have not the slightest inclination and wish to come East and pass some time with us.

I have no news from the other side, (Germany) and we are thinking often of grandmother Emma, Willy, Valeria, and their children. What a terrible time they are passing through! Are they still amongst the living and what will be the news?

Well, keep healthy and cheerful and be heartily greeted and embraced by your father.

Mother couldn't go home to her parents in her condition. She soldiered on. Was she in denial? If so, it would not be the last time she walled off impending disaster.

Early in August she wrote about her first trip to Yellowstone. Despite gas rationing (and four months into pregnancy), Mom traveled through the park with Willard, Elaine, and a professor from the University. She was thrilled to see a moose and reported great success fishing.

Mother was always proud of the fact that she "held her pregnancies well." I remember her bragging that she never showed with her first pregnancy till she was nearly six months along and that when she carried me, her weight never topped 132 pounds. In a black-and-white photo taken during that trip, she looked quite svelte with a string of fish held in front of her stomach.

Interestingly, Mother had begun corresponding with the US Department of Justice; Immigration and Naturalization Service. She had filed an application for a certificate of derivative citizenship which precipitated a lengthy paper chase between New York and Wyoming. The certificate was sent to Basin, Wyoming, county seat for Big Horn County—the county shared by Sheridan and the CX Ranch. At some point before she left Wyoming in October, she must have returned to the CX. But she missed this important document and asked that it be sent back to New York City. "I'm planning to be in New York City in April or May '44, but am not sure where I'll be between now and then," she informed the Immigration Service.

From August 1943 till December, the record of Mother's whereabouts, thoughts and feelings dries up. Even photographs lack dates or labels. An unexpected note dated December 11, 1943, slipped out of one of her journals to reveal her state of mind:

> To my parents,
> You will not read this unless I am dead and this concerns my last wishes regarding such an event.
> I do not want to be buried in a graveyard. Is that clear? I want to be buried all alone out west under the sagebrush and where no other graves are. Failing that I wish to be buried away from other graves in the woods or else thrown in the ocean.
> I do not want any church ritual of any kind said over my rotting bones. Don't put me in a funeral parlor or keep me lying around the house. Get it over with. Don't ever burn me. Let the mice eat me, they want to live too, and when my soul passes into another incarnation I won't need this body any longer.
> No crosses over my grave please, they give me the creeps.
> No weeping. This is not a sad affair, merely the passing of a soul from one body to another.
> Now as to my property. There isn't much. If I have no children, distributes my things among my friends. There will be a list of them enclosed with this letter. What is left and what there is of money give it to some needy child or some orphan home, or to Matilde Walter if she is still alive.
> All I ask for the benefit of my soul and my immortality is that my friends remember me kindly.

My mother stayed remarkably true to these wishes. After her death, we found similar notes scattered throughout the house. She was determined that her children would have no excuse to fail her in her last wishes. By then, however, she had come to accept cremation as the preferred disposal method, and she commanded that her friends gather and make merry by drinking all the remaining liquor in the house. Nothing should go to waste.

Mother's November 20th birthday greeting from her father hints at a brief face-to-face visit but expresses concern and bafflement about her whereabouts. He wrote the letter, but hung onto it for several days, waiting to hear from her and to divine where to send the greeting. She would have been about seven months pregnant by this time—and showing, no matter how badly she wanted to obfuscate the facts.

> *Dear Yry,*
>
> *Let me wish you many happy returns of the day, success and what is most important contentment which can be reached only by learning slowly to harmoniously adjust oneself to life, a difficult task, a goal fraught with bitter and overt experiences. You are not just an average person; you live your life through your heart, and this will cause you many a heartache in your life.*
>
> *I was very glad to see you after so many years and to find that the association with self-satisfied mediocre people of unlimited selfishness could not kill in you the core of an inquiring and searching mind and will, and that under a seemingly hard and abrupt exterior there is a beating heart of understanding for poor humanity and its problems, still somewhat full of preconceived prejudices and generalizations but willing to investigate and to learn. I comprehend your inclination to love animals. You have not yet learned to drink of the well of human suffering, selfishness and egotism, and to*

Wyoming, August 1942

assimilate what there is good in contact with our neighbors who give us constant food for thought and create in us the hunger for inquiry and exploration in the realms of godly of humans." [The lecture continues ad nauseam.]

I am enclosing a cheque for $20 as a birthday present, the other $20 a weekly allowance and from today to be followed weekly. I hope you will have a good time and will enjoy your liberty and youth, and your studies.

Don't be too hypochondriac. There is no being who is feeling one day as good as another. We are all influenced by emotions, even the animals, to a certain extent, weather, events impress us and influence our bodily well-being. ... And let us hear from you. Your mother is thinking of you all day, misses you and is looking forward to every line you may and will write her. She is nervous and unfortunately worries too much about the house; so don't forget to give her the pleasure of hearing from you.

With many good wishes and hearty greetings, lovingly your father. [Note from Norah on back] *We received your letter of the 25th and I am writing soon. What are the results? You have not told us. My love to Elouise and regards to Jim. Much love to you my Dear write soon again. Lovingly Norah.*

It does sounds as if perhaps she made a quick trip to New York City, which is why the correspondence from Immigration and Naturalization got so tangled. But she was clearly holding her parents at bay, withholding information, details, probably too nervous and exhausted to deal with their reactions to her situation.

My Life With an Enigma

Yry & her victim, Mrs. Greer - 1942

Yry at the CX Ranch

Part V: Back on the East Coast

"If you ask me and my sister to describe our mother, you'll get two totally different mothers, and neither one of us is lying. Memory is a form of fiction, and we can't help that. So we are very much the creation of the stories we tell ourselves. And we don't know we're telling stories." Michael Ventura, *We've Had a Hundred Years of Psychotherapy – And the World's Getting Worse.*

Between December 1943 and March 1944 Mother lodged at The Frederick Hotel, room 308, in Huntington, West Virginia. She spent Christmas with friends Eloise and Jim and their kids. It was a simple environment. No explanations needed, gentle understanding available, and Eloise, having been through childbirth twice, was a mother-in-absentia during the challenges of the last trimester of a first pregnancy. Mom still had every intention of a quick return to Wyoming, where she felt her life's work was yet to begin.

In her journal, Mother vented energetically in a tirade against the proposed Austin-Wadsworth National War Service Act, a form of Civilian Selective Service, which would have imposed mandatory two-year domestic work assignments for women ages 18-50 and men 18-65. The theory was to mobilize an untapped workforce, thus freeing up men from critical industry jobs for military service.

> *To live and work on a ranch, the free and open life and association with living things, the physical exercise which brings joy and satisfaction of mental and spiritual nature has become a necessity to my life. In fact it is the only thing I have to live for; take that from me and there is nothing left to live for. I am now thirty and too old to put off my life work any longer. I do not have the time to fool around with factory or office or any other kind of work so it would be useless for me to volunteer for anything as these city jobs are all immaterial to me...and what dirty politician would take the trouble to help me get to ranch work 2,500 miles out westward from here when ranch work is not even recognized as proper work for a woman. Yes, women can work drills and what not of heavy work in factories but let one try to punch cattle and the laugh is on, though the actual work is no harder.*
>
> *Put me on my honor and I'll work; Force me and I'm the mother of rebellion itself. That's the way I'm made, the pioneer spirit of my ancestors come to light again, maybe. That is probably why I got on so well with westerners, because they still have spunk enough to stand up and fight for their free rights and tell a usurping government where to get off ...*
>
> *I was planning for more study at U of W next winter, but of course this bill would upset that entirely since study would not be considered an exemption at my age. Anyway, I'm returning there as soon as my business in NY is completed by hook or crook, even if I have to turn a criminal to be there.*

This explains why my mother held Rosie the Riveters in contempt. She considered their contributions frivolous.

On Christmas Day, Herman wrote a chatty letter informing her that since they were still without household help, he and

Norah had chosen to dine out for Christmas Eve. They'd encountered a clutch of couples whose robust holiday cheer spurred them to finish their meal without hesitation and move on to the Christmas service. He ruminated about religion and faith and hoped she'd had a good holiday.

The next letter acknowledged the end of another year, and as always, included some tidbits of Herman wisdom, encouraging Mom to make the best of life by rendering it useful. "What we so often desire we must learn to renounce!" he chided. And, "we should not hunger after that what we are denied." A check for $125 was enclosed with the letter.

The Arrival

At the end of January 1944, Yry again visited Dr. Ratcliff, as evidenced by a $75 receipt. On February 5, an unnamed female baby, #8237-44, was born to Mrs. Allen Wilcox in Cabell County, Huntington, West Virginia. On February 28, Mrs. Allen Wilcox paid the final $25 on Dr. Ratcliff's bill. What was Yry going through between Christmas and the end of February? The emotional toll must have been enormous, the decisions momentous, and the apparent solutions no less than monstrous. There are few breadcrumbs to follow.

A congratulatory letter, of sorts, arrived from New Jersey on February 16, 1944. This scolding letter from one of her friends is a window to Yry's state of mind leading up to the birth.

> *Congrats. I expected it much later ... Are you mad thinking of giving the baby away? And I was so proud of you that you were going through with it—that you didn't have an unnatural abortion. Don't give the baby away. If you have to fight the whole world to do it, keep the baby. You can run away from many things, but you can't run away from your conscience. Your conscience would kill you in the end. As it is, your nervous system is the weakest part of you ... You've disregarded conventions all your life, don't start thinking of them now ... you better plan on giving her a religious upbringing so she won't have the spiritual void you have ... You*

won't be able to live in a hotel with an infant. You will need to find a rooming house to rent. After a few months you'll be able to find a day nursery to care for the baby and you'll be able to get a job. From now on, you have to think of your baby. You've always lacked emotional stability, and your baby ought to make you kinder and more charitable in your opinions.

Your letter of January 10th bothered me a lot. Now I know why. You were full of plans, selfish plans that didn't seem to include your baby. You were going to NY and then west again and nothing about the baby. Never did I realize that you could be contemplating giving your own flesh and blood away. Do you think you're the first mother to have a baby out of wedlock? ... You won't be able to keep your baby a secret, not for very long, anyway. So you better decide on a story you want to tell the world. With all the men in the service, you might say that your husband is a soldier in the service overseas. Later you can say he was killed. It's better to lie, than to give one's baby away. You'll have to decide for yourself what to tell your folks. You may tell your mother the truth or some such story as I mentioned. Your folks are lonely and in time they'd be happy to have a grandchild. I'm sure they'd help you all they could. You've been willful and unkind to them. You've blamed them even when they were right and you were wrong.

The next startling clue to Yry's despair is the carbon copy of a letter that was witnessed by a notary public on February 29, 1944, two weeks after the birth of her child.

State of West Virginia
County of Cabell, To Wit:
To Whom it may concern:

Whereas, I am the mother of a female infant born February 5, 1944, being unable to provide personal care for the said child, I have agreed that it be placed in a boarding home by the Division of Child Welfare, Department of Public Assistance.

I further state that the board for the said child has been paid by me to the Division of Child Welfare who in turn will pay the boarding parents.

It is understood that the said child is placed temporarily and will be returned to me if I can make suitable plans for her.

Signed: Mrs. Allen Wilcox.

Yry's room was paid through March and she used her Huntington library card to check out books through March. She had assumed that she could push out a baby and hand it over to adoptive parents. But life tangles intricately with love. After long hours of pain, she briefly held the child that emerged from her womb. That embrace changed her life. Previous plans evaporated. She needed an entirely new strategy. With her baby temporarily entrusted to foster parents, Yry swallowed enormous pride and visited her parents.

Herman and Norah, waiting for her to step off the train, embraced her with joy and uncharacteristic warmth. For several days, Yry stepped gingerly around the topic uppermost in her mind. Eventually she confided to her mother, half expecting to be disowned. The response surprised her. Norah, sympathetic to youthful scandal, was ecstatic at having her only child at home again, especially at a time of such need. The presence of a grandchild was an unexpected bonus.

Yry and Norah sat together in the living room with Herman. Choosing their words judiciously they took turns explaining the situation. They expected fireworks and recriminations from this analytical and rather sanctimonious man. But he, like his wife, was delighted by the prospect of another generation springing, one-step-removed, from his loins. And to have Yry home again, managing the household for Norah, would solve that untenable problem that had nagged him for years—the lack of adequate household help.

Back to the concrete prison

And so it was that Yry returned briefly to West Virginia to gather up her babe, say her thank-yous and good-byes to Eloise and Jim, and return to the trap she'd been so determined to escape. Now, though, the baby distracted her from failed hopes and dreams. There was more to live for than "physical exercise which brings joy and satisfaction of mental and spiritual nature." She would return to the west when the time was right.

Despite the circumstances, motherhood thrilled her. She'd always wanted a child—a piece of herself that would reflect the unconditional love that she'd yearned for in her own life; and this little being was an enduring legacy of her deep love for Dallas. She was irrevocably tied to him now, even if he didn't understand or acknowledge that fact. Determined to raise a strong and healthy child, she foreswore prepared baby food, opting instead to grind her own meals for the baby. She sewed tiny tops and bottoms and dresses trimmed with bric-a-brac. She even made a toasty-warm, woolen coat for Joan. Now she daydreamed about the day her child would first straddle a horse. She kept copious notes for the baby book, recording weight and size, and noting each developmental step: first smile, first fingernail clipping, first fever, first successful, unassisted roll-over, first attempt to crawl, then to stand, then to walk.

Perhaps the biggest surprise was how easily her parents embraced Joan. The baby had drawn her closer to her mother. In a moment of rare confidentiality, Norah revealed her own youthful scandal. Yry was shocked to learn that her very upstanding and conventional parents had never officially married. Norah had fled her first marriage to a syphilitic husband, and being Catholic, was unable to remarry in the church.

Back on the East Coast

Herman was besotted by his grandchild. Tossing dignity to the wind he'd come home from the office and immediately collapse to the floor, mindless of damage to the knees of his business trousers. He'd mime, cajole, and coax giggles and joyful shrieks from the baby. Yry stuffed back little jabs of jealousy at how her father doted on Joan, enduring drool and spittle and completely abandoning dignity. Herman was home more now, traveled less, and enjoyed the luxury of being fully engaged in the baby's progress. How different her life might have been if she'd been that important to him when she was a baby.

Fall broke the shimmering heat of New York City. The trees in the park began their seasonal wardrobe change. Yry's time evaporated in the endless and mindless tasks of grocery shopping, cleaning, laundry, ironing, and meal preparation. Her refuge, once again, was the park. Pushing the pram with Joan tucked inside and dropping peanuts for the squirrels as she went, she pondered the future, wondering how soon she could make the transition back to Wyoming.

~~~

An undated issue of the *Yry Press* reveals the tale she and Eloise concocted. This missive was not distributed until November or December of 1944, nearly a year after she returned to the east coast. This version of the story differs slightly from what she told me and from what she was prepared to tell Joan.

Hello all of you Western Friends!

I've been silent as the prairie and I'll bet you think I've forgotten you all and decided to stay back here. Well, guess again, because it's not so. I've thought of you, every one of you, often and of our beautiful country but my return there has been delayed for the "duration." You see, nature took a hand in my affairs, but to explain that I have to go back a little.

I was married while out west, but we kept it secret, or at least intended to do so for quite some time, as I didn't want any objections from home. My dear parents would have raised the usual remonstrances about a son-in-law whose family and person were both entirely unknown to them and I'd had enough fighting on a similar subject once before. But here is where nature took a hand—result, my baby daughter whose name is Joan. At any rate she took care of the objections by so conquering their hearts as to make her grandfather at least, seem at times to be quite crazy. She's blue eyed and fairer than I, at present at least; and most people say she looks like her grandma, I can see mostly her daddy in her. Of course, it's hard to tell in a young baby just what or who they look like.

How does the Scotch folks song go?
Oh where and oh where is your highland laddie gone?
He's gone to fight the fee for King George upon the throne
And its ooh in my heart that I wish him safe at home.

Well, that ought to be our theme song, mine and Joan's 'cause Daddy is fighting the war in the Pacific (not so pacific now I should say) and we plan for a ranch and a peaceful, healthful life when it's all over.

For the present I'm with my parents. I don't think a baby should be toted around all over, children have a right to a home, security and regularity, but she's going to be a rootin', tootin' little westerner. (I can't wait to put her on a horse). So you see I've really been busy since you saw me last.

The summer in NY has been excessively hot and humid. ... City life is rottener than ever. People hereabouts are all very bad tempered, unfriendly and uncivil; labor is short in every line (the stores are begging for part time housewives and offering the moon as compensation) and consequently the performance of employees is bad. My mother remains without help in her home as she would rather have none than bad maids and have them leave every 2 weeks as happens to her friends.

How often I dream of such edible delectables as thick western ranch cream, fresh butter, and meat aplenty, T-bones, pork, pheasant, and elk steaks, not to forget freshly laid eggs and vegetables picked an hour or so before consumption. If any of you envy me my city life, take a glance at my city diet: [she goes on about the travails of finding passable food with rationing coupons, black market, etc.]

What's worse is worrying about my husband being constantly in danger of his very life; but there again is Joan claiming my time and attention and there's nothing like work to keep a man's soul healthy and his mind from being morbid.

(Note to Laramieites and Casperites) It wouldn't take much to make NY as sooty and dirty as Laramie and as windy as either Laramie or Casper. We are on the Hudson River where the wind blows like 60 and howls thru the apartment and the elevator shafts like on top a high mountain. (I'm the only one that doesn't object to the howling. It makes me feel at home); and the tankers etc. come in to stock up and overhaul, besides the increased size of the factories on the Jersey side—and from all this one gets clouds of black stinking soot (soft coal) billowing over NY and into one's home.

Greet Wyoming for me; I miss it painfully and hope to hear from you all soon. Tell me about the grass, the cattle, the weather, the crops, the college, and your personal doings. I hope this "masterpiece" will make up for my

> neglect to answer letters etc. and I hope my readers are all well and spend a happy Christmas and a happier New Year.

In later years, Mom opened up to an assortment of friends and relatives, each of whom heard slight variations of this story. I think she rather got a kick out of shocking people with her former transgressions.

Global Chaos

Yry's troubles paled in comparison to the misery of millions around the world. Newspaper headlines screamed from overseas. There was no news from the German relatives. The British dodged bombs, searched for food, and tried to stay warm and dry. Only a few hastily scribbled notes dribbled out of England to confirm their existence. The Russians kept pushing the eastern front, crowing about the miserable conditions of the retreating German soldiers. Was Yry's cousin Hermann one of those sick, scarecrows in tattered clothes fleeing the Russians? And what about food? Did the family have enough food? Were they safe? Had they survived the winter?

The world rejoiced in May of 1945 when Hitler abruptly disappeared. Allied forces entered Berlin. Herman immediately barraged the US State Department with pleas for information about his brother and family in Germany. Letters began to trickle out.

Herman's parents had survived five years of bombing. Berlin was a smoldering death trap with few intact buildings—those that stood, did so precariously. Willy and Nelly were grateful for their windowless home with tattered roof and no utilities. It was a base from which to scrounge for a living. Their stick figures shivered in frigid dampness. Heating and cooking fuel were dear as an honest politician. Categorized as "old and unskilled" by the Russian regime that controlled their sector of Berlin, they received less than 1,248 calories worth of rations per day. Their daughter, Yry's Cousin Lore, left her parents alone in Berlin to commence a harrowing journey through the war-torn landscape to locate her brother, Hermann, who languished in a military hospital in the south. Word had arrived that his leg had been amputated and he was in critical condition. Lore set out to find and help her brother, even though that meant leaving her parents to fend for themselves.

Norah's English relatives fared little better than Herman's in Germany. Food there was also scarce, nerves as well as buildings, shaky. A cousin of Norah's expressed a sentiment common to the citizenry of both war-ravaged countries.

> *I am sure the peoples of this earth do not, as individuals, wish to fight each other. It seems to be the respective governments which conduct us to our graves; to wit, the recent Moscow Conference. To realize our position here today would fill pages. In a word, it is not England anymore, and is fast becoming a "Zazi" state; that is almost unbelievable after fighting against such a doctrine for six years.*

Through a Swedish business contact, Yry's father arranged to have care packages smuggled into Berlin from Sweden. Each week, he gave Yry $200 for supplies. She'd trudge to the store, often pushing Joan's pram and loading it with non-perishable foods, warm clothes, and blankets. Back at the flat, she boxed everything up to ship overseas, some to England and some to Germany. Then off to the Post Office she went—all without the use of a car. Sometimes she used a two-wheeled shopping cart, which worked well while the weather was good. But jerking or pushing that load through snow and ice was a challenge.

After a harrowing journey through four national occupation zones, Lore located her brother Hermann and nursed him back to the world of hope and determination. When he was well enough to leave the hospital, she helped him relocate to Langen, Germany, where the southern Pauls still lived in their modest home. To this crowded venue, came Willy and Nellie from Berlin. Lore could then care for her entire family from one central location. The rural setting around Langen made it easier to find and dig up abandoned potatoes, and to offer an extra pair of hands to farm women whose husbands had not returned from the front. The rewards were milk, eggs, and occasionally meat and vegetables.

~~~

Years later, Mother told stories about those grueling shopping trips. She'd gaze at her hands and remember her fingers—cracked and split from wrangling cardboard boxes, folding and cutting paper, and wrapping string around each box. The packages she couldn't fit into the shopping cart, dangled from sore fingers.

In my youthful arrogance I'd dismissed much of what she said, judging her descriptions of bloody fingers as hyperbole. Having seen her fly off the handle in histrionic fits of rage, I mistrusted her penchant for drama. By the time I realized how important, how real her stories were, it was too late. Between my inattention and holes in my memory large enough to devour a planet, I've spent the better part of my adult life flogging myself for the loss of details I once had such easy access to.

Fortunately, Mother was a hoarder and a compulsive list keeper. Scattered through her things after she died, were lists she'd scribbled in the margins of junk mail, the backs of envelopes and bank statements. She had lists of lists; and they hid from her inside shoe boxes, folders, books, bags, and purses. During that period of post-war mailings, my mom kept fastidious records of what she purchased for the relatives. Partly she was accounting to her father how she'd spent his money. But she also listed the contents of each box to compare with what actually arrived. She followed each mailing with a letter listing all the items she'd sent.

At both ends of the transaction, the family marveled at what survived layers of hunger, temptation, and larceny along the journey. Often two thirds of what left New York City, disappeared before reaching its destination.

This passage from a letter dated, 24 June 1947 is a typical accounting of goods gratefully received.

> *Received the wonderful gift parcel that was mailed 13 May from New York. It arrived on 20 June. Inside: 1 pound rice, 1 pound bacon, 5.5 ounces Pate e Foie, egg powder, coffee, chicken spread, 1 pound honey, Mazola oil, Spam, Cocoa mix, black tea, Kraft American cheese, Boneless chicken, and nuts. Many thanks for sending it. It is nearly impossible to get anything eatable or otherwise from the shops here these days.*

~~~

A trail of letters from the CX Ranch to Norah dates to early 1944 and indicates that the Cormacks had no knowledge of Yry's pregnancy. Dallas was mentioned only in recounting a private airplane crash that he had survived. In the fall, Claire wrote about George's campaign for sheriff and included this reference:

> *Norah, of course we hadn't heard of Yry's marriage and it seems very strange. The baby must be like you if she has beautiful hands.*

To Yry, Claire sent holiday greetings and pictures of the ranch, horses, and new foals.

In July and August of 1945, Yry escaped the city heat to visit the New Hampshire resort where she'd often vacationed with her parents. At 18 months, Joan toddled around investigating the grounds, the guests, the cats, dogs, and whomever wasn't quick enough to elude her embrace. She charmed everyone, including Bozo, her first equine pal. Like her mother, she loved to swim.

In a letter to Yry, Norah complained about the city coming to a complete halt for two days to celebrate VJ Day. And she was scandalized by her doctor's suggestion that a nasty rash might be a result of her Elizabeth Arden, Paradise Pink nail polish. Norah's chatty letter included a $200 check to cover Yry's and Joan's expenses.

The bliss of the woods couldn't last forever. Yry and Joan returned to the city, Joan to charming her grandfather and Yry to shopping, wrapping, posting, and cooking.

Post-war communication stabilized; letters chased each other across the ocean. Written on every inch of onion skin sheets, family members added their personal greetings to each letter, receipt of which was treasured equally on both ends.

Despite dismal conditions, letters from Germany were peppered with whimsy and graciousness. In December 1946, Cousin Hermann who, with his sister's help, was adjusting to a new body, wrote with pragmaticism and philosophical wisdom.

> ... I changed my study for there is no more research of chemistry and so I study special engineering for building big bridges. That will have a good future for there are still only a few good bridges here. During my free time I study philosophy. I always wished to become a researcher of the atomic sciences and to see the last limit of human thinking of our time. It's wonderful to comprehend the last connections of our life. So I try to think in an absolute manner about our living and being human. Politics are only things of moments and occasion. Sciences exist eternally in nature. We live only a short time and it is our own task to exhaust it completely.
>
> You can't imagine the life here nowadays. Sometimes I think about Spengler's book, "The End of the Evening Land." That's how it is, and best is to laugh about all, for

weeping doesn't have any purpose. My sister (Lore) says, "More laughing! When you laugh ten minutes it will have the same value as eating an egg, and since we have no eggs, we laugh!"

When I first saw Eastern Europe and Russia (as a German conscript) I couldn't comprehend the possibility of living in such a primitive manner. Now we ourselves do so ...

Four months later he wrote:

My dearest Iry,
Thanks for the packages! ... The chocolate bar disappeared at once. Lore, Hedi, and Verena could nourish themselves on only chocolate!

You can't imagine the arrival of a parcel containing clothes. It is opened by our "three" with a noise that would make Apaches jealous! The stockings are cheered like a newly elected president after a big speech. Aunt Emma is sitting down weeping and laughing about her excited girls. Afterward I have a private modeling show as the three parade in their new clothes.

Tomorrow the new semester begins. I hope it will be as successful as possible, for it is difficult to get glasses for the laboratories, caused by the iron curtain. (The big glass plants are all on the other side.) Despite all the pains of Marshall, the Moscow conference has brought hardly a success and that is a strong brake for starting the engine. ...

Spring gives new hope and strength. The apple trees in the garden are flourishing wonderfully. ...

The letters always included greetings to her parents and to little Joan. Frequently the references to Joan also included allusions to the tragic loss of her dear father, indicating that the father issue had been resolved when his ship sank at sea. I wonder how many other unplanned pregnancies were resolved in a similar fashion during the 1940s.

Meanwhile, worry gnawed at Herman's health. Not one to share his concerns or to complain, he grew gaunt. Joan's liveliness brightened an otherwise dour household. As the decade closed, Yry was still putting together care packages for the German relatives, but less frequently. The packages now coincided with birthdays, anniversaries, or holidays.

Yry and Joan spent hours imagining themselves into exotic scenes in life-like dioramas in the Museum of Natural History. Or they went to the Zoological Park where Joan giggled as the elephants suctioned peanuts from her open palm. They spent hours together in Central Park; Joan patiently chummed ducks, geese, and squirrels with peanuts and breadcrumbs while Yry fiddled with her Leica, perhaps imagining yet another career possibility. The two of them formalized their outings by creating a botany notebook where pressed flowers and photos of plants illustrated their shared research projects. Yry's papers contained countless references to nature.

> *I have found great satisfaction in studying nature, as I have great longing for contact with the earth. I think we would all be saner if we would know nature better and understand more fully our place as one small particle in a great complicated and wonderful universe.*

During the summers Yry and Joan escaped to New Hampshire or upstate New York where they could swim, pick berries, and ride horses. Occasionally Herman and Norah joined them, but Norah's severe arthritis and bouts of depression made travel difficult.

Joan dove into the world of language and books. Precocious and well mentored by her mother and grandparents, she was reading by four and by age five she meticulously printed letters to the delighted relatives in Europe.

~~~

Back on the East Coast

With her 40s looming, my mother ignored impertinent questions about her marital status. But schoolgirl notions of love lurked in her heart. Mother never shared stories of her courtship with my father. Given her melodramatic ways, I mistrusted anything she said about him. Certain facts can be corroborated by my birth certificate, which I didn't see until days before my own marriage. Others can be inferred from letters and from the numerous short stories that Yry penned, and which corresponded quite miraculously to my birth.

This one was dated May 1951.

> As I read back thru these pages, I see my faults, I see my groping, clumsy attempts to attain happiness, the rainbows I've chased and the ignorance of human nature which led me astray more than once. I see also the ever pervading sense of loneliness, the striving for being loved which runs thru all my sentiments, (a thing I remember from earliest childhood) After being burned and seared and disappointed, I approach the middle years of my life and find that in my heart which I thought had gone dead and barren, blooms a new love. This knowledge like a stroke of lightening, making me tremble with dizziness. At first I was afraid and skeptical. Would love play me false again? Now I am hopeful and happy and very, very humble and grateful that yet another chance has come my way. And I pray, "Oh God, make it right this time. Let him love me. Let me be right for him and he for me. Guide me in the right path to deserve his love and bring good things and happiness into his life."

The entry goes on to talk of all that her love has brought her. Friendship, companionship, and FAITH! Oh, and now she discovers that Judaism holds the tenets of all she has held true.

Marriage

I spent my childhood puzzling over where I came from. According to the official story, Mother had been married before, so Joan's father was different than my own. That was supposed to account for our entirely different looks—chubby Joan's angelic blond hair, blue eyes, and dewey skin was such a contrast to my scrawny physique, thin, freckled face, with a prodigious nose, and lank brown hair. But it didn't fully account for the fact that I lived in a household of three people, not one of whom shared a single feature.

I had never seen a photo of my father. In the midst of one of our epic battles when Mother was out of the house, Joan yelled something about my father. I don't remember the details. I'd probably threatened to go find him and live with him or some such nonsense, which typically flew from my mouth in the heat of combat. What I remember is spittle gathering in the corner of Joan's mouth—a sure measure of her excitement, "You want to see what your Faatheh looked like? Huh? Huh? You just wait little sister; I've got a photo of him." She dashed out of the room and returned too quickly.

"Here, take a look. Look at your Faatheh!" She jammed the photo at me and despite my obscene curiosity, I clamped my eyes shut and squirmed free of her grasp, determined not to look. I sensed that if there was something Joan wanted to share with me while we were treating each other like gas and matches, then it was meant to do maximum harm. There was something about my father I shouldn't see, at least not at that moment and in that manner. I visualized a two-headed monster, one of whose ugly mugs I'd inherited, much as Mom sometimes accused me of having inherited his "god-damned stubborn streak."

Family resemblances unsettled me, a reminder of my own aberrance. My best childhood friend was the twin of both her younger sisters. Even my high school best friend with white-blond hair and baby-blue eyes resembled her dark-haired, dark-eyed sister. But I looked like I'd been dropped into my family as an afterthought. At least that was the way I felt until I finally met other members of my family during a visit to Germany with my Mother when I was 27.

Mother had asked me to join her on this epic journey to the old country, her first since she'd left Europe at the age of eleven—my first ever. Finally the names on aerograms and greeting cards metamorphosed into warm bodies. We were gathered at Tante Nelly's flat in Duisberg, Germany for a celebration of our arrival. Cousin Lore and her mother lived comfortably together in this little flat. We spent the day sightseeing with Lore, while Tante Nelly spent the day cooking. In the evening Cousin Hermann and his very chic wife arrived, and we six sat around a large round, beautifully-laid table to feast on Nelly's home-cooking. She'd been to the market and purchased fresh white asparagus—a beloved German delicacy—and had prepared the most divine homemade chocolate pudding I'd ever tasted.

After the dishes had been cleared and washed, we pushed the dining table to the side and relaxed on a small sofa, an easy chair, and the dining chairs. Out came Schnapps and Punktion, Lore's private term for that special punctuation at the end of the meal—rich dark, Belgian chocolate with a red wine chaser.

The conversation slipped effortlessly into German. I sat, the silent observer, listening and watching; straining for telltale clues from talking hands, and listening deeply to sieve the few stray German words I recognized and string them together, trying to tread water in the conversation. With ears on high alert, I noticed how my mother's German speech differed from theirs! Though she was fully fluent, there was a slight—a nearly imperceptible accent—not the typical American accent that garbles the German language into a horrendous guttural gack. Her accent—my God! I realized it was the exact same indefinable accent that infiltrated her English speech! I grinned with recognition and thought about what distinguished my mother from convention.

Not only were Mother's speech *patterns* different from those of native Wyomingites, but her pronunciations were different as well. First, she *pronounced* words—all the sounds and syllables, unlike the slurred western tongue that stretches some vowels, while combining others, and runs words one into another. Mother didn't have a British accent. Nor did she have a German accent, or New York, or East Coast accent. Mother's speech was an amalgam of all the places she'd lived baked into a unique, layered confection that set her apart no matter where she was.

I considered how strangers had shocked me by claiming that I have an accent. But my accusers struggle to establish the nature of my accent. *Do I sound like my mother?* I don't think so. As a child, my peers bullied me into proper pronunciation and word choice. It's crick not creeeek; ruf not rooooof. It was never a couch, it was a sofa; not an ice box but a fridge.

As my mind strayed, Nelly noticed my vacant gaze. *"Ach, die Liebe Linda! Wir mussen auf English gesprachen!"* Ach, dear Linda. We must speak English!"

"Nein, nein," I replied, struggling to form a sentence. *"Ich verstehe etwas."* I understand some. Then, trying to prove my clever ability to decipher, I repeated back what I thought they had been talking about. Giggles erupted. I was way off. A pattern that continues to this day.

So, for a while, the conversation switched back to English. But eventually, complex ideas took hold and they slipped seamlessly back into German. Hours passed. I was intoxicated and exhausted, yet entranced.

Suddenly, I was again the focus of Nelly's observation. She was speaking German, but looking at me as she did so. I picked up "so like Willy." Nelly was commenting not just on my physical features but also upon my expressions and attitude. Willy, her husband, brother of my grandfather, uncle of my mother, had died many years ago. I'd seen photos of him. He was a thin man with a mustache, pointed features, a large beak, and sunken eyes. Of course, I hadn't really considered it at the time, but I'm sure those images recorded a man who was on the point of starvation just after the war.

One of the many war stories that repeatedly surfaced was of the first care package to arrive in Berlin. Mother had included cooking lard along with tins of meat and veggies. No one had consumed animal fat or protein in ages. Uncle Willy eagerly devoured a tower of lard on a slice of dark bread. The richness landed in his stomach, did a 360 flip, and came back up. The poor man made a mad dash for the outhouse and lost his false teeth along with the lard. As I write this, I question my memory. Is it real? Right or wrong, the story is a symbol of what war and starvation mean.

In any case, at that moment, with all eyes directed my way, heads nodding in recognition and respect, I felt as if the warm rays of god's light were streaming through the clouds and had landed squarely on me. I had already recognized Lore's stark features as my own. She wore her looks so gracefully that I felt ashamed of my own vanity. All those years of ruing my thin, lifeless hair, thin lips, and hawkish nose seemed frivolous in the light of this strong woman who had lived through astonishing atrocities and come through with a serenity and joy for life that was a model for lesser human beings.

And then there was her mother, Nelly, with a nose every bit as large as my own, beautiful as she approached the last years of a long and difficult life. Her dark eyes flashed under thick, dark eyebrows that remembered the original color of her curly white hair. Dressed in a simple black dress with a pair of gold necklaces for trim, she imbued a quiet elegance inside and outside the domain of her kitchen. And she beamed at me with unmistakable delight, seeing in the tilt of my head or the look of concentration knitting my brows, a flicker of her beloved husband come to life before her eyes.

I looked again at Hermann and at Lore. Yes, we all shared something—a hardness around the jawline that draws to a point at the chin, narrow faces, small and narrow eyes—in short, there is a shared angularity in our features. I am too good at masking my feelings. I'm quite sure no one in that room comprehended the seismic shift that began in my soul that night.

But what of my origins? Mother spared no grace when speaking of my "faatheh." She hated him enough to refuse to accept child support, to refuse to let him know where she was taking his daughter, and to enroll me in school using her maiden name rather than his name as it appeared on my birth certificate. Aside from my teenaged temper tantrums during which I raged that I would just go live with my father as I slammed the bedroom door behind me, I never gave the man a thought. Later, when friends seemed shocked that I wasn't curious about my father, I considered the prospect of finding him. But then I sat myself down and thought about the 21 years that my mother had been my shelter, my support, my conscience, my counselor, my nurse when ill, and my whipping board when angry. Where had he been when I had the measles, the mumps, the teen devil? He could have found me, had he really wanted to. My mother had not made it easy, but anyone can be found. The ruse of her maiden name was not all that clever. And so I continued to consider him a nonentity—a sperm donor.

But reality is not flat. Truth is never black or white. His story remains untold and that is inherently unfair to him. I was shocked to learn, many years after my mother's death, that Joan had adored my father. She felt that Mother had shrewishly driven him away. All those years, I had assumed that she shared Mother's dislike of the man. Reality is round, shaped by the players within and the audience without. And so, as I recount the years after my arrival on scene, I offer a view from both without and within, but it is only a glimpse. There are many more threads, many more stitches in the story.

In 1951 Mother was pushing 40. She'd been mulishly tuning out admonitions of friends and family. Settling down was for someone else. However, she was still a vibrant woman with needs and desires. Between household chores, caring for Joan, and corresponding with the relatives in Germany, she made room for a social life. She longed to fill the cavernous need in her heart. She thought she knew what that need was, but each time she seemed close to satisfying it, it slipped away—a shimmering mirage on the horizon. Now, once again the mirage was dancing, promising friendship, companionship, faith, and cleansing of wounds.

Perhaps today's psychobabblers would suggest that the mirage was her father's love, the need for warmth, acceptance, and physical closeness that had always been missing. But psychobabble was not de rigueur in the fifties. Nor would she have heeded the warning, had it been available. My mother was destined to follow her heart no matter where it led.

I have only one side of the story. I never met my father or any of my father's people. His side of the story is buried along with him in some grave or urn which I've been too disinterested to disinter. When I graduated from high school, my mother dug a couple of savings bonds out of hiding. They had been bought for me by my paternal grandmother upon the occasion of my birth. These were modest bonds, nevertheless, I was touched to realize that there were people I'd never known who had once entertained high hopes for me.

But I delay. It is not easy to broach a topic that should be so important and yet about which one knows so little. Predictably, Sidney Keschner was ten years Yry's senior. He was Jewish, and according to her, when they met he was still living in a flat with his parents. When he and my mother started dating, she began studying Judaism, hoping that this religion could answer the cosmological questions that Christianity had failed to address.

On April 5, 1952, Yramiris H. Paul married Sidney R. Keschner at the Stephen Wise Free Synagogue, Rabbi Edward Klein presiding. They had dated for over two years, and Sidney had seemed to Yry, as well as to her parents, like a modest, easy going gentleman. Their ideas and tastes seemed to mesh, and Yry felt that at last she had found her soulmate. He and Joan got along well. They had decided to forego birth control. They moved into a five-room apartment at 219 W. 81st Street.

But, according to her, there was no honeymoon. By the end of their first week together, before she'd even finished unpacking, Sidney's character reversed; he became sullen and snippy. When pressed, he belched out a list of petty offences that convinced him he could not live with her. Astonished, she apologized and thanked him for telling her what was wrong so she could learn to please him. (This is a completely uncharacteristic response, one which I never observed in my years of living with her.) Harmony ensued for a few weeks until he fell into another sullen spell and more fights erupted. Was my father bipolar?

Interestingly, it wasn't until I began posting chapters of this book on my blog that I heard from a Keschner. Out of the blue, a comment appeared, alerting me to some errors in my assumptions about my father. According to this potential cousin, Sidney was not bipolar. He "was an incredible, wonderful, generous, charismatic man, who lived a great life and was a sensational uncle." There is another side to the story, but since this is Yry's story, I will tell it as she revealed it. Sidney's story is for another book.

Mother described a confining relationship in which dinner was to be ready, delicious, and piping hot no matter what time Sidney arrived home from work. I am so ignorant of this father, that I do not even know what his work entailed. As my mother described the situation to me, what Sidney expected of marriage was a mother with a vagina. My mother was willing and able to provide the later, but indignant by the first expectation.

As she told it, barely a month after the marriage, just before the New York City heat bloomed, Mother prepared an extravagant dinner for Sidney. She'd scraped and saved for two weeks to augment her shopping budget for a pair of steaks and a nice bottle of wine. The evening got off to a bad start because, as usual, Sidney was late getting home. The vegetables were overcooked, and the meat not yet cooked because Mother didn't want to risk ruining the expensive steaks. Sidney fumed and pouted while Mother quickly broiled the steaks, further heating the small apartment.

After dinner, Mother brought out a custard that she'd prepared according to her mother-in-law's recipe. Sidney had already pushed away from the table and marched into the living room to hide behind the sprawl of the evening newspaper. He growled that her damned radio program was too loud. She scurried back into the kitchen to turn off the serialized radio drama that kept her company during her time alone in the apartment.

The magical evening that she'd envisioned evaporated in more acrimony. Exasperated by the way the evening was evolving, she spilled the reason for her special efforts.

Sidney's sharp response: "Do you really think we should be having a child when we clearly aren't compatible?"

Stunned, she wondered just what he was alluding to. It was a bit late to debate the merits of having a child at this point. Taking a few minutes to compose her thoughts, she responded.

"Sidney, marriage is not something that happens magically when a priest or rabbi pronounces some words over you. It takes time—years of sharing, caring, and trying to please each other and meeting each other halfway to work things out."

He snorted.

Three months into the marriage, her pregnancy was confirmed. Several days of relative calm would invariably erupt in another round of accusations and complaints: her cooking was killing him, she was rude to his friends, she was spending all his money (this despite the monthly stipend that Herman pitched in to pay for Joan's expenses). They traded insults, and each threatened to leave, but argued over who would get the apartment.

One July night he became a raging bull. Hurling insults, he pulled his mattress and bedding through the apartment to the spare bedroom which housed Yry's books and Joan's toys. Screaming profanity and lobbing things into the hallway, the neighbors grew concerned at the racket. Then he demanded proof that the baby in her belly was his.

Joan tiptoed out of her room, white-faced and solemn. Neither Mother nor daughter could sleep, so they curled up together in Joan's bed and read for an hour or so and stayed together the entire night. Yry was unsure of what danger lurked behind Sidney's violent mood swings.

The next morning, Sidney's mother called and asked why she hadn't seen Yry and Joan lately. Yry confessed all that had transpired during the past few weeks. Even Sidney's parents agreed that, given these conditions so early in the marriage, there was no hope of it lasting.

Reno

I battle the urge to belittle my mother for suckering up to the promise of love. That a woman approaching 40 would again turn to her father for help assaults the very notion of independence that this same woman ingrained upon me. Love is the wild joker of life. Love shapeshifts and disguises otherwise untenable personality disorders. A woman of my generation and economic stability can endure the luxury of falling under the spell of misbegotten love. But previous generations of women lacked economic independence, *especially* once they had a child or two to take care of. My mother was fortunate to have parents who could afford to help her. Although tender words and touch may have eluded the parent-child relationship in this stiff-upper-lip household, my grandparents showed their love of their only child in other ways.

Back on the East Coast

Divorce laws in the 1950s were strict and heavily weighted in favor of husbands. A heavily Catholic state like New York required substantial proof of adultery before divorce could be considered. After adultery was proven in court, couples had to wait for a year after filing for a divorce to be granted. Divorce laws in Nevada, however, were streamlined. A resident of Nevada could file for and be granted a divorce in the same day. Grounds for divorce included desertion, failure to provide the necessities of life, and mental cruelty. Reno, catering to the Hollywood elites and wealthy Easterners, earned the nickname of Divorce Capital of World.

And so in the fall of 1952, my mother, accompanied by Joan, and financed by her father, was at last back in the west and awaiting her six-week residency requirement. She had a room at the Palomino Ranch, one of many other rollicking dude/divorce ranches that circled the town of Reno. Nightlife spilled over from downtown Reno. Some of the guests—both male and female—brought their next-in-line with them, strategically introduced as brothers, sisters, or cousins. For women without the next pot lined up, Nevada cowboys eagerly strutted their stuff, hoping to land a rich divorcee.

Several cowboys clustered about Joan, vying for attention by romancing the kid as a means of getting to the mother. By day, Joan got to ride horses, twirl a rope, and tie together three legs of an upended goat—practice for rodeo calf-roping. By night, Mother, carrying her pregnancy with taut stomach muscles, sparkled on the dance floor. And while everyone back home in New York huddled under oppressive gray skies and howling, bitterly cold, arctic blasts of wind and snow, the Nevada sun baked pink skin under relentlessly blue sky. Tall mountains cradled evening shadows, a dramatic backdrop to the raucous neon lights of Reno.

The divorce was granted on December 3, 1952, details finalized January 21, 1953. Mother was awarded all household furnishings plus $600 cash. Prenatal and birth expenses were to be paid from funds received as wedding gifts. Sidney was to pay $15 per week for child-support. He was to be informed at all times as to the residence and whereabouts of "the child." Visitation was scheduled for every Sunday between 2:30 and 5:30 plus one extra weekday afternoon. As soon as the baby was old enough, Sidney had the right to have the child with him for two weeks each summer and for three days during the Christmas holiday. Sidney escaped alimony, maintenance support, and paid no court fees.

Mother liked to brag that she'd been out dancing the night before contractions began. On December 23rd, she called a taxi for a ride to the hospital. I arrived the next day. The ranch provided adequate supervision and care for Joan while Mother convalesced impatiently for a few days in the hospital. When she arrived back at their room with me bundled in hospital togs, Joan was eager to see what manner of thing I would be. She gazed in fascination as she unraveled the layers of blankets and cotton wrappers that the hospital staff had diligently cossetted me in. Disrobed, I was a tiny, red, wrinkled raisin. Joan was a quick study with the diaper and eagerly took over Linda-watching. We were the hit of the ranch. Beautiful ladies came by to baby-gaze and twittered amongst each other about that crazy woman who was exposing her poor child to frostbite, for heaven's sake. Mom stubbornly insisted on setting the pram outside the front door with me perched atop a pile of blankets, rather than under them. "She needs vitamin D," my mother asserted to the naysayers.

So, I entered the scene, with a contrary mother and an eager sister. Mom loved to brag that a week after I was born, she was back on the dance floor to ring in the new year. She left Joan to look after me, the first of many such occasions. After she left, one of the know-it-all-neighbor ladies—probably disappointed to be dateless on New Year's Eve—popped in to check on things, convinced that a nine-year-old child was incapable of caring for a newborn. This well-meaning biddy wrapped me in swaddling till I was a boiling, screaming mass of messed diaper. Then she proceeded to change my diaper, a task which Joan had mastered on her third try. This lady was not the expert she thought she was and managed to get shit everywhere. By the time Mom returned to our room in the wee hours of the morning, poor Joan was a nervous wreck and I was screaming bloody murder. A nice way to ring in 1953.

When I was a month old, Mother wrote her parents with a detailed accounting of her finances and ending her letter with:

> *Well, this baby is an expensive item, more so than Joan. I hope she will be worth it. She's a cute little tyke. Her face is getting sunburned. She's awake, lying on my tummy sucking, squirming, and looking around. She must have gas.*
>
> *Love to you both, Yry & Linda*

Mom lingered at the Palomino Ranch for three months. It was a blissful escape from the reality of life in New York. She received a steady stream of congratulatory cards and letters. One of her school chums offered wise consolation:

> *After two failed marriages I finally found Bob. If you can do as well as I did the third time it is worth it. Don't feel too badly about the divorce. I'll bet Joan likes riding and the west. She must be quite a young cowgirl now.*

A note in her diary reveals that she was devouring a book by Joseph Wood Krutch. The opening pages of *The Desert Year* moved her deeply. She wrote that his words *"illustrate what I felt when I first came to Wyoming and what I have felt all the time I was away and then felt anew with overpowering force when I returned to the west, this time to Nevada."*

She mourned the promise she'd made to return to New York. "It was so terribly hard to leave this second time after an almost ten-year absence, especially when I knew deep in my heart that I was returning to trouble and much difficulty." She dreaded Sidney's visits to a child he never wanted.

Back to New York

> *And now the vows are broken*
> *And time has passed and soothed*
> *My revolted spirit, my volcanic hate,*
> *I can even learn to laugh*
> *At this stupid hypocrite*
> *Who comes to view his undesired offspring*
> *To fawn and smile and bribe an innocent babe*
> *Not for love of the poor little one*
> *But for hate of me*
> *For this Jekyll and Hyde*
> *That could be so sweet and yet so raw and mad*
> *Are bound under one hide.*

Penned in a journal, these musings reveal Mother's perspective on the failed marriage as she wistfully returned to New York to resume her responsibilities. She lived like a draft horse, trudging to and from the grocery store, tugging the shopping cart behind her through a sludge of tired, gray and brown snow puddles in the winter, and wilting in the sauna summers. Now she was shopping for five, cooking and cleaning the upper west side flat, providing increasing personal care to her ailing mother, while parenting two kids with vastly different needs. And there were the weekly "father" visits. At first Sidney arrived every Sunday, but as time passed and his arrival was met with cold aloofness and hard looks, the visits dwindled. Lying heavy on Mom's mind was that stipulation that when I was old enough, Sidney would be entitled to take me for two weeks during the summer.

I don't remember much about our New York years. Mother would say that is a blessing. I can relate to her hate for the traffic, the noise, the congestion, the stench of diesel and ripe ocean. If I crawl deeply inside her head, I can also imagine that life in the city embodied the deep, unavoidable disappointment of failure. She was still a striking woman in her fourth decade, but the bloom of youth was fading. She was living with her parents. She had no means of supporting herself, let alone two kids. She was wholly dependent upon the generosity of her father, a driven, self-made, man with high expectations.

Her relationship with her father was tense. A history of poor judgment shadowed her. How would she provide for his two grandchildren once he was gone? He threw himself into his work at the office with the vigor of a man far younger than his 72 years. The work left him drained and nervous. His reward was coming home to Joan, a child who blossomed with fair beauty and the eager, alert mind of a budding scholar. The love he showered on Joan was different from the classic, German, discipline model he'd used with Yry when she was a child—a predictable grandparent phenomenon. As a child, Mom was taught to be seen and not heard. Yet she was pushed to perform flawlessly when asked to learn German, then French, then Spanish. She was expected to excel academically—and even when she did, there was no fanfare for her efforts, merely caustic reminders to strive harder and to reach higher. There was no warmth in letters he sent to his eleven-year-old daughter when she was homesick and lonely in Switzerland; there was only a ceaseless standard of excellence to meet.

Herman's lax attitude toward Joan flabbergasted Mother. They argued over Joan's behavior and how she should be disciplined. By this time, Norah battled the relentless pain of rheumatoid arthritis. She was cranky, easily disturbed by noise, and fully embraced the notion that children follow all the rules of proper manners and decorum. On the other hand, Herman's romps through the flat with Joan were anything but quiet. He snuck treats to the chubby child—again, against Mom's wishes. And now the flat was filled with the needs and shrieks of an infant. Joan stepped into the role of big sister like a pro. She'd had lots of experience with her dolls, and my squirming self was that much more challenging and engaging.

After long, grueling weekdays at the office, my grandfather looked forward to Saturday morning walks through the park with Joan. They'd feed the birds and the squirrels and indulge in fresh popcorn or hot roasted nuts for themselves. Mother relished telling a story from these days: After a particularly rambunctious game of hide and seek, Herman's ever-present fedora slipped off his head at the precise moment that a pigeon flew over depositing a moist, chalky gift smack in the middle of his balding pate. As he mopped at his head with a handkerchief, Joan fell to the ground in a cataclysm of giggles.

It was after one of these Saturday outings in the spring of 1954 that Herman's exertions got the best of him. When they entered the flat, it was obvious that something was not right. Joan ushered her grandfather in, guided him to the couch, and yelled for her mom. Mother found her father sheet-white, beads of sweat gathering on his forehead and lips stained blue. She called for an ambulance, ignoring her father's remonstrations. He never walked out of the hospital.

In looking back, his colleagues and partners pieced together bits of insight and realized that he had been having small mini-strokes during the weeks before his death. Joan was devastated. Her nights were filled with lurid visions of ambulance drivers bursting into the apartment and scattering stuff all over, hovering over her grandfather, and inserting needles and tubes. No one hinted that she could have had anything to do with Herman's collapse. But that idea may have niggled her—a heavy load for a ten-year old. In the dark recesses of her mind, she even wondered if her mother's financial burdens had contributed to her beloved Vovo's demise.

Letters of shock and condolence arrived from friends and family the world over. Norah was bereft. Their union had weathered immensely trying times and events, but their love was as deep and true as it had been the day they met. I suspect that no one, including Norah, expected her to outlive her robust and energetic husband.

The rest of 1954 gave itself over to grieving and consultations with the partners and lawyers over settling Herman's business affairs. Mother worked especially hard to normalize the holidays without her father's presence. She decorated the flat, bought and wrapped gifts, and baked cookies with Joan.

Perhaps having a toddler cavorting around was therapeutic. There are photos that document the happier times. Joan loved playing dress up and I was a wonderful, if squirmy, subject for her imagination. There were doll parties where each of her many dolls was dressed in finery that was sewn by Mom, with Joan's help—Joan was developing new skills through these play sessions. The dolls were assembled around a table set with Joan's play dishes, complete with tea and tiny sandwiches.

My grandmother, Noni, as Joan called her, lingered for another two years. She suffered from debilitating anxiety—which I believe had plagued her throughout her life—and severe arthritis. She was bedridden during her last months. As I think back on this, I wonder how in the world my mother managed. There was no household help, no home health nurses, no hospice, just my grandmother's darkened room and the screams of pain that echoed through the apartment every time she moved. In my memories, my grandmother, when she was still standing, was comma-shaped, with flaming red hair, lips drawn into a grimace, and harsh words for anyone who stepped into her path, said the wrong thing, or made too much noise. I was frightened of her.

Escape!

Norah died in April 1957. True to form, Yry raised eyebrows in the wake of her mother's death. No lengthy, black-clad, grieving for her. She had plans. Her father's business partners, Fred and Ernest, knitted their brows and wrung their hands the day she strode into the office and announced that she intended to sell her inherited share of the company. Ernest had promised Herman that he'd look after Yry and the girls in Herman's absence—a promise he was discovering would be difficult to live up to.

"But Yry, what will you do? What will you live on?" asked Fred.

Ernest chimed in, "You're worn out, dear. You need some time to recover from the shock of losing your dear father and now your poor mother."

"You're right, Ernest. I am exhausted. But I've no intention of burdening you two with my ineptitude. I have no interest in trade. I never did. I have no role in this business. I want to be free of it."

"But Yry, of course you have a role here. You've been a wonderful help to us whenever we needed you during inventory or tax time. We love having you here in the office with us. Everyone loves you. You must think of your future ..."

"Thank you, gentlemen, for being so concerned about my welfare. I'm sure my intentions come as a shock. My fatheh loved this business." She raised her hands to encompass the conference room in which they sat. "He devoted his life to it. I think he gave his life to it. But this was his dream, not mine. I've waited long enough to get on with my life. I'll not wait a moment longer."

Fred interjected, "You're not thinking clearly here. You mustn't rush to make rash decisions that will impact your life forever. ... And your children. You must think of them ..."

"Ha! My children! Do tell." She pierced first Fred and then Ernest with flashing eyes. "I'm doing this for them as much as I am for myself. No child of mine will grow up trapped in this concrete fortress. My children will know the sky, the sunshine, the mountains, the prairie sage! My children will play on the back of a horse, not in a grimy alley." Her nose wrinkled with disdain. "My children will thrive and grow strong, breathing crystal clean air. You must understand, Fred and Ernest, that this is no rash decision on my part. I've been thinking about this ... well, all my life, actually. My hands were tied until now."

Yry closed her ears to the Stein's remonstrations and to those of her and her parents' friends. Oppie, her father's attorney, prepared the necessary documents for the sale of her share of the partnership, which would be split into three payments, spread over several years. Meanwhile Mother packed household items, sorted and disposed of things she couldn't take with her, and re-established contacts in Wyoming. She contacted Mr. Dever, an insurance agent whom she'd met while taking courses at the university. He owned some rental properties in Laramie and was well informed about the local real estate market. Yry wired $500 to Mr. Dever, to be used as earnest money for the purchase of a house. She gave him free rein to find the appropriate property that met the following conditions: an older, single-family property; within walking distance of a school; must have a private yard; and preferably near the university campus.

Her lawyer swallowed hard when she announced that she'd hired a moving van to pack up the furniture. "To where will you be moving, Yry?" asked Mr. Oppenheimer.

"To Laramie, Wyoming," she announced breezily.

"Where is Laramie?"

"About 130 miles northwest of Denver, Colorado."

"But what on earth will you do out there? My goodness, that's wild country. Are you sure you want to go there all alone?" he asked, brows furrowed.

"I won't be alone. I'll have the kids." Her eyebrow arched, a signal that further conversation would be unwise. "After I get established—get the girls into school and learn the lay of the land—I'll get into ranching." She ignored the half-smile that Oppie squelched by clamping his lips against each other.

"You know you'll be violating the divorce agreement by taking Linda out of state. Sidney will no longer be required to pay child support."

"Which is another splendid reason for removing myself from this hellhole. I don't need or want his money. I don't want to see him or hear from him." She paused for a beat, locking eyes with old Oppie, then practically hissed, "And I do not want *anyone* telling him where I have gone or giving him my new address. His perfunctory visits upset all of us, including his child."

Her next order of business was to locate a car. She'd never needed nor desired to drive in New York. She admittedly knew next to nothing about cars, though she had learned to drive a stick shift while living in Sheridan. She instructed Fred to find her a reliable used car that could deliver her across the country. Fred reluctantly laid out $750 for a three-year old Chrysler sedan.

With huge, antique furniture—including her mother's grand piano—packed into the Gray Line van and on its slow journey west, Mother stuffed food, clothing, Joan, and me into the Chrysler, characteristically using every available square inch of space. Fred shoved a AAA membership into the car, along with a stack of maps and AAA trip tics outlining a safe journey across eight states. In late June 1957, the Stein brothers and their families waved goodbye and murmured prayers for a safe journey. Yanking the heavy driver door shut, Yry moved her inexperienced right foot from the brake to the accelerator and released the clutch to launch the car into a crow-hopping gallop down the street while her worried onlookers waved and blew kisses, shaking their heads in disbelief that she was actually following through on this folly.

So began our great adventure. I was four and half years old; Joan was thirteen.

Part VI: Wyoming

I'm not sure of our route. The Interstate, merely a year after President Eisenhower signed the Federal-Aid Highway Act, was barely in its infancy. We traveled small roads between New York and Laramie, which was frankly all Mother ever traveled, given the choice.

It would take at least two weeks for the vans filled with our furniture to arrive in Laramie. Mother approached the cross-country venture like a field trip. I have vague memories of stopping at gas stations to fill the car and empty our bladders. This was a good time for Joan and me to swap positions from front seat to back seat; the front being where all the action was—a first-hand view of what was coming; the back seat view was the gray wall of the back of the front seat. But there was enough space back there for me to curl into a ball and sleep.

The first distinct memory I have of the trip involved a storm like nothing I'd ever witnessed. I think we were in Iowa. We'd been driving in steady rain for a while, but suddenly the storm intensified. The windshield wipers thwacked furiously at sheets of rain. The car crept through a womb of gushing water. Wind buffeted the car. With jaws clamped tightly shut, Mom fought to hold the car on the road as bathtub-sized puddles conspired with the wind to eddy our ship-on-wheels off course. Occasionally random debris or a branch surfing the wind slapped against the car.

While the storm raged outside, the inside of the car was silent except for an occasional exclamation or shriek of wonder. My sister and I had engaged in plenty of arguing and bickering, but the fury that raged outside doused our antagonism. Joan's silence was, in fact, nearly as dark as the storm. While she was eager to return to the west, to a life among horses and open sky, she was wary of Mother's judgment. She missed her grandfather and at this particular moment was convinced that were Vovo in charge, we would have stopped when the weather had changed. For over an hour we'd been following a hog truck that stank to high heaven. Joan grumped and mumbled, envisioning us upside down in a flooded borrow pit, drowned and dead. *It would serve her right!* she fumed under her breath. *But why should I have to die just because I have a nitwitted kook for a mother?*

Mother stayed a conservative three car lengths behind the truck in front of her. It did stink, but its comforting bulk was a moving landmark to keep us on track when the windshield wipers couldn't keep up with the sheeting rain. The truck turned off the main road. Then we were on our own on the straight, flat road. An occasional car approached with its lights on, spraying a fountain of water as it passed. One car passed us in the opposite lane then slowed to a stop. It turned around and began to follow us. Mom's knuckles grew whiter on the steering wheel. From my vantage point in the back seat, I saw flashing red lights on top of the car. Mom pulled to the side of the road, expecting the police car to go on by, but to her dismay, the flashing lights pulled up quite close behind us and, after waiting for what seemed like forever, the driver's door opened, and a dark form emerged. The officer's hat was tipped against the driving rain with one hand clamping it on his head. As he hunkered down to speak, water poured off his hat like Niagara Falls.

"Ma'am, haven't you heard the weather reports?"

"I don't listen to the radio. I'm not fond of the music they play."

"There's more than music on the radio this afternoon, ma'am. There's a tornado-watch. No one should be out on the roads. A twister's on its way right now. It's not safe out here at all, ma'am."

"Well, what do you suggest I do? It's not like I have a root cellar under the car here."

"No ma'am, I'm sure you don't. You don't have kin around here?" he ventured, taking in the absence of a man and the car stuffed with pillows, suitcases, toys, and kids.

"Nope. I'm on my way to Wyoming." Her voice always sang just a bit on that last word.

"Hmmm, well there's a little town up the road a few miles. It's called Osceola and they have a few motels. I'm sure you can find yourself a place to stay for the night. This storm isn't likely to let up for several hours and it'll probably get worse before it gets better."

"Well, I wasn't planning to quit so soon, but maybe it's a good idea. Thanks."

She started to roll up the window, but he leaned down a bit further, huddling his shoulders together as he did so.

"Excuse me, ma'am? I would also suggest that you listen to your radio now and then if you have one. Ya never know ... and also, it might be safer for you if you turned right on 35 up past Osceola. You could get up to Des Moines and take the state highway nearly all the way to Wyoming. It'd be safer, you know. There's services, and motels, and... " His voice trailed off as she continued rolling the window up.

We crept down the road. Osceola was small and looked as drenched as the policeman had. The first motel had a no vacancy sign as did the second. We pulled into the parking lot at the third motel.

"Wait here," Mom growled as she cinched a scarf over her hair and struggled into a raincoat. As she slammed the door on her way out, a horrendous clap of thunder reverberated off the parking lot tarmac.

"What's a twister?" I asked my sister as she twisted her head in all directions to examine the sky. Joan plunged into a dissertation about mid-western weather patterns.

A few minutes later Mom scrambled back to the car and threw herself inside. "We got their last room," she announced victoriously. She parked in front of #4. Carefully planning what bags to take inside, we orchestrated our move and dashed to the front door, which was protected by a broad overhang. Mom fumbled with the key and then we tumbled into the room, soaked and dripping. We opened the curtains and watched the rain slashing against the window and splashing off the car. Bright streaks of lightening lit up the sky. In spite of the lost time, Mom was glad to be off the road. The wind whipped furiously at the shrubs beside the building.

After hanging our wet clothes to dry in the bathroom, Mom looked around the room and sighed. She handed out snacks from her bag of goodies and we played games until howling wind and slapping rain lulled us to sleep.

We woke to a cloudless, pale, blue sky. The metallic smell of the night before was replaced by the just-washed smell of dirt and hay. Delicate bird twitterings filled the still air. The only sign of yesterday's mayhem was the pond-sized puddle in the center of the parking lot and the broken limbs and battered leaves and trash that littered the ground. Staring out the back window of the car, I watched as the clean white motel with the pink and turquoise neon strips around the top of the office grew smaller. I wished we could have stayed long enough to sit in the colorful pairs of sculpted metal lawn chairs that sat before the window of each unit.

My other memory of that multi-day journey in the old gray Chrysler is the heat of Nebraska. It was the first week of July—the heat-stroke days of summer. Nebraska was experiencing triple-digit temperatures as we steamed across the state in our oven-on-wheels. Air-conditioning was rare in restaurants and motels and practically unheard of in automobiles.

As I look back on it now, I wonder how we survived. I think this memory is so deeply ingrained because my mother lost it and actually yelled at Joan. Perhaps she'd done so in the past, but never, to my recollection, in front of me; and to my child eyes, Joan knew everything and did no wrong.

I remember sitting up front with Mother. Joan was in the back seat with the runny remains of a bag of ice we'd gotten at the last filling station. By turns, she rubbed the ice on her forehead, chest, and arms, and nibbled it. She was inconsolable when the ice ran out. We were all hot. Even I had water running down my face. How my mother kept her foot on the accelerator, I'll never know because she was notoriously hyper-sensitive to heat. But we do what we must, and she pressed onward—windows rolled down and fan cranked high to blow more hot air at us.

Joan fussed and fumed from the back seat, whining about being too hot. "I'm going to die," she moaned. I turned around to peer over the back of the seat at her. She really did look awful. Her peaches and cream complexion had turned radish-red, her steel-blue eyes were bloodshot, her lips sagged; if she'd had enough moisture to produce spittle, I think she'd have been drooling. Mother tugged at my leg and told me to turn around and sit properly. The last thing she needed was for me to start antagonizing Joan. But I honestly felt sort of sorry for her.

"Mother, I need ICCE!" she wailed, then whimpered.

Silence.

"Moottther, I have to have IIICCCE!"

"Joan, you're just going to have to tough it out like Linda and I are. There is no ice, as you well know. We'll stop at the next little town we come to and we'll get more ice. But I am not a magician! I cannot turn your tears into ice. Believe me, if I could, I would...gladly!"

"Mother, you're going to kill us all with your crazy ideas."

"Joan, I'm warning you. I've heard enough. Now shut up."

Mother told Joan to shut up? Wow! Unbelievable. She must be *really mad*, I thought, as I wiggled down into my seat, trying to become invisible. Lord knows, I didn't want her venom turned on me.

The racketing of the hot-air fan filled the car, along with the roar of wind whipping through open windows. I rubbed my face, surprised to feel hard grains of salt under my fingers. A nauseating whiff of mint wafted through the car from a nearby field and Joan began whimpering again.

"Stop. Just stop the car. I'm going to be sick."

Mother's jaw wobbled. She suppressed a sigh. The car coasted to the shoulder of the road. Joan stumbled out and stood leaning toward the borrow pit. A semi whooshed by, kicking up a spray of hot road dust. Joan stood, moaning, mopping her wet forehead.

"Well?" Mother had no patience.

More moaning from Joan. Without air brushing across the radiator, the engine heat gushed back at us like oven heat that steams your glasses when you crack the door for a peek at cookies baking. My hand reached for the door handle. Mother snatched my arm. "You're staying right where you are, young lady. Joan, get back in the car right now. We're all just going to get hotter sitting here." Like an exclamation point, another semi thundered by, disrupting more heat waves.

Feeling sick, but unable to purge the nausea, Joan dejectedly turned back and slid into the back seat. "Just stop at a motel for God's sake." she mumbled.

"The motels don't have air-conditioning. We'll be more miserable locked in some dingy room than here in the car where at least the air's moving. Besides, it's too early to stop."

"But we could stop at one with a *swimming* pool," she persisted.

"*Mein Gott nochmal!*"

Oh dear, here comes the German, I thought, shriveling a bit more. She pounded the steering wheel, "Joan get a grip. I can't take this anymore. I'm just as God-damned hot as you are. Linda is too. We're not whining about it. Now just shut up. There's not one damned thing I can do about the weather."

I felt an unfamiliar flutter of pride that Mother had used *me* as an example for Joan! As grumpy as Mom was, I could fall off my short little pedestal in the blink of an eye if I said the wrong thing, so I continued my invisible trick. Our thoughts roared through the car on the hot waves of air that whistled in through the windows. There was no more conversation till a small mid-western town came into view.

"Oh, God Mother, you passed the gas station!" Joan shrieked.

"That one's too expensive. We'll see what the Shamrock station is charging."

Loud and belligerent groaning from the back seat. I was disappointed too. I liked the Sinclair stations the best because they had cool, gigantic, green dinosaurs. Finally we found a station that suited Mother. We filled up on ice, water for the radiator, gas and oil, got the windows cleaned, and hit the road again. We skipped the bathroom break. None of us had drop of liquid to spare. When Joan's ice supply ran low, I shared mine with her. For a few short hours that day, I felt very strong and grown up. For a change, I was not the one who got yelled at. We did eventually pull over to a motel with a swimming pool which revived Joan instantly.

Motels with swimming pools were a treat. l loved the novelty of the big blue pools, sometimes with funny shapes. Joan especially loved the water; Mother said she was a fish. She could swim anywhere, in the deepest water of the biggest pool or in the ocean. She could dive and loved to hold her breath and swim along the bottom of the pool. She'd grab at Mother's feet and try to upend her, which Mom resisted with good humor until Joan succeeded. Then Mother would shriek about getting her hair wet. Joan never got cold. Mother said that was because she carried her own layer of insulation. I, on the other hand, was skinny as a pool cue and it seemed no swimming pool would ever be warm enough for me. Rarely were the motel pools heated in those days. Even on a triple-digit day, swimming pool water turned my lips blue and set my teeth to chattering uncontrollably.

Joan made fun of my chattering. She wanted to horse around and have fun. Mom and her infernal hair got boring, so she was on to me for entertainment. She would start out in her reliable, helpful older sister routine, demonstrating how to move my arms and my legs to swim.

"First you need to be able to float, Linda. It's really easy. Just lie on your back and let your arms and legs hang loose." She'd flop onto her back to demonstrate how easy it was to float. It looked easy enough. I tried it. Over and over, I tried it. But as soon as I lifted my feet off the bottom of the pool I'd start to sink. I was terrified.

"You have to arch your back. Let your head go back," she instructed. "The water has to come all the way up to your ears."

It just wouldn't work. I felt like I was pushing my belly button to the sky, but she'd be yelling at me to arch my back even more. Then she'd tell me to lie across her outstretched arms. "I'll hold you up. Just relax."

Ya hell, you'll hold me up! I knew better. She'd keep her arms there just long enough for me to think I might live, then all of a sudden her arms would disappear and down I'd go, snorting a lung and a half of water. I was wise to this trick. On my back, above her arms, my body was like a two-by-four. But it was more like a two-by-four of steel than of wood, because there was no way it would stay on top of the water like Joan's prone body did.

After a while, Joan would get bored with her unsuccessful tutorials and she'd pester Mom for a while. Mom'd run her off and then, more excited and rambunctious, she'd start tossing me around like a pool toy. This was supposed to be fun. I was supposed to be laughing as I gulped gallons of water and suffered hot needles of chlorine jabbing all the way through my sinuses. I hated it, and in no time I'd be howling and screaming, and Mother would have to step in and tell Joan to leave me alone. Yes, swimming pools were fun. The idea of swimming pools was fun. When you're dripping Nebraska sweat, the sensation of ice-cold water enveloping your bare skin seems like a great idea. But the reality of swimming pools was always a mixed blessing as far as I was concerned.

Years later, when I was in grade school, Mother enrolled me in all sorts of swimming programs in the hopes of mitigating my water phobia. I bless her for that wisdom. The pool sessions did teach me a few things. Deep water no longer triggers instant panic. I know enough different strokes that I could plod my way across a lake. I can tread water with the best of them. Oddly, I fell in love with diving. After pushing past the horrendous fear of the first leap off a high diving board in high school, I discovered how quickly my streamlined body found the bottom of the pool where I could rocket to the surface long before I needed a new breath of air. And once I was confident of the recovery, I discovered the exhilaration of being propelled through the air like a missile. And there's nothing more powerful than slicing the surface of the water like a Torpedo Gannet fixated on a school of sardines below the surface.

But that is where my proficiency and my confidence end. Swimming along the bottom of the pool? Forget it. Four attempts to roll out of a whitewater upset in a hard-shell kayak? Forget it. The past reaches out for me with hot fingers, panic drowns logic, and once again I'm that helpless little kid, getting dunked and tossed by an overly helpful sister.

Home, sweet home

Return

The years have been long.
My exile in city canyons is ended.
And now I am back in Wyoming

> *where my heart has been.*
> *The skies are so blue,*
> *the stars so bright,*
> *the sun so light,*
> *the air so pure.*
> *I smell the sage on the prairie*
> *the pines in the hills.*

Mother's prose reveals how her mood improved along with the elevation. The state of Nebraska tipped upward the farther west we traveled, and the air grew thinner, dryer, and cooler. I can only imagine the quickening of Mom's blood as we approached the border. Wyoming—the very sound of it conveys something wild.

It was late when we pulled into Laramie. Mom stopped at a motel with a horseshoe sign and a small swimming pool at the north end of town. I think this is where we stayed for several days until our furniture arrived. I know we were there long enough for Mom to make friends with the motel owners who had a daughter about my age.

The next day was Sunday. Mom knew the address of the house she'd purchased but did not yet have a key. She was excited and chattered with the motel owners. They knew the house and assured her it would be easy to find. Her eyes sparkled as she danced us out to the car so we could have a look at this first house she'd ever bought. For the past twenty years, she'd lived in apartment houses, her comings and goings monitored by doormen and nosey neighbors.

The motel people were right. Our house was a snap to find. Early on Sunday morning, we went about 10 blocks from our motel on 3rd Street, turned left on Garfield, drove another six blocks and there we were! We had passed only one car along the way.

Our "new" house was a seventy-year-old, two-story, the lower half of which was a dull pink stucco, the top was painted, white wood. It perched in a sizeable patch of grass on a corner lot, with a grade school cattycorner and a small neighborhood grocery across Garfield Street. Not only was the grade school a spit away from the house, but Joan's high school was one block west. The location couldn't have been better.

The first thing I noticed was the triangular window in the front door. It was too high for me to look through. Mom was first to peer through the window, then Joan. I was bouncing up and down, trying to grab a peek, too. Joan lifted me up so I could peer into the darkened hallway on the other side of the door. What I saw next excited me beyond belief. Stairs! With a fancy banister, painted in shiny red! Oh, I couldn't wait to see more. We walked around the house, peering into windows where we could. How did we get through that long Sunday—able to look at, walk around, touch, kick, and lick this new home, but unable to go inside?

Our kind hosts at the motel saved the day. Mrs. Hill put together a lovely picnic basket for us while Mr. Hill instructed Mom on how to get to the Snowy Range, 35 miles west of town. The drive was fun. Gone was the heat of Nebraska, the torrential rains of Iowa. Now all we battled was a ferocious head wind. We drove past a lonely looking shack that said "Brees Field Airport." Mom wondered if someone didn't know how to spell "breeze." The windswept landscape was flat and treeless. The prairie grass that rippled in the wind was fading from spring green to khaki. Occasionally we'd see a herd of cattle or some horses grazing. In the distance, two ranges of tree-covered mountains parted ever so slightly to advertise a startling patch of white mountains behind them.

Our straight, flat road suddenly dropped into a verdant valley bisected by a tree and shrub-rimmed river that fed rich hay fields. At the end of the valley and just before the climb into the mountains, lay a tiny little village called Centennial. We stopped to look at a quaint little museum and to peer into the fancy western-themed restaurant called The Old Corral.

Then we were off again, winding up the twisty, turny road that lead to those snowy mountains we'd been ogling all morning. It was beautiful, indeed. At the snow line, the road had been plowed for several miles, then we came around a corner to find a huge pile of snow blocking our path. So much for the plow. We got out and marveled at the smoothly cut walls of snow that towered above our car on either side of the road. And COLD! It was so cold that we grabbed our coats out of the car. Not only was the wind cold, but the air was cold, too cold! We turned around and retraced our route till we got to a beautiful lake where we munched our lunch between chattering teeth. The snow-covered peaks behind the lake were duplicated in the mirror surface of the water. Tiny striped chipmunks dashed before us like moths darting to a streetlight. Joan tried to chum them closer with crusts from her sandwich, but, unlike tame urban squirrels, they darted at the very blink of an eye. By the time we got back to Centennial, we'd thawed enough to stop for ice cream before driving back to Laramie.

Back at the motel, I was fascinated but intimidated by Ramona, the motel owner's daughter. I had never played with kids my own age. Joan was so much older than I that she was more adult than kid.

Ramona seemed worldly. She had the run of the motel. She could go anywhere she wanted, whenever she wanted. Or at least that's how it seemed to me, who had never been out of sight of my mother or Joan. Ramona's toys even seemed worldly to me. She had the kid version of a car—a shiny, red big-girl tricycle, which she rode with wild abandon across the motel parking lot, down the sidewalk, careening around the corners as fast as she could go. She was obviously bored by my lack of sophistication as I stood there, gnawing on my fingernails and watching her in wonder.

Meanwhile, Mom was networking. The motel owners had lived in Wyoming for about ten years and had connections around town. They'd been ranchers in South Dakota, and they moved easily in western social circles. Mom, on the other hand, had "dude" written across her abundant chest in fancy filigree stitching and pearl snap buttons. This is not to say that people in Laramie didn't wear pearl snap buttons, because they definitely did. But their shirts and blouses were simple plaids and neutral colors. Mom's were extravagant primary colors with contrasting stitching and fancy, decorated pockets. She wore heels where other women wore simple loafers or oxfords. She turned heads wherever she went. Validation from the locals would help establish her in this more practical community.

On Monday morning, Mom met with Mr. Dever, whom she'd wired earnest money to for the house. Mr. Dever escorted us to the house and opened the door. Oh my, the excitement. I would have my very own room! Joan would, too! The stairs were magnificent. There was also a dark, scary staircase that lead to the basement which had a fireplace. But it smelled musty down there and I wasn't too crazy about it. Mom wasn't too crazy about the décor throughout the house which consisted of wallpaper, wallpaper, and more wallpaper ... all in different colors and patterns with huge swirly flowers—even different patterned wallpaper in the same room. But Mr. Dever pointed out that wallpaper could be stripped or painted over. I think we were all delighted by the possibilities of this, our first house.

So began our new life. A life that for me seemed carefree and full of wonder. A life that for Mother was the first step towards her dream of becoming a rancher. A life that for Joan substituted pets of every size and shape for the love and adoration of her grandfather and the nagging of her sick and cranky grandmother.

My small hand no longer clutched in the nervous paw of an adult each time I stepped out the door, I expanded into my new freedom. I flew up and down the stairs like a marathon runner training for hills. I was allowed to enter and exit the house whenever I liked, as long as I didn't let the door slam behind me. I had the run of our yard but was still forbidden to go further without prior approval. We spent the summer exploring our new terrain, meeting the neighbors, and fixing up and painting our new home. It was a big house with tall ceilings, and it bore the scars of multiple make-overs. Mother came to rue the previous owner, who was, coincidently, the high school shop teacher, and who had muddled nearly everything he'd touched. Beautifully carved wooden moldings had been rudely painted over and, on some doorways—but not all—stripped away. The house had been rewired, as Mother would come to find out—incorrectly. The plumbing had been reworked and misrouted.

So during that summer of drop cloths, paint brushes and rollers, and paint in the eye, Mother became the star client of the electrician down the street and of the plumber, Mr. Tracy. It never occurred to me to wonder about the frequent visits of the plumber; it seemed that our old house was just a bit of a lemon.

With the house remade, Mother began exploring our environs. Loading Joan, me, and a trunk full of gear into the car, she'd find some dusty old logging road. Minus air-conditioning, we traveled with windows open. Dust tornadoed inside while I sat in the backseat, growing progressively more ill with each hairpin turn. Mom's compensation for the dust only further aggravated my churning stomach. She'd brake beside a patch of sagebrush to harvest a pungent branch which she placed atop the dashboard where the sun baked the oily sage smell. To stave off my nausea, I'd flop across the big, upholstered bench seat where dust stored from previous trips boiled out to mingle with new dust. If I could fall asleep until the car came to a stop, I avoided the otherwise inevitable shriek: "Stop, I'm gonna puke!"

The old logging roads had a way of leading to nowhere. Mom would go for miles and miles with no clear idea of where she was going. Her Triple A road maps were worthless in the backcountry and I never saw her use a topo. The destination was not the goal. Mom sought the peace that comes from penetrating the landscape. I don't think we ever got seriously lost. But I do remember incidents that involved backing the car a quarter-mile or more down a serpentine, two-rut path with rocky wall on one side and sheer drop off on the other side, either because an out-bound logging rig had stared us down, or the path before us simply petered out.

She'd bought a forest-green, canvas, A-frame tent; two oversized, zip-together, down sleeping bags, which kept the three of us toasty warm; and a cast-iron frying pan that required two fists to lift. Pitching the tent was a black comedy, inducing screaming fits between Mom and Joan. The tent never collapsed, but there were times when it leaned alarmingly windward. The tent smelled bad—not moldy but tenty. If you've ever smelled an old canvas tent, you know what I mean. It's a musty, turpentiney smell that floods my mind with memories every time I catch of whiff of it.

Once Mom forgot to bring matches. We had the fire all nicely constructed, and the only potential spark was the cigarette lighter in the car. Mom crinkled some newspaper and held the lighter to the edge of the paper, blowing gently to coax a small flame. But the lighter would cool before the spark had a chance. Or if she cajoled a small flame, it died between the car and the fire pit. I understood Jack London's *To Build a Fire* on a personal level. We ate cold, canned green beans that night.

On another adventure, she remembered the matches but forgot the fire-starting paper. Having no paper other than dollar bills and books, the only choice was to gather dry pine needles, which surprisingly didn't want to catch a flame. Eventually Joan made a ball of dry grass and managed to produce a wobbly little fire.

On another camping trip, the privies in the campground were so dark and terrifying that I seized up every time I went to pee. After a full day of bashful bladder I began whining that I had to pee.

"Well, go to the outhouse you little nitwit."

"But I can't go."

"Whatever do you mean, you can't go? March yourself down there and pee."

"But I can't. It won't come ..."

Suspiciously, "Have you peed since we got here?"

"No Mother, I can't. I try but I can't."

So she dragged me to the outhouse, opened the door, releasing a fetid blast of air, and ordered me to sit there till I peed. Terrified of falling through the hole into that menacing pile of dark stink below where flies buzzed angrily, I was crying and yelping all at the same time.

"You're not going to fall through," she said. "But you are going to get sick if you don't get rid of the poisons in your system. You'll get sick and I'll have to haul everything back to the car and we'll have to drive all the way back to Laramie and put you in the hospital. I may just leave you there for being such a silly ninny. I can't afford hospital bills. Now, pee, damn it!"

By now, my urine had reached the boiling point. Every time I almost got a stream going, fire assaulted the tender skin down there and I shrieked and clutched once more. This battle went on for a long time—long enough that after I finally succeeded in letting loose a ferocious, blistering stream of yeasty urine, it was nearly as dark outside as it was inside that nasty old stinkhouse.

Looking back on this event, I wonder why she didn't just have me squat and pee in the bushes. Of course, that was just as unappealing to me, but surely it would have been an option. Maybe this was her way of forcing me to face my fears.

Mother, a single woman in charge of two children, was proactive. Though she disapproved of firearms, she owned one. I don't remember the long tale of how the old blunderbuss made it into her hands. Nor do I know any details about the weapon, other than that it was a pistol which she kept hidden most of the time and, according to her, it was unreliable—in that it might or might not fire when the trigger was pulled. Or rather than firing, the barrel might explode. Why in the world would she lug around a menace like this? To fend off creeps. But that old gun and its implications planted a seed of the macabre.

Wyoming

One night while we were snuggled into our sleeping cocoon, I had a violent dream in which a stranger sliced through our tent with a huge hunting knife. (Mom had one of those, too.) Dreams confuse the chain of events, but somehow the knife ended up in my mother's hands and she sliced off the hand of the intruder; I woke with the stump of the man's arm waving before my eyes. For the rest of that camping trip, I kept circling the tent to convince myself that there was no evidence of foul play.

Behind our house on Garfield Street, an elderly, single lady lived in one side of a duplex. With short, tightly curled, gray hair perpetually corralled by an auburn hair net; wire-framed glasses that distorted her eyes; and clunky black shoes; she became my surrogate granny. She spent her days in an upholstered chair beside the window, her swollen ankles propped on a low ottoman, a television flickering black-and-white advertisements, Jack Parr, soap operas, and in the evening; news, then Mitch Miller and The Honeymooners. Her hands were perpetually in motion, either with a pair of knitting needles or a crochet hook. There was something tragic about her life that I never fully understood. I remember whispers about her husband, who had died many years earlier, and her grown son, who ignored her.

On the south side of our house, facing Ninth Street, was a completely different situation. That stark, two-story house trapped three lives. Old man D___, with a long, narrow face, lined like a topo map of the Colorado River tributaries, ruled over his boxer dog, his daughter and grandson. They lived secretively behind curtained windows and locked doors; their grassless back yard was hidden from prying eyes by a six-foot, wooden fence. The only sign of life was from the boxer who frothed with rage at the neighborhood kids who walked down the alley, dragging a stick along the boards of the fence to stir up trouble. Occasionally, the big wooden gates to the alley swung open and all three D___s plus boxer would emerge in a rickety blue pickup truck and disappear for the weekend.

It took a while, but Mother eventually befriended the daughter, Virginia, a tall, angular woman with long, straw-colored hair, metal-framed cat-eye glasses outlining steely blue eyes. Not only was Virginia's stiff-shouldered appearance intimidating, but her voice was harsh and cold. She frightened me. Her son, several years younger than I, was never allowed out of the back yard or even to play in the grassy front yard. Instead, he was caged, like the dog, in that dusty back yard or inside the fortress of a house. Occasionally Mom would drag me along for a visit. The two women would sit at the kitchen table, kibitzing over cups of coffee while I was assigned to play with Alan on the bare, wooden dining room floor. I never liked that floor because I feared getting a splinter from the rough wood, but it was surgically clean. Virginia had only a few rag rugs which she beat mercilessly with a broom because she didn't own a vacuum. She swept and washed her wooden floor every day, along with practically every other surface in the house. She had little control over her life, but what she did control, she ruled fanatically. One day she glimpsed me rolling one of Alan's toy trucks over the top of his head to his giggling delight. She barreled out of the kitchen and grabbed me by the arm; jerking me to my feet, she yelled that I should know better than to put that dirty, nasty toy on her boy's head! I was shocked. I had no idea that a kid's own toys could be considered dirty and that there was a right or wrong way to play with a toy truck. Heck, I had no idea how to play with a little boy, period. Alan's giggles ceased instantly, his shoulders rounded, and he stared mutely at the barren floor.

Like me, Alan had no father. There was some awful story about him being a drunk or a gambler or something. I don't know if he was banished or if he had simply vanished from the rigidity of that household. I suppose this mutual manless state was the glue that cemented Mother and Virginia's friendship. It was hard to imagine that a husband could have been any worse than Virginia's father. We never visited when he was home, and we could often hear him, from inside our own house, berating his daughter with unmentionably cruel words and an occasional resounding slap.

So, I dreaded visits with Alan, looked forward to visits with old Mrs. "Boring," who often lured me with a plate of oven-warm cookies, and eventually I met some of the other neighbor kids. Before that first summer came to a close, a chain-link metal fence encircled our yard. It served the dual purposes of marking my boundary of freedom and containing our constant and mercurial hodgepodge of four-legged housemates. Some of my new friends seemed to think I was a prisoner, as I stared out from behind those metal strands of confinement. But they had no concept of the big city prison that we'd escaped.

And it seemed that our plumbing would never be reliable. Mr. Tracy continued to visit our house. He was a kind, older gentleman who never failed to notice me and to say something funny. I loved it when the doorbell rang, and I'd open the door to find Mr. Tracy standing there with his toolbox and his Dick Tracy hat.

Mom was fussy about food. She wanted only "fresh, farm eggs—preferably brown," and was convinced that homogenized or pasteurized milk lacked vital nutrients. She loved the thick rich cream that formed on top of fresh milk. We established a ritual of driving ten miles west of town to the Talbot dairy ranch every Sunday to pick up a dozen still-warm eggs and two gallons of fresh-out-of-the-udder milk.

Besides the dairy operation, the Talbots ran beef cattle, sheep, and had a pig or two who roamed freely along with the chickens, turkeys, and even a pair of peacocks. Tragedy always accompanies lambing season, and so it was that Joan's first 4-H project was a pair of bum lambs from the Talbots. The ewe had died birthing her twins; the Talbots were out of surrogate ewes to pair the orphans with, so two tiny lambs came home with us in a cardboard box that smelled of barnyard, tinged with blood and lanolin.

That first night, the lambs were painfully tiny, their pink noses and hypersensitive pale-blue eyes made them look tender and vulnerable. Even their bleats were faint. We set them up in the linoleum-floored kitchen where it was warm, and we could easily block them into the one room. Ebony, Joan's little black dog, who was secretly expecting a litter of puppies, sniffed at the lambs with interest but no animosity.

For the first few weeks, our lives were consumed with learning the ins and outs of bottle-feeding bum lambs. Leah Talbot answered panicky phone calls with an endless supply of advice. One of the first disasters occurred after the lambs grew strong enough to jerk while feeding. The rubber nipple slipped off the glass rim of the pop bottle, sending Joan and her baby in opposite directions and spewing formula across the floor. It was a constant adjustment process as the babies grew stronger and more curious. Soon they were crashing through barriers and bleating through the living room. And when we put them outside for sunshine and fresh grass, they assaulted Mom's hollyhocks—despite the wire borders that marked the boundary between lawn and half-wild flower beds.

"With all that grass, why do they have to pick on my flowers?" Mom complained. "If I'm hosting vegetarians, I shouldn't have to be worrying about mowing that damned lawn." Neighborhood kids—and parents—lined up on the other side of our fence, staring in bewilderment at this misplaced spectacle of barnyard in the middle of a nice, clean residential area. Joan derided these city kids who should know better than to ask: Why we had them? Where were their mother and father? What did they eat? Would we be able to ride them when they grew bigger?

I was appalled by the docking procedure, but it was necessary if Joan were to show her charges at the State Fair in August. Wyoming sheep men have no patience for dirty sheep bottoms and tails getting in the way of ewe's troublesome deliveries. Heavy rubber bands are applied to the lambs' tails. With circulation to the unwanted appendage hampered, the tail eventually drops off like a loose baby tooth. I dreaded walking through the house or yard and finding a disembodied tail.

We had barely weaned the lambs from the comfort of the kitchen when Ebony delivered her little surprise. Four squirming pups showed up in the dirty clothes basket one morning. Yes, we were learning all about life ... and death. One of the pups died shortly after we moved the litter from the clothes basket to the obligatory nursery box in the kitchen.

Meanwhile, Mom was still coping with faulty plumbing. Who knew so many things could go wrong with toilets, faucets, and pipes? I have described Mr. Tracy as an older man, which to me he was. But, time plays funny tricks with age. As I look back now and do the math, well ... he was in his 50s. And Mother? She was thirteen years younger than Mr. Tracy. Virginia, the neighbor so abused by her father, with her dated hair and glasses and utter lack of make-up, looked Mother's age but was probably in her late twenties. They all seemed so o-l-d! I think about these things now and realize that my sterile little neighborhood was thrumming with hormones and pheromones—good heavens! Even old lady "Boring" was probably not a whole lot older than I am right now, though she looked and seemed ancient with her powdered wrinkles, cheap old-lady perfume, and compression hose.

One day returning from my friend's house down the block, I was surprised to find that our house had acquired yet another pet. By this time, in addition to the lambs, we had the dog and her pups, two cats, and now a bird! Jerry, was a beautiful, blue-green parakeet. To keep him out of cat claw range, Mother hung his cage from a plant hook screwed into the ceiling. Jerry's story was a sad one. Apparently he had belonged to Mr. Tracy's nine-year old daughter. But since Mrs. Tracy had died recently, Jerry, the parakeet, was not getting enough attention because Mr. Tracy didn't have the time to care for him. Or some such story. I was excited because I thought Jerry would talk. But he never did. He just sang off key whenever Joan practiced the piano.

I never paid a lot of attention to the fact that Mom was frequently gone after dinner. At first she'd send me next door to keep Mrs. Borher company. But eventually, she was gone for longer and longer in the evening and she'd come home to find me asleep on Mrs. Borher's couch and Mrs. Borher rubbing nap-bleary eyes. So she began leaving me at home with Joan in charge. I loathed these evenings, as I suppose Joan did too. We invariably ended up in a spat and sometimes circled each other like mismatched boxers.

Mother had joined a few clubs. These were her excuse for being out at night. Of course, as I said, I never thought to wonder about her disappearing acts. The notion that she might be on a date was the farthest thing from my mind. My mother was asexual. There was no talk of dating or husbands or any of that nonsense. As a matter of fact, some of the women she knew were desperate to get out of marriages. At one point, Mother had skipped town to avoid a legal summons from a pair of her friends who were slamming each other around in divorce court. Mom didn't want to be forced to take sides, so she simply left town for a week to avoid being served a subpoena. Joan stayed with a friend and I got to stay with my best friend down the street. It was a grand week during which I indulged in delicious PBJs on Wonder bread with smooth Skippy peanut butter and smooth Welches grape jelly. As I look back on it, I wonder, did she really visit the Red Desert alone, as she said? Or did she have company?

The innocence of childhood

Illusion *(1958)*
I gave my heart to my love
And asked only to be loved.
Then I found to my amazement
My Love was someone else's love.
I'd given my heart into a void

Wyoming

And there was nothing, nothing but emptiness for me.

Sometimes only a dated poem documents what, as a child, I was blissfully unaware of. I never noticed when Mr. Tracy stopped coming to our house. It was inevitable that our plumbing would eventually get sufficiently updated and repaired. As the years piled up, I'd occasionally hear Mother's rumblings about small-minded people in small towns. She claimed that all the women were scared to death that she, the new "divorcee from the East," was out to steal their husbands. That notion was so preposterous to me, on so many levels, that I never took her seriously. I assumed that she was exaggerating as usual. Just like I assumed she was imagining things when she would jerk me along beside her as she practically ran from store to store downtown, muttering that so-and-so dirty old man was ogling her. *Oh Mom,* I thought, *who do you think you're kidding? You, with your old-fashioned hairdo, sheltered from the Wyoming wind with a silk scarf in the summer and a woolen scarf in the winter? Why would any man look at you a second time?*

When I started school, I realized that my mother was as old as my classmates' grandmothers. Even though she was not yet 50, her fashion sense froze in the styles of her ingénue days. Her hemlines were too long, her waistlines too exaggerated, and her hair was Greta Garbo when everyone else was Jackie O or Nancy Sinatra. My mother was impervious to trends and cared little about what other people thought of her. She never failed to embarrass me by confronting my beleaguered teachers and lecturing them on how they weren't doing their jobs. It's true. I was slow. I must have appeared like a complete dolt compared to Joan who had skipped two grades because she already knew so much when she started school. I, on the other hand, was always one of the last to reach academic milestones. But I enjoyed school. I enjoyed my teachers who were invariably kind and encouraging to me. And I enjoyed getting out of that house and away from Joan.

Mother didn't believe in Kindergarten, so in September 1959 I got my first taste of school. I had dreaded that first day as much as I dreaded going down the dark staircase to the even darker basement to retrieve something from the pantry for Mother. My friends had learned how to write their names already. I knew how to feed a baby lamb and clean the cat box. But first-grade teacher, Mrs. Tracy, a short, broad woman with the obligatory old lady shoes, was kind and generous with me. Oh how quickly I fell in love with my first teacher!

And oh how ignorant I was! I never put together in my child head that Mrs. Tracy might be attached to the famous, recently widowed MR. Tracy! Then one day, Mrs. Tracy must have left something at home, or perhaps needed to sign an important paper, because our class had a visitor! Mr. Tracy, the plumber, knocked on the door. I could see his head in the glass window at the top of our classroom door.

"Mr. Tracy!" I squealed with abandon—charged and ready to leap from my chair and rush in for a hug. But Mrs. Tracy abruptly clapped her hands and told the class to take out our crayons and start coloring the handout she'd given us earlier as she strode to the door, exited, and firmly closed the door behind her.

And poor Mother, when I got home that afternoon. How could I have known what my excited chattering about Mr. Tracy's visit to our classroom felt like to my mother? How could I have possibly dreamed of the complicated gyrations of adult friendship, love, loyalty, and impatience? How could I have known that the sudden appearance of Jerry in our house was not because Mr. Tracy no longer had time to care for the bird, but because *the new Mrs. Tracy* wanted nothing to do with Jerry. The bird had been given to Mr. Tracy's daughter by her mother before she died. There was a ton of emotion wrapped up in that one small ball of feathers.

It would be years before I finally connected the dots to realize that upon initially arriving in town, my mother, lonely for male companionship and sick to death of caring for people, had enjoyed a quick, hot, romance with the newly widowed plumber. He, attracted to the exotic new legs in town, was eager to lasso a new bride. He needed a wife. He needed a mother for his young daughter. His need was urgent. But my mother, having been unlucky in love, was cautious. She no longer had the luxury of a devoted father who could erase her mistakes. She was aware of whispers around town about the rich new trollop who'd moved into that house on Garfield. She was also aware of her inheritance, which could not be jeopardized with a hasty liaison. So she said "not yet" to Mr. Tracy's over-eager proposal. How it must have pained her to discover two months later that Mr. Tracy had married—that he had married a short, dumpy-looking, first-grade teacher who took over his house, his life, and his daughter without a backward glance—and then had the gall to steal *her* youngest child's heart as well!

Expansion

Life goes on. Mom, prideful and distracted by demands of single-parenthood, licked her wounds quietly. During subsequent years, our menagerie grew, as did Mother's real estate holdings. The sad day arrived after the fair when Joan had to load up her 4-H lambs and return them to the Talbot ranch where they would be slaughtered, and their meat would fill our freezer. As recompense, Mother purchased the little white stud colt that Joan had been admiring from the Talbot herd. On the heels of that purchase, Mother succumbed to the clownish antics of a little brown colt that came nibbling for attention each time we went to the pasture to visit Joan's young, Blanco. And then there were two colts.

1960 was a pivotal year. During the '59-60 Christmas holiday, we rode the train to New York City to visit Mother's friends and business partners. On that endless trip, I lost interest in the novelty of passenger trains, growing cranky and red-cheeked. The porters tried to entertain me with ice creams and a collapsible cardboard piggy bank in the shape of our train. But something was off.

We arrived to a robust welcoming committee comprised of the Stein brothers and their families, who whisked us off to Fred's home in the suburbs. After a quick consultation, the adults concurred that I had the measles and was to be isolated—left to rest in a dark room with little distraction. Nevertheless, a faceless, nameless string of teenagers snuck into my room one at a time, bringing tantalizing fluids like Kool-aid, games, and books to read to me. I rather enjoyed all this attention. I spent most of this visit sequestered in someone's bedroom, which freed my mother to conduct whatever business she was up to.

With that measly trip behind us and another installment from the sale of Herman's business in the bank, Mother felt a little financial leeway and she began investing. She purchased 60 acres of dry land just a few miles from the city limits. The property included a house, barn, and corrals. She also purchased an old pickup truck with hand-made wooden stock racks and, later, a single-horse trailer that had been made as an FFA project. With this combination we brought the two colts to their new home. Mom rented out the house on the property, and also rented stall and pasture space to college students and other citified horse-owners. Then came the addition of my elderly half-Welsh pony, Jessie, who would become teacher to me and a slew of neighborhood kids, as well as surrogate grandmother, babysitter, best friend, and confidante.

Mother's herd grew by one or two per year until we had more than a dozen of our own horses and several stabled horses to care for. At some point she considered getting into the sheep business; not a particularly welcome past time in Wyoming cow country. But the income stream of sheep ranching was enticing—not only is there the meat product, but all that wool! And, perhaps there'd also be money in lanolin made from crude wool grease. Fortunately, this idea flitted in and out of her head without any investment or disappointment.

All the while, Mom was also purchasing rental property in town. She rented to a river of college students. Each spring and fall she geared up for the student turnover. It was a time of elbow grease and paint. The work was a family affair—a way for us girls to learn the value of sweat equity. She kept the units as well-maintained as possible and fretted over a lost month's rent. She chose tenants by the look in their eye and never signed lease agreements. When one group graduated, their friends eagerly replaced them. In later years she was often not quite sure who was living where.

Mom's property management sometimes involved a dose of parenting to kids naïve about lawns, furnaces, and gas stoves. She ministered to tearful girls who'd fought with their best-friend roomies and couldn't come up with the rent money, and she lectured brawny boys on the necessity of cleaning up the lawn after a party. Occasionally her heart broke when young married students ran into hard times with broken promises or unexpected pregnancies. She was known as a soft-sell, and miraculously she rarely got stiffed. She represented something old-world and slightly demented—a talisman of luck to passing generations of students. I think she charmed people into behaving the best they could toward her.

The rental properties were Mom's job. She used her inheritance to expand her real estate empire so that by the time I moved out of state, Mom was managing a dozen or more rental units. Although I was one of only two or three kids in my class who was raised by a single-parent, I was the only one whose parent was home every single afternoon and for every single lunch hour—for which I was expected to come home, rather than to eat in the expensive cafeteria with its food of dubious nutrition and quality. No latchkey kid here. I was supervised.

In between property management crises, we entertained the neighborhood with an unofficial and impromptu zoo. After the bum lambs came the orphaned foal. One of the bizarre ways in which Mother conserved resources was to collect grass clippings to augment the hay and pasture for our horses. She couldn't bear to see waste. Grass clippings dumped into the landfill represented a waste of nutrition. We spent Saturday mornings driving up and down the alleys in search of freshly discarded clippings, which we gathered with the aid of cardboard vegetable crates and dumped into the trunk of the sedan.

We developed a routine of ferreting out the ritzier homes that had high quality clippings (and of course rich classmates who watched Joan and me as we scrounged in the alley, just ahead of the smelly garbage truck.) I don't remember that either Joan or I complained about this chore. Mom made it into a lark, like a treasure hunt, a contest to find the most and the best clippings. We learned to detect clippings that had sat too long in the hot sun. If you plunged your hand into a heap of green and felt warm breath on your skin, it was best to leave those clippings behind. Fermented grass expires into deadly gas in the tender belly of a hungry horse.

With the trunk full, we'd hurry out to the ranch to mix our bounty into dry, dusty hay to lessen the chance of it overheating in the summer sun and of the horses gorging too quickly on this rich salad. But one day, our methodology failed. Around dinner time, the tenant of the house on the property called Mom to inform her that the mare with the foal was down and thrashing around.

We hightailed it out there to investigate. Sure enough, the little four-week-old, sand-colored filly was standing aside, watching her mother alternately rolling from side to side, pawing at the air with her hooves and wringing her tail in an agony that brought deep groans from her throat. Mom borrowed the tenant's phone and called the vet.

"Get that mare movin' and keep her movin'. Don't let her go down cuz then her intestines'll twist and she'll be beyond all help," he warned. "I'll be there as soon as I can."

With one of us in front tugging on the lead rope and two behind pushing her tail end up, yelling, shrieking, clapping our hands, we got her onto four shaky legs. She stood splayed, eye's glazed, sweating despite the gathering cool of evening. We coaxed, we begged, we pleaded with Jewel to move, to walk. We would lift each leg in its turn inching it forward just a bit, pushing and tugging. Finally the vet showed up. He stirred a tarry-smelling concoction into a metal pail, then grabbed a six-foot strip of rubber tubing and snaked that through Jewel's nostril and down her esophagus. We could see the progress of the nasogastric tube wiggling down her long neck. When it was properly positioned, Dr. Allen lifted the bucket high above his head to let gravity draw the liquid into the mare's stomach. I don't know what the magic potion was; maybe it was horse-sized Gas-X.

By now it was dark in the corral. The other horses all stood huddled in a corner, watching the circus with trepidation. Dr. Allen instructed us to keep Jewel moving for as long as it took. The gas had to work its way through her system and out the back end because horses don't belch.

It was the longest night of my young life and the first time that I escaped the dreaded command to go to bed before the excitement of the evening was finished. The tenants, feeling sorry for us, brought out hot chocolate and sandwiches. We worked by flashlight and occasionally shone the headlights of the car into the corral for a better view. Around 4 AM, Jewel groaned and pawed the ground, wrung her tail, and collapsed like a broken sawhorse. She was done. We were devastated, each of us.

Mom went down with her, echoing her groan of despair. "Oh Jewel, Jewel ... I am so sorry. The grass was supposed to be a treat, not the death of you. Oh Jewel, why did you have to eat so much of it? Never again ..."

"Come on, Mom," Joan's voice was huskier than usual. "It's over. We can't do anything more for her. But we gotta do something about Sandy, there," she nodded toward the corner of the corral. "We can't afford to lose two in one night." Jewel's dazed and hungry foal stood off by itself, the other horses nearby, but unable to offer solace or sustenance.

My Life With an Enigma

The loss of Jewel was not my first experience with mortality. By this time we'd lost a few puppies and kittens and, of course, Joan's lambs. When I was about seven, I'd come across the body of a little stillborn lamb dropped unceremoniously by its dam in the corner of one the Talbots' corrals. Kids take their cues from the adults around them, and I was surrounded by ranchers who viewed livestock as a responsibility—to be nursed, fed, and watched over until it was time to slaughter them. There was a tacit agreement that the animals would ultimately pay for their protection, food, and comfort by, in turn, feeding the provider. The circle of life was small and close to the bone.

I assimilated the fact that life and death are both connected and final. Contrary to some beliefs, I learned that you get born only once. You don't get another chance. And you die only once. You aren't coming back after that last puff of air leaves your lungs. Ranchers are not cruel or hard-hearted because they harvest animals for food. Ranchers are pragmatic. They live within the circle, coaxing life into the world, going so far as to stick an arm, pit-deep into the back end of a horse, or a cow, or a sow to pull forth new life that's headed the wrong way. And, at the other end of that infinite spectrum, ranchers muster the strength and the courage to kill quickly and efficiently when it is necessary. I knew that my mother and Joan were both devoted animal lovers. And I knew that they were both correct to fold that remaining gift from Jewel into the backseat of the car and bring her home to live with us in town. We focused forward on the life that was here rather than on the life just lost.

This unblinking approach to death may not have helped on those nights when sleep dueled with the anxiety that I might never wake up, as I lay in the dark, shivers tickling my spine, and my brain fussing over what death feels like. It did nothing to allay my anxiety on those occasions when Mother spouted off about riding into the mountains to shoot herself when her time came. And it didn't prevent that knot in my throat or the ping in my chest when we looked at little Sandy and remembered the last hours of her mother's life.

Jewel was the first horse we'd lost, but she'd left a legacy. The small sandlot-colored filly came home with us to a new bottle routine. Our experience with the lambs was but a shadow of the knowledge we would need to keep this month-old filly alive. Mare's milk is a unique mix of fats and proteins, so Mom had to figure out how to doctor up fresh cow's milk and make it, not only palatable to the little horse, but also properly nutritious. And Sandy had to learn how to take milk from a pop bottle with a rubber nipple attached. And the neighborhood kids had something new to gawk at, more stupid-assed questions to ask, and disbelieving parents to show off to.

Sandy lived in our yard through the summer, fall, and winter. As longer days signaled the approach of a brief Wyoming summer, we took Sandy back to the ranch where she learned to hold her own with the big horses. She never grew very large. At two, she was barely taller than my pony. But she thrived and charmed people with her expressive brown eyes and quizzical gaze. She was always the first horse to approach a person with or without a bucket of grain, and she followed us around like a collie. Eventually Mom sold her to someone who wanted a small cart horse.

One spring afternoon my best friend from down the street phoned. "Linda, you won't believe what dad brought home from hunting! Come see," she ordered breathlessly.

I arrived to find a large cardboard box with four squirming puppies inside. They all looked alike, with downy, prairie-brown fur, blue eyes, and round button black noses. "What the heck? What kinda dogs are these?" I asked.

"They aren't dogs, stupid, they're coyotes!"

"What? Why'd yer dad bring home coyote pups? What in the world is he gonna do with 'em?"

"He found them in a cave," Terry explained. "They were all alone, so he rescued them."

"Cool! But what are you gonna do with them?" I asked.

"I think he's gonna keep one and find homes for the others. You want one?"

"Oh man, I'd love one! I'll go ask Mom," I yelled as I dashed back to my house.

Upon my enthusiastic explanation of the situation, my mom exploded. "That man!" she grumbled. "He is an idiot, a lunatic, a truly ignorant SOB!" she thundered.

Her response shocked me, but when she pointed out that the pups were alone because the mother was probably out hunting and that he should have left them where he found them. I glimpsed the light at the end of the tunnel.

"Hell, he probably shot the mother, then followed her tracks to the den. He's probably planning on selling those pups to baiters or a zoo or something."

Her logic made painful sense. Mr. H was not known as a kind or cuddly sort. Resembling a beardless Earnest Hemingway, he was a beer-drinking, braggartly, loudmouth who never let anyone forget that he suffered the disappointment of having three daughters and no sons. It was hard to picture him oohing and awing over a den full of coyote pups.

"Well," I ventured cautiously—when Mom was on a rant, it was wise to just let her go till the steam ran out, but I was too excited. "But ... the pups are here now. I don't suppose he could take them back to the den even if he wanted to. Probably the mother would reject them, right?"

"Yeah. I'm quite sure Mr. H would never return those pups, even if he could," she muttered.

"Well, if he's giving them away, can we take one?"

"Linda, what in the world are we going to do with a coyote pup? Those puppies may be cute right now, but they're wild animals. They'll grow up to be big coyotes, predators. Do you understand what that means? They will hunt mice ... and cats and dogs. The city is no place for a coyote."

"But ..."

"Go along, now. I'm busy. We are not taking in a coyote, for God's sake. What do you think this is? The Paul Petting Zoo? Get out of here. I won't hear any more of this nonsense."

I ran upstairs, angry, sad, confused.

Later that evening, my mom got an unusual invitation from Terry's mom to come over for a visit. I was not invited—which annoyed me to no end. Mom, of course, knew the H_s, but she didn't socialize with them, so this invitation and her acceptance of it triggered alarm bells. I lay awake for a while, but I never did hear Mom come back home.

The next morning I found Mother and Joan crouched over a box in the kitchen, the familiar barricades were in place in the doorways. Joan's dog Ebony was standing on two legs beside her, peering into the box at a frightened little pup. "Shall we try it?" Joan asked Mom.

"We don't have much to lose," Mom replied.

Joan gently placed Ebony inside the box, keeping one hand on her back, just in case. Ebony was between puppy litters; the fuzzy, mewling ball of fear jumpstarted her maternal instinct. She approached the pup slowly, licking her chops, her tail stub waving slowly. She sniffed the nose, then the belly and the business end. Then her long pink tongue began to massage the baby's fluffy coat, imprinting her own smell on her new adoptee. Before long, she was curled in a protective ball around the now silent pup.

I'll never know how the H_s changed Mother's mind. Was it Mr. H_'s suggestion or Mrs. H_'s pleadings that caused Mother to rethink her resistance to taking on a coyote pup? Maybe it was the adorable and fragile look of the puppies that convinced her that the pup had as good a chance at life with us as he did anywhere, now that he'd been yanked from his mother. Once she'd caved in, though, she was as devoted to the coyote as his own mother would have been.

The coyote pup required doll-sized baby bottles which he adapted to quickly. Before long he was scrambling out of the box and investigating the kitchen, staring intently through the barricades at the rest of the house and at the cats who watched in disdain from a safe, but enticing distance.

As he outgrew the kitchen, the pup began to explore the rest of the house. He blended right in and surprisingly, paper trained more quickly than any of the domestic puppies we'd had. He earned his name, Thumper, from his excursions behind the couch, where he loved to hang out, his long tail thumping the wall in rhythmic contentment.

Thumper lived with us for almost a year, during which time Ebony had another litter of pups of her own. Would Thumper be jealous of the new kids on the block? Not at all. The adolescent coyote identified the pups as part of his pack. When the little guys were big enough to romp outside with Uncle Thumper, he watched over them and withstood their playful fight bites with nothing more than an occasional yelp of pain. When I played with him, Thumper would ever so gently mouth my wrist and lead me to his favorite hideouts under the bushes of our lawn. As the coyote grew, Mother worried constantly about him getting loose or jumping over our three-foot high fence. If no one was outside with him, Thumper had to be chained to a stake in the yard. He created a perfect crop circle where his padding feet wore out the grass. The pups would tumble out the door and race for Thumper's food bowl at the edge of his circle. He'd sit patiently watching while the puppies scarfed down his food.

There were no regulations in Laramie barring wild animals from private property. Kids of all sizes strolled by on their way to school and stopped to gawk at or play with and sometimes to cruelly tease Thumper. Teachers and parents worried. And so did my mother. Thumper was so sweet and so gentle, but he knew us. His feral instincts were unfathomable. Would that quiet pool of trust and acceptance one day boil into rage and frustration as some loud teenage boy tried to assert his superiority over a young wild dog? Or would Thumper defend his pack against the meter reader or the mailman some day? And what was to become of a coyote so habituated to people? Thumper led an unnatural life, no better than the life of a zoo animal, worse really, because he had no possibility of a mate and his life in our front yard contributed nothing to a practical knowledge base about his species.

I was aware of the Thumper dilemmas. Mr. H_ had only kept his pup for a few months before he announced it turned wild and bit him. Mother grumbled that he'd turned it wild and that it bit him because he deserved it. I heard the rumor that he'd taken the pup out into the prairie and shot it through the head. The other two pups from the litter had mysteriously disappeared, supposedly to one person, but we never knew any details. Thumper was the last of his litter and he was rapidly approaching the age when young male canines start sniffing the air for a girlfriend. The last thing we needed was for him to catch wind of somebody's bitch in heat and dash off for a quick tryst in the alley. When I came home from school one day, Thumper was gone. His chain and stake had been removed from the lawn, his bowls were gone.

I ran into the house, yelling, "Thumper, Thumper, where are you?" my voice on the edge of hysteria.

Mom came downstairs and looked me solidly in the eye. "Thumper has gone to his new home."

"What new home?"

"Some friends of the Talbots agreed to take him out to their ranch. They run cattle. There are no sheep anywhere nearby. They agreed to turn Thumper loose out by their corrals. They'll throw food to him as long as he hangs around. Eventually he'll figure out how to hunt his own food."

"Can we go visit him?" I asked, knowing better, but testing the waters anyway.

"No. It's best that Thumper make a clean cut. He needs to stop thinking of us as his pack. This is the best thing for him. It's not safe to have a wild animal in town. Eventually he'd get loose and either someone like our Mr. H would shoot him on sight or he'd get run over by a car."

I was disappointed, but not surprised. By the following spring, Thumper's circle had been reseeded. It sprouted an oddly bright shade of green. As the years passed, I often wondered about Mother's story. The more I thought about it, the more implausible it seemed. What Wyoming rancher would volunteer to turn a tame coyote loose on their property? I still wonder if this was just a story my mom told me to make me feel better. Perhaps instead, she took Thumper to the vet and had him euthanized. I almost think that would have been a better ending for him.

Not long ago, I watched a DVD of old converted 16mm film footage that Joan had shared with me. Herky-jerky images immortalize me playing with Thumper, him playing with the pups, him running circles at the end of his chain—first in one direction, then in the other direction, gazing longingly toward the house, over and over. My throat constricted and my temples throbbed as I recalled watching crazed bears trapped in too-small enclosures in zoo displays. It's no wonder that my mother was fodder for behind-the-back chatter. She must have seemed like a lunatic to old-timey residents of Laramie. Raising a coyote in that confined space was not right. What should we have done? Should we have just refused to take the pup from Mr. H? Perhaps it would have been better if Thumper had never known the back side of our couch.

And what did Thumper teach us? Perhaps he demonstrated the limits of well-intentioned kindness. I learned that animals respond to the way in which they are treated as infants. Spare the rod, nurture the loyalty. Mr. H's pup responded to his ill-mannered roughness by biting the hand that fed him. Thumper responded to our love by gazing at us with adoration and watching his adopted litter mates devour his food.

Thumper was the last of our bizarre household pets. Joan would soon graduate from college, get married, and move away.

Lovers of drama and dress up, Joan and Mom lived for the summer parade ritual. With a keen desire to show off her horsemanship and business acumen, Mom hung out a shingle for riding lessons, which formalized what happened more or less organically with family friends. Jubilee Days, Laramie's version of Frontier Days, kicked off the first week of July. The Jubilee Days Parade was a perfect venue for free advertisement of the "riding school."

As she acquired more horses, Yry also kept an eye out for tack, particularly black bridles and saddles which would look sharp on her white and palomino horses. Yry pulled out all the stops, buying us matching cowboy hats and boots, and sewing matching fancy western shirts for the three of us. The riding students (or friends) were matched with mounts and rode down the streets with us. If there were more students and friends than horses, the extras were loaded into the hay-filled back of the pickup adorned with a sign for the riding school.

The days leading up to the parade were filled with nervous energy; the horses had to be groomed and preened; the tack cleaned and oiled; and the pickup got its yearly wash and was decorated with signs and ribbons. The morning of the parade, everyone got up early and drove to the ranch on Skyline Drive. Everyone had to pitch in and fully tack their mount. Then we rode the horses two miles through an open field and through city streets, which triggered every dog on every block to a frenzy of barking. The house in town was a few blocks from the start of the parade and served as a final staging area. Invariably the night before the parade, at least one of the white horses would take a nap in a pile of manure, prompting a last-minute bleaching session at the house.

At first, I suppose I was excited about the hoopla. But as I grew older and school friends would point and laugh from the sides of the streets, I began to feel like a butterfly pinned in a display case. We looked so hokey. It was a nerve-wracking couple of hours as we prayed for no disasters on the slick pavement. The last thing we needed was for an unexpected noise or firecracker to spook one of the horses (or all of them) and for one of the students/friends to crack a skull on the pavement.

The Pet Parade was another beloved feature of Jubilee Days. Joan and Mom collaborated for weeks to dream up clever ideas for me and one of our pets. Their creativity transformed me into anything from a princess to a tin man. I quickly graduated from walking a dog for a pet to riding a horse in the Pet Parade, thus stealing the thunder of the poor urban kids with their cats, gerbils, and collies.

At some point during her college career, Joan's horse, Blanco, had his own walk-on role in a university theater production. And a production it was, bringing a full-sized stallion through the green room and onto the stage, praying all the while that he'd not be moved to leave a trail of hot green marshmallows in his wake. Calm, as always, he performed his role with dignity and graced the audience with his presence during the curtain call.

Joan moves on

Joan graduated from high school in 1960 and sped through college with a double major, graduating Magna Cum Laude in 1964. Shortly after graduation she got married. Her wedding was a big deal—an opportunity for Mom's naysayers to see her in her element, to see that she was not crazy and had not ruined her life or the lives of her children by fleeing the big city in favor of the Wild West. After surviving the short, roller coaster flight from Stapleton International to Brees Field, Mother's wide-eyed, green-jowled, East Coast guests stepped shakily down the wheeled, steel staircase, grabbing hats and hairdos in surprise. The blast of Wyoming wind was the first jolt; the nothing was the second shock. To a one, the dudes—as we thought of them—stopped as soon as their feet hit solid ground. Then came the slow pirouette, as their eyes scanned the upside-down blue bowl of sky, searching for some reference point to indicate they were still on planet Earth. Nothing greeted them but wind and pale land that curved upwards somewhere far away as it reached for the sky.

Guests arrived from both directions, Mom's East Coasters and the groom's West Coast friends and family. Mother's Cousin Hermann arrived from Germany. Mom's greatest accomplishment was to coax her reluctant guests onto the back of a horse. Even Cousin Hermann, with his prosthetic leg (which Mom always referred to as wooden, making him all the more unnerving to me), relented to Mother's persistence; he clambered stiffly from an upturned tub, to the back of the pickup, and then carefully slid his rigid leg over the saddle and pulled himself into position atop one of our most dependable horses.

My memory is fuzzy about much of the goings on, but I do remember giving up my bedroom for the sake of some lucky guest. In exchange, I had the run of the basement. Oh, yeah, this sounds like a wonderful reward, eh? But remember, that basement was dark and spooky.

The stairs leading down were bad enough—nothing more than 2 x 12s set into notched railing with no finished risers and no handrails. Negotiating those stairs was like running over the top of a sewer grate; the spaces between the stairs offered a dim view of "stuff" stashed beneath the staircase. I had no idea what the stuff was, but it lurked like goblin eyes, waiting for a false step.

I dreaded being sent to the basement for a can of green beans or to bring up the laundry. A bare light bulb hung at the very top of the stairs, doing little to illuminate the stairwell. Typically I'd dash down the stairs, at the bottom of which was a cement wall. I'd bounce off the wall and swivel to the left into the utility/laundry room or to the right, where I had to creep through a dark, unlit passageway leading to the rumpus room and unfinished kitchenette where we stored extra food.

Another stairway led from the end of this room up to an exterior doorway that opened onto the driveway behind our house.

The rumpus room wasn't bad, in itself. There was an old couch and bookcases and a brick fireplace which we never used but for the mantle that held family photos and do-dads. It was a long, narrow room with only two skinny windows at ceiling level that blocked more light than they let in. For the week of the wedding festivities, this rumpus room was my home. I nested with a pillow and sleeping bag on the couch. A small lamp on a side table above my head allowed me to turn off the overhead light without being doused into total darkness and I could read for as long as I wanted without scrutiny. Once through the dark passageway and into the rumpus room—with the lights on—I convinced myself that it was kind of a cool hang out. That is, until the night I felt a spider walk across my face! I leapt out of bed, stumbling to untangle myself from the sleeping bag and to find the light switch. By the time I was upright with the light on, the spider was long gone, nevertheless I tore the couch apart looking for it. I'm not afraid of much—but spiders. I ripped the cushions off the couch, reluctantly slid my fingers down the crevices of the couch, grimacing at the thought of what I might find; I shook my pillow, removed the pillowcase and vigorously shook that, beat the sleeping bag to within an inch of its goosey life, and inspected the floor, the walls, and everything near the couch. Long after I had remade my couch-bed and gingerly crept back into the sleeping bag, I could feel that spider's many legs tip-toeing across my cheek. My heart raced for a long time. Eventually, I decided I'd probably scared every spider in town, so I turned off the light.

Funny that this is my primary memory of my sister's fancy church wedding. I also remember that I was supposed to be a flower girl or some other such ridiculous role. I was to walk a funny way down the aisle and to pace myself properly to the person in front of me. I didn't like any of those responsibilities and

I didn't like the frilly dress I was supposed to wear. But I took it all with relative grace, I think. I simply reminded myself that Joan would be GONE in just a few days! No more big sister! No more big sister telling me I was a stupid ninny. No more big sister embarrassing me in front of what few friends I had. Surely this reward was worth wearing a frilly dress and enduring a spider walking across my face.

The year after Joan left, I brokered my way out of the piano prison that I had innocently stepped into years earlier. Joan was taking piano lessons before I started school. The ivories and ebonies of my grandmother's piano lured me like a fish to a spinner. I begged to play the piano. Once I began first grade, Mom granted my wish. I learned to read music before I learned the alphabet.

Initially I was entranced. My teacher, Miss McKay, lived with her aging mother, in an old, two-story house on a tree-shaded street within walking distance from our home. Once a week I walked to her house and up the stairs to her music room, where I sat at her upright piano, feet dangling in the musty air, and thumped out simple right- and left-hand exercises and pieces from the *Francis Clark Library for Piano Students*. Miss McKay peered at me through rose-tinted, wire-framed spectacles. Tightly curled steel-gray hair framed her spinster face. I basked in her kindly attention. Aside from her mother and her students, her life revolved around church, where she was the esteemed organist.

Before assigning a new piece, she'd demonstrate it and, if it had words, she'd sing along with the piano. "Oh, you'll recognize this one, it's a favorite with my Sunday schoolers," she'd say. As she demonstrated, her voice sweeping the cobwebs off the ceiling, I'd stare blankly at her. "Don't you know that one, dear?"

"No. I never heard it before, Miss McKay." I'd fidget, mortified by my ignorance, but even more mortified by how silly the songs were.

Twice a year, all Miss McKay's students had to perform in a recital for the parents, held downstairs in her white-carpeted parlor, where her grand piano gleamed with anticipation. The evening began with the newest, least proficient students and progressed to her top pupils who were playing "real" music like Liszt etudes or Chopin waltzes and nocturnes.

It didn't take long for the new to wear off my piano lessons. Worse yet was the practice I was supposed to be doing between lessons. The half hour chained to those leering keys was torture with the background chant of my friends' playing ball or riding bikes around the neighborhood.

"Mom, I'm tired of taking piano lessons."

"But you begged and pleaded for them. I've spent plenty on those lessons. You need to buckle down and practice. Make the most of this opportunity."

"But I don't wanna to play anymore."

"That's too bad for you. This is a lesson in life. You must finish what you start," Mother snapped.

So, how was I going to "finish" this project? Did I have to become the last student to perform in Miss McKay's recitals? That was never gonna happen. Then one year, the string instrument teacher for the entire Laramie school system visited our school. With all the fifth graders gathered on the floor of the gymnasium, Mrs. Gillespie began her recruiting session by playing Prokofiev's *Peter and the Wolf Suite*. She had one of each string instrument: a violin, a viola, a cello, and a string bass, which she demonstrated and allowed each of us to fondle.

I rushed home that afternoon and breathlessly announced, "Mom! I wanna play the cello!"

"Really?" Mom replied. "The cello? Well, that's a big instrument to lug around. And guess what? We already have a víolin." Her pronunciation emphasized the first syllable. "It'd be perfect for you. It's a three-quarter sized víolin that my grandfather played when he was a boy."

"Okay! Cool! But, if I play the violín, can I stop taking piano lessons?"

"Oh, so that's your plan. Well, young lady. We'll have to see about that. You play the víolin for two years. Then, if you want to continue with the víolin, you may drop the piano lessons. But, understand, that you will have to continue with one or the other instrument."

"That's not fair, Mom. You didn't make Joan continue with the piano ... and besides, it's not a víolin, it's a violín."

This was not an argument I would win, on either level, so I ran up to my room to supposedly do homework.

I don't know why I enjoyed the violin more than the piano. Perhaps it seemed more exotic. Or maybe it was a more social affair. I met new kids, and, as we screeched together, we laughed good-naturedly at our excruciating failures. And I liked Mrs. Gillespie a lot more than Miss McKay. *And*, recitals were not one-on-one terrors, but were concerts in which individual mistakes could be drowned out by the rest of the group. (Or so I presumed.) At last I dropped piano lessons to focus on the violin. As luck would have it, in the ninth grade, just as I was getting really fed up with the violin and the embarrassment of lugging it back and forth to school, I participated in my first all-district music festival, where we played the first movement of Beethoven's First Symphony in a full-sized orchestra with a drop-dead gorgeous man as conductor. I was hooked!

Mother and I drew closer together after Joan left. Between the ages of eleven and fourteen, I was an only child, just as Joan had been an only child until I was born. After she left, taking her dog and two cats, the house expanded. Mother and I began eating out more often. She purchased a TV—a portable black-and-white set. I would be surprised to find her watching *The Days of Our Lives* when I came home for lunch. She asked if I'd like a kitten of my own. *Would I?* We went to the pound where I picked out a beautiful tuxedo kitten. I thought he would look cool beside my black and white dog, the only puppy of Ebony's that we'd kept. Mom chose a shy gray kitten and later rescued a pair of scrawny Siamese kittens. We had fun playing with our new litter. There was more oxygen in the air. It seemed like overnight I had become a person worthy of talking to.

I began to like my mother just a little bit. Things were simpler with just the two of us. With little preparation we could load two horses into the trailer and head for the hills. Initially we drove to the Medicine Bow National Forest between Cheyenne and Laramie. We explored miles of dirt roads and paths that crisscross this high country plain, interspersed with huge outcroppings of rock and spindly, wind-blown juniper forests. Later, as we grew more confident, we ventured farther taking the tent and camp stove for overnight trips to the Encampment and the Cache La Poudre areas on the Colorado/Wyoming border.

We learned together on these overnight adventures. Fearful of rope-entangled equines, we tried hobbling them at night. The next morning Mom stepped out of the tent and shrieked. The campsite was empty. A virtually untouched pile of hay lay where the horses had been the night before. So before breakfast, we had to track down our errant equines who had caught the scent of a lush meadow several miles away, over a hill and through the woods. Hobbles? No problem. They figured out a three-legged dance that barely slowed them down.

I suspect it was through these outings that I began to absorb Mom's love of the mountains. Once out of the dusty backseat of our car that had made earlier outings a trial, I absorbed the warm sunshine on my arms, the scent of pine forest instead of over-ripe radiator sage, and I daydreamed to the hypnotic rocking of the saddle. Atop a horse, miles from home, where the unexpected could always happen, I learned to focus on details. I felt responsible for the safety of my mount. And, I began to recognize that Mother was learning lessons right along with me, and that she didn't necessarily learn them as quickly as I, nor did she anticipate trouble until it was upon her. Without even realizing that it was happening, I began to take the lead. I worked with our horses, making sure they'd trailer load without objection. I monitored their hooves and made sure that they were properly shod or trimmed before we headed for the hills. I augmented the organic knowledge that grew from experience by reading books and magazines about horsemanship. And I developed a keen sense of adventure—that penchant to discover what is just over the next hill.

Mom and I got along remarkably well during this time. She respected my diligence and responsibility, and I recognized some of the sacrifices she'd made in order to make this life possible for us. And yet, beneath my grudging approval lurked the knowledge that my mother did not fit in with her surroundings. Just as she sat a horse too stiffly to feel a storm lurking beneath the saddle, she looked and talked like a dude. When we met grizzled old hunters or fisherman on our backcountry adventures, I cringed at the questions she asked and the pompous comments she'd spout. Her highly articulated speech set her apart. I don't think she was even aware of the impression she made.

She still wore her dark hair capped close to her head, with tight, frizzy curls rimming her scalp like the collar on a coat. It was so 1930's during this time of bouffants and beehives. Forget the cowboy hat; Mom cinched a scarf over her hair to protect it from the unrelenting Wyoming wind. Though she complained bitterly about her big boobs and the men who loved to ogle them, she insisted on wearing form-fitting, tailored blouses and dresses which emphasized her abundance—this in a time when Twiggy and shift dresses were the rage. Then there was her handbag. For a while she actually carried a small hard-sided suitcase that resembled a lady's travel toiletry case. I have no idea what all was in there, but I know she always had room to stow away extra jam cartons, sugar packets, and napkin-wrapped leftovers when we went out for dinner. Her heavy handbag, coupled with the weight of her double D cups—overflowing a C bra—pulled her upper half over, giving her an upside-down L shape as she marched purposefully around town.

Occasionally I'd bemoan some exasperating social incident from school. I felt alien from my classmates and Mom's anachronisms drew attention to my geekiness. She sewed most of my clothes and what she didn't sew, she bought from the bargain racks at the end of each season. By the time I got to wear them the next fall, they were already outdated. I just wanted to look like everyone else. I argued my hair into stylish pageboys or bouncy flips, but my thin, lank locks quickly sagged straight when they weren't flying into space. Mom's solution was the *Toni* home-perm which produced a premature Afro. I complained about these trials. And when I complained, I always got the same response:

"Linda, don't be in such a hurry to grow up. Before you know it, you'll be wishing you could go backwards in time." Or:

"Don't be led by others. Be yourself. Be proud of who you are and stop being a baa, baa sheep all the time." Or:

"I don't know why you keep picking on yourself. You have lovely brown eyes. Just concentrate on those." Or, when I moaned that my face disappeared behind my nose:

"Wear your nose with pride! Look at Jimmy Durante. He's made a living out of his nose!"

After that, I searched for Jimmy Durante's name in movie marquees just to see what the ol' duffer looked like. And when I finally figured out who he was, I was even more mortified. *My own mother compared me to Jimmy Durante?*

The Pope Springs property

During these years, Mom continued to amass her real estate holdings. In 1964, the year Joan married, Mom worked with her local attorney to close out the last of her shares with F. H. Paul & Stein, Bros. She was to receive yearly payouts for five more years—the amounts declining as her shares decreased. She leveraged her buying power with the collateral of the ranch and our house in town. Dipping into savings, she'd put down large down payments on inexpensive homes near the college campus and quickly rent them out to college students or new professors. The *coup de grâce* was the purchase, in 1965, of a 360-acre ranch property five miles south of town.

The ranch had an old, heavily remodeled and expanded log house, plus a 1940s vintage main residence. A grove of cottonwoods sheltered the houses. The most remarkable feature of the property was an artesian well that supplied the sweetest drinking water I've ever tasted and fed a small pond in one of the pastures that was just deep enough on one end for a horse to swim for about four strokes.

The place was magnificent. It was vast compared to the measly 60-acre place we'd been using for the horses. Like the king on a chessboard, a full-sized prairie barn anchored the property. The barn was covered in rusted red metal sheeting and stood watch over extensive smaller sheds, corrals, and three pastures. Fortuitously, faint lettering on the front of the barn read "PAUL." We never figured out the origins of this coincidence. The floor of the barn's loft was as reliable as a nonagenarian's teeth; many of the cross boards were missing or soft, so the safest path across the floor was from joist to joist. The only light came from between the gaps in the floor. It smelled musty, redolent of some long-ago time. A few old relics scattered about served as clues to its past: an old notebook with grain purchases penciled in; an old bible, whole pages missing or stuck together; an old wooden rocking chair whose seat was as soft as the unreliable floorboards. My friends and I would sneak up to the barn and pretend to be early settlers. I felt a special ownership of this property. It was the first place in my life where my sister had not preceded me and had not been instrumental in decision making and management. I knew the ins and outs and the quirks of the place like I knew the palm of my hand.

In typical fashion, Mom rented both houses. We continued to live in our house in town, where I could walk to school and—sigh—still come home for lunch every day. Each afternoon after school, we drove out to the new place to feed and ride the horses. We had about ten of our own, plus several other horses that we boarded for townies. My friendships revolved around the horses and the ranch. If I wanted to spend time with other kids, it had to be on my mom's terms. My friends had to come out and help me with my chores. In return, they learned to ride. I began to relax. My grades improved. Life was good and complete, as far as I was concerned.

Perhaps not so much for my mother. During my life, thus far, if Mother had any romantic notions or desires, I was completely oblivious to them. She was *old*—an old withered prune, way beyond love or romance or dating.

How foolish, how naïve I was! True, she'd been a single parent for over thirteen years. But when she bought the Pope Springs property she was in her early 50s. I understand now, that she had only put a temporary stopper on her emotional and physical needs. But oh how shocked I was when one fall day, Mom announced that we were going to Mr. Tracy's house for Thanksgiving dinner. Mr. Tracy's marriage—to my former first-grade teacher—had disintegrated. He and his daughter were batching. His sister, Aunt E.D., drove up from Ft. Collins to prepare the holiday feast.

I was propelled into a new paradigm—primarily the importance of NFL football. When we arrived at Mr. Tracy's house, the TV was blaring from a darkened living room. I remember only the name of one team, the Green Bay Packers. The name stuck because it sounded cool to me. But I had no understanding of, nor interest in, the antics that looked a bit like uniformed ants colliding on their way back from foraging.

I met Mr. Tracy's daughter, Glenda. At 19, she was ever so mature. She had a driver's license and smoked cigarettes. She was in her first year of college and was struggling to learn a bunch of Latin terms for a biology class. After the meal, the two of us huddled in her small bedroom with me grilling her on the terms she had to learn for an exam. At 14 I was fascinated by anything that related to the insides of an animal. The terms were easy; I had already put together an Invisible Horse for a 4-H project and had volunteered at the veterinarian's office. I was surprised to realize what a struggle it was for Glenda to remember the Latin words. She grew increasingly frustrated as the evening wore on, making memorization even more difficult.

From that day on, Glenda and I spent a good deal of time together. She confided in me that she had never liked her stepmother. By this time, I had actually forgotten that Mrs. Tracy was my teacher. I mean, I *knew* my first-grade teacher was called Mrs. Tracy, but I'd forgotten about her connection to *Mr. Tracy*, the plumber. And, of course, I was still oblivious to my mother's earlier thwarted romance with Mr. Tracy. Glenda further admitted that her Aunt E.D., who had cooked our Thanksgiving meal that day, drove her nuts.

"She's nice and she means well. But, geez. When Dad and I moved into this house, I set up the kitchen and I've been cooking for us. Dad seems happy and I like taking care of him. I've been doing all the household stuff, cleaning, laundry, shopping. But here comes Aunt E.D. and she has to empty the drawers and cupboards and clean everything and rearrange it so after she leaves, I can't find a blasted thing."

Aunt E.D. was a hoot. She looked like a Daddy Longlegs on two legs. Her black leggings clung to skinny, knobby-kneed, bowed-legs like a second skin. A large, men's, white, button-down shirt disguised her top-heavy, upper half with room to spare; the tails of the shirt flapped in the breeze as she scooted around the house cleaning invisible dirt. Her head stuck up above that white shirt like the shiny, dark carapace of an insect. Aunt E.D. really worked at her cleaning. She'd get down on all fours and scrub as if her life depended upon it. She smoked a lot of cigarettes, so the hard, physical exertion brought on fits of coughing and left her heaving, her cheeks flushed.

Aunt E.D.'s husband was a sweet, loveable old guy with a heavy Swedish accent. His passion was dog racing, and he regaled us with exotic stories about the track. Uncle Rudy knew enough to jump when E.D. said to jump and to do so with joy in his heart and a smile on his face. Standing beside her, his small, wiry frame and bald head seemed gnomish; and oddly enough, I would come to discover that Aunt E.D. had a collection of garden gnomes in the postage-stamp-sized yard of her Loveland mobile home.

Mother's burgeoning romance shocked me. Till now, I'd been oblivious to her wild side. But, to be honest, I could see great advantages in this liaison. For one thing, her energy was completely absorbed by romance. I slipped off her radar and basked in freedom and autonomy that I'd never experienced before. Glenda's kindness to me was another comfort. She became the big sister I'd never had but always longed for. The fact that she had a driver's license and bright red Ranchero to cruise town with was another source of delight. Mother had always micro-managed my friendships and denied me the time and freedom to hang out with other kids, but now she relaxed her hold on me. Whenever Glenda wanted to go for a drive, she generously invited me along. We'd cruise Grand and Third Street and stop at Scottie's to order a coke and fries at the drive-through. I had no allowance and no money, but Glenda always had a supply of cash. If she wanted to go to a movie, she'd hit her dad up for a twenty and off we'd go. She'd buy our tickets and treats and pocket the change. What a racket!

As we all grew more comfortable together, Mr. Tracy became Glenn. All four of us would go out to the ranch on weekends. Supposedly Glenn had grown up on a ranch and knew horses. But he never looked particularly comfortable on a horse. Glenda had no experience with horses but was thrilled by the opportunity to ride. With encouragement from my mom and me, she learned quickly. When the tenants vacated the main ranch house, Mom didn't bother to advertise it. Instead, she and Glenn made plans for an addition to the house. They announced their engagement and told us to prepare for a big trip. All four of us would be going on a cruise to Europe. Glenda and I were beside ourselves at the prospect.

Time spurted forward. The addition was coming along nicely. Glenda and I planned how we'd decorate our two rooms that faced each other across a small hallway to our shared bathroom. Glenn, knowing how to charm a teenager, had presented me with my very own record player for my birthday. Mother promised Glenda a horse of her own. It was a yearling that I would saddle break for her. She'd have to wait until the colt was old enough to ride, meanwhile honing her horsemanship skills on our other horses. She was enthralled and spent every possible moment fussing over her little gelding, Fireball.

Besides gaining a big sister and a handful of new aunts, uncles, and cousins, I also gained a big brother and sister-in-law. Glenda's older brother, Bob and his wife Vivian, also lived in Laramie. But it was hard to think of Bob as a brother. He was 17 years older than Glenda, making him more of a fatherly age for me. But he was kind. All these new family members were easy to get along with. There were no hidden mine fields, no animosities. If there were differences of opinion, they were kept silent. Debate and argument did not exist.

The addition was completed in late summer and we began the exciting move from the town house to the ranch house and the mingling of two families. The old folks got the new bedroom with private bath that had been added to the back of the house. To our dismay, the trip to Europe was tabled. But we were mollified by the prospect of the old folks' impending honeymoon during which time Glenda and I would stay alone at the ranch. Woohoo! We were both good kids, so it wasn't a big leap of faith to leave a 14-year-old and a 19-year-old on their own. But it was a big adventure to us, and we were prepared to savor it.

Although I barely knew how to boil water, Glenda's domain was housekeeping and cooking. She wowed me with a delicious goulash. We had to celebrate with a bottle of wine, of course. What a lovely evening we had. Life was good—until after dinner when we were cleaning up. Together we washed the dishes, Glenda washing, me rinsing. We'd used my favorite of Mom's many sets of wine glasses—antique cut-glass with rose-colored bowls. I gently set each of them in the drain board. When

I placed another item beside them, one tipped over, breaking the bowl off sharply at the stem. We cried out in unison and covered our gaping mouths with our hands like a pair of monkeys in cahoots.

Remarkably, there was no finger-pointing, no accusations, no scapegoating. We were in this together. The next day, Glenda brought home a container of super-glue. We carefully patched our booboo, marveling at the luck of a sharp, clean break which was easy to glue. We let the glue set for 24 hours then carefully positioned the wounded glass at the very back of the collection of wine glasses. This infamous supper cemented our quasi-sibling relationship and loyalty.

A wedding and a honeymoon

> *I love you, my Love*
> *With my whole heart.*
> *There is a fullness to this love*
> *That I have not known before.*
> *There's a pleasure and a joy*
> *That carries me on evenings of ecstasy.*
> *And in giving you myself, my love*
> *I am filled to bursting full*
> *With the joy of living.*
> January 1965

As usual, there was much that flew over my young head. I didn't fully grasp that the European honeymoon collapsed in a double trap. The plumbing shop was looking a bit droopy and Mother, always eager to put money to work, agreed that it made more sense to invest in a facilities upgrade than to spend an exorbitant sum on travel for four to Europe.

Then there was another reality that hadn't quite registered with her yet. Her new husband was not cosmopolitan. A lengthy boat ride across the Atlantic to a foreign country did not thrill him. He wasn't keen on learning new languages or eating new foods. His idea of an exciting adventure was Las Vegas, where they could stay cheaply in a fancy hotel and he could play craps and blackjack. I wouldn't learn till many years later that Glenn had lured Yry to Vegas—a city she inherently loathed—on the assumption that they would also visit the vast southwest landscape, which she'd always wanted to see. The Grand Canyon! Zion National Park! The newly established Canyonlands National Park! Off they went to tie the knot in Vegas, of all romantic settings. Mom, disturbed by the bright lights, smoky environment, and endless racket, spent most of her time in their room, reading. Glenn plunked himself at the slots or around the gaming tables, pleased by everything that disgusted his persnickety bride. Eager to be seen with her, he cajoled her into attending glitzy, live entertainment acts with him. She fumed silently as she thought of the live opera she might have seen in Europe, but tried hard to compromise and play nice for Glenn so that he would reciprocate for her when they visited the natural wonders she was looking forward to. Their stay in the Sin City dragged on, cutting into the time she had assumed they would spend exploring the great outdoors.

When they did finally leave the high life of Vegas, the adventure through the landscape was rushed. Yry felt cheated. But marriage is a compromise. It is rare for a couples trip to play out exactly as each partner envisioned it.

As the school year progressed and more of my friends learned about my mom's unexpected marriage, I became the object of curiosity. Friends asked probing questions. Teachers quizzed me and looked at me as if a time bomb was ticking just behind my pupils. It seemed that I should be feeling something. Hurt? Rejection? I analyzed the situation and decided that since I was a teenager and had lived all my life without a father, my mother was now being selfish, and I should resent her. So I tried on a new tough girl act. I mumbled pat little passive aggressive comments. "Yeah, my mother doesn't give a shit about me anymore.

She's all gaga googoo over her new husband." This was pure BS and drama. Deep down, I knew it. But the added attention was fun.

In reality, Mom's marriage was the best thing that could have happened to me. For one thing, a vexing worry that had plagued me for a long time disappeared; if something happened to my mother, I would end up in the care of Joan. Now, though, I knew I would be absorbed into Glenn's family, no questions asked. Also, Mother's attention was off me and all her energy was deflected into playing the role of wife. As her time and attention shifted from the horses, I seamlessly took on more responsibility. Living on the property afforded much more time with the animals and I loved every minute of it. I spent hours feeding, grooming, and working with our horses as well as conferring with tenants who boarded horses with us. During the summers I spent most of my daylight hours riding. There were always plenty of young horses that needed work and exercise, so I thought nothing of riding one horse for several hours, returning and exchanging it for another, and after lunch, yet a third. There was absolutely no quibbling when it was time for me to start driving because my mother didn't have the time or the energy to chauffeur me into town for school and orchestra practices. By the time I was 16, I no longer bothered to suggest that we order more hay or schedule the farrier. Flexing adult muscles, I simply took on those responsibilities.

Many years later, after I'd graduated from high school, quit college, gotten married and moved to Idaho, Mom began her yearly visits to her children. Glenn preferred to stay home, watching over the plumbing shop and the property. These journeys were Yry's vacation away from a marriage that had not lived up to its promise. Tentatively exchanging married-girl secrets, I began to realize just how difficult that transition from single to married had been for my mother. And it would be many years, and two failed marriages of my own, before I would fully appreciate my mother's disappointment in yet another failed romance.

Within a year of her marriage to Glenn, Yry's luxurious, dark hair began falling out in clumps. "It's those damned permanents!" she exclaimed. "My system just can't tolerate all those poisons." When Yry and Glenn first began dating, she'd finally updated her hairdo. With his encouragement, she visited a hair salon and had her hair professionally styled and permed. She looked great. But she resented the necessity of this change. Her hair was not the only adaptation the marriage required.

Our house in town had been an old-fashioned house with high ceilings and vast reaches of wall space. Old, heavily-framed artwork plastered every bit of those walls. A royal-blue carpet covered the expansive living room floor, while the rest of the house was carpeted with dark red Persian rugs. Mother loved primary colors which were abundant in the slipcovers and curtains she sewed on her portable Singer sewing machine. The family furniture that had traveled from Europe to New York, then to Laramie, was antique, big, bold, and ornamental.

Glenn, by contrast, favored earth tones, simplicity, and an uncluttered environment. Mom tried to reign in her flair for flamboyance. They purchased new bedroom furniture, the first new furniture my mother had ever owned. On the main floor of our combined living space, Mom curbed her desire to hang every painting she owned. She agreed to beige walls, solid-colored and demure draperies, and cardboard-brown, wall-to-wall carpeting.

Then there were issues of diet. Mother, like her mother before her, suffered from mysterious digestive problems. She had learned to barely manage these by means of diet. I never understood what that diet was. I do remember that she refused to mix starch and protein in the same meal. She'd have the last laugh at the current pop dietary recommendations: lots of fruit, vegetables, and protein, with little starch, and few refined carbs. Mom could prepare an elaborate meal centered around Szechuan Duck, or roast goose stuffed with veal, but for the life of her she could not make biscuits or gravy, let alone both together. To further complicate matters, after a lifetime of cooking with gas, she now struggled with the all or nothing heat elements of an electric stove, which she didn't have the patience to master. Oh, the burned pans, the smoke drifting from the kitchen into the living room; oh, the curse words!

Glenn was a meat and potatoes Midwesterner. He'd grown up on a truck farm near Fort Collins. He expected meat at all three meals and feared spices other than salt, pepper, parsley, and sage.

As if décor and diet weren't problems enough, Glenn hated cats. At the time of their marriage, Mother and I had three cats and one dog. Glenn was fine with the dog. As a matter of fact, Glenda also had a dog. However, cats in the house were non-negotiable. This was Glenn's ultimate deal breaker. He would tolerate working cats outdoors, but even those he hissed at on sight. "The wilder they are, the better they hunt." This was devastating to Mom—and to me. A compromise was arranged. Our three cats would be relegated to the basement where Glenn never trod.

Diet, décor, and cats. Those, unfortunately, were only the outer shell of spiraling incompatibility. There was also the issue of money. Having invested a chunk of cash in the remodel and upgrades to the plumbing shop, Mom expected the business to grow. The shop looked lovely, with more open space and a bright, clean showroom for fixtures and even a line of luxury towels. Glenda was hired as a receptionist along with a new apprentice plumber. Mother knew and accepted that this was a long-term investment. Meanwhile, she enjoyed free plumbing service for her growing list of rental properties, an arrangement that stuck until her death some 15 years after Glenn's. Nevertheless, she was disappointed that expansion never translated into increased profits.

So, décor, diet, cats, and money. Those were not the end of Mother's disappointments. The move to the ranch and the addition to the house were based on Mother's assumption that Glenn was a rancher at heart and loved to ride horses as she did. Both of which weren't exactly correct. His boyhood experiences on the farm had provided no experience with saddle horses and precious little with other livestock. Laramie, at an elevation over 7,000 feet, is not farming country. However, Glenn did love animals and he planned to raise cattle, hogs, and sheep on the ranch. But if he'd ever raised these animals on that farm so long ago, he retained little memory of animal husbandry.

There is no doubt that Glenn loved the animals. They were his pets, his children. But he made horrendous mistakes that further tweaked his compassion for them. He bought a couple of weanling steers one spring. Eschewing the idea of cutting or sawing off the budding horns of his steers, Glenn decided to use a more humane method: a caustic paste that cauterizes the horn tissues and prevents growth. But he failed to read the fine print warnings on the can. After he applied the paste, a summer rainstorm washed the chemical mess into one calf's eye. Poor Glenn came out the next morning to find the critter with a festered and oozing eye socket. He never forgave himself. Responding to Glenn's backrubs and handfeeding, the one-eyed calf grew into a bovine Bunyan and following him around like a Saint Bernard on steroids. This baby beef earned permanent residency, safe forever from the butcher's block.

Next, Glenn purchased a young brood hog. Blossom was cute in a pigly way. And she ate anything and everything, including—if we weren't paying attention—the pie plate on which we delivered table scraps to her. Like Glenn's steer, Blossom grew enormous. When it came time to give birth, she could barely fit her entire body into her small covered pen with fresh straw spread across the dirt. Blossom valiantly birthed eleven piglets in an hours-long process that Glenn observed from outside the pen, like a distraught father. And he had good reason to be distraught. The babies, camouflaged in the loose straw, resembled hard-shelled puppies, tiny, pink, but strangely firm. Each time Blossom struggled to her feet to examine a new babe, she would step on another piglet whose squealing protest rattled her into a spinning dervish of tangled feet and piglets. Just three of her brood survived the improper farrowing pen.

Then Glenn purchased a mini herd of pregnant ewes. Our property was surrounded on three sides by the largest private sheep producer in the county. It would have cost nothing for Glenn to quiz Dick Strom on precautions he should take for his young, pregnant ewes. But what Glenn gained in love of his animals, he lacked in curiosity, nor was he one to consult the library. He simply turned the ewes into the pasture and wished them well. One by one, the ewes dropped their lambs alone and untended in the cruel Wyoming winter. The herd dwindled one-by-one till no one returned to the paddock for feed. In the spring, after the snow melted or blew away, I rode through the sheep pasture and, over time, located all six sheep carcasses, their babies nearby or not yet fully emerged.

Glenn was a kind, gentle man. He did not drink or gamble to excess. He could be very thoughtful, and he was generous to a fault. Shortly after completing the eighth grade, like many young men his age, Glenn had quit school to find work and help support his family. Mom was shocked and disheartened to realize that she had married a man who loved horses only from the ground, who would not read—perhaps due to a reading disability—even to improve the condition of his beloved livestock. His idea of entertainment was Lawrence Welk, the Lennon Sisters, Jackie Gleason, and a great Vegas show. His range of travel ended in Vegas or in Denver where his sisters lived.

No wonder my mother's hair fell out in handfuls. I calculate backward in time and realize that she was also juggling the whims of menopause. Although "the damned chemicals" may have played a role in Mom's sudden hair loss, I am convinced that this vexing problem was also a result of enormous stress, disappointment, and a cacophony of mixed-up hormones.

After many failed romances and one divorce, Yry came to realize that her heart had once again overruled her head. Difficulties aside, she knew she had a good man. He was loyal and honest. And she was resigned to lie in the bed she had made, which frankly was probably the best part of their union.

Finding her stride

Aside from rancher Leah Talbot, most of Mother's friends were connected with the university. Did she fit in better with academicians? Or did she just think she fit in better? I asked her once, why, when she had the entire West to choose from, did she decide to settle in Laramie, such a windy and desolate choice?

"It was because of the University," she explained. "I wanted a place where you kids could be exposed to the things that a college has to offer: the arts, the lectures, the intellectual stimulation. Sure, northern Wyoming is beautiful, but there is less culture there, fewer opportunities."

I suspect this wasn't a sacrifice on her part because she, too, needed people with a broader world view than the typical farming and ranching communities that shelter in the rural west. For a while Mom was active with a rock hunting group. Rockhounds are a breed apart. But they were friendly and enjoyed traipsing around outdoors. Through this group, Mom met people in the UW geology department. After Joan enrolled at the University, Yry began to meet some of Joan's favorite professors in the history and English departments. And Yry was more than a landlord to her tenants; students and young professors who rented from her often blossomed into friends.

Leah was involved in county land-use planning, sitting on several boards and agencies. Mom sometimes accompanied her to Farm Bureau meetings or, at Leah's urging, spoke up in council sessions. She observed Leah's strength and leadership in these organizations and when the time came, Mom, too, stepped into the role of leadership. The issue that lured her in, however, was far more controversial than zoning or acre-feet of water.

Although the State of Wyoming lagged in national trends, the University was the heartbeat of social and progressive ideology. During the late '60s, tentative anti-war protests on campus baffled the locals. So did long-haired men in sandals with bellbottoms and flowers in their hair. New attitudes toward love, sex, and equal rights electrified Mom. She fully supported young people's social protest and rejection of the status-quo. Some say that the availability of birth control contributed to the free-love movement. However, in our town, as in much of the west, I'm convinced that birth control measures gained traction on the heels of the sexual revolution. This of course, was just the topic to kindle Mom's passion for action.

Learning that University students, as well as young women throughout Wyoming, had difficulty obtaining affordable birth control measures, Mom joined with a handful of much younger women to establish a family planning clinic in town. With much encouragement and admiration from her young friends, Mom screwed up her courage and began speaking out for women's health rights. The voice of an older woman—and a mother, at that—leant credibility to the cause. At this time and in this place, birth control was still a relatively novel concept. Many adults knew little about preventing pregnancy besides abstinence and condoms. The old codgers equated a family planning clinic with abortion. Mom's foremost interest was in preventing unwanted pregnancies. However, when the issue of abortion rose from the crib, she embraced a woman's choice on that matter as well.

I was in high school at this time. Glenda had moved out of the house in search of her own path. Glenn's health was diminishing. My energy went into music and caring for the horses. Mom was flexing new muscles. She'd return from late-night meetings, fuming at the stupidity of people who thought any unwanted, unplanned pregnancy was a gift from God. She was indignant that men controlled the type of medical care and procedures that women were *allowed* to receive. She fumed about population control, resource management, and the shrinking planet. She was a heroine to a cohort of young women who saw her as the voice of reason and experience in an otherwise deaf community.

Glenn was uneasy. Never comfortable as the center of attention and unwilling to engage in controversy of any type, he watched my mother's growing notoriety in silence. I never heard him contradict or reprimand her or even ask her to step away from the mission. But I sensed his discomfort and the growing chasm between them as he retreated to his private thoughts and endless television shows.

By now my mother had lived in Wyoming for over twenty years. Her reputation, I'm sure, differed depending on various prisms through which she was viewed. To the ranching community, Yry was, and would always be, an outsider. Like the college community that mostly passed through town on their way to loftier careers, she brought her past with her. Her history was tainted by the otherness of the larger world. Her views were not necessarily trustworthy because, try as she might, she was foreign. She could read and recite the history of the west, of Wyoming, of Laramie, even of her own property. But she had not *lived* that history. The history that resided deep in her bones was alien. She dressed differently, she talked differently, she ate differently, she straddled a horse differently. Even the horses she bought were different: showy palominos and, of all pariahs, a collection of albino parade horses. These animals stuck out like peacocks amongst the squat, muscular sorrel and bay Quarter Horses favored by the Wyoming ranching community.

I'm not quite sure how the town folk viewed my mother. Among them were many natives: people whose families had arrived in the early days of the railroad, who had ranched, or sold to ranchers and shared the ranching perspective. But there were also college transplants, outsiders like herself, prone to a wider world view. Among them were people who had come from the outside and stayed despite the harsh wind, short growing season, and bi-seasonal climate. These residents had been captivated by the same things that lured Mom to this place in the middle of nowhere. They came for the wide-open spaces: that endless sky, the fresh air, and pure water. They came to escape the frenzy and fumes of population density.

These people—the academicians, the professors, the graduate students—appreciated Mother's passion. Her larger world view did not frighten them or diminish them. They admired the crazy, weathered woman who stood before a crowd pleading for money to fund a small clinic to support family planning practices in Albany County.

One afternoon Mom came home and breathlessly announced that she'd been elected Executive Director of Albany County Family Planning Services. "Oh lordy. I never expected this. I so hate talking before a crowd."

"Really? Why do you do it then?" I asked.

"Well, Linda, you can't let fear rule your life. Sometimes you just have to swallow your pride, your prejudices, your fears, and stand up for what you believe. And, on a personal level, it's good for me. If I didn't push myself I'd be a hermit. I'd have no friends, no people to talk to. That's not healthy. We can't live inside our own head all the time."

"Well, I'm way too shy to talk before a crowd," I said. "I'm okay with a few friends, but don't put me in front of a podium. God!"

"You know," she said, "that madman Hitler got away with genocide because shy people like you and I were afraid to stand up and talk. There are bad things going on in the world right now. People are turning a blind eye to massive poverty in countries where religious zealots deny women the right to control the size of their family. There's not enough food, women helplessly watch baby after baby die of starvation and disease just because some male is privileged to scratch his horny itch every time he feels like it. Right here, in this country, women die hunched over a toilet with a coat hanger stuck up their vaginas."

I was surprised to hear my mother describe herself as shy and uncomfortable, but I was familiar with her graphic language. I felt a rant coming so I headed out the door to do some chores. Mom was certainly different than the other demure mothers I knew. I couldn't stand her soap box sermons, which often ruled the evening meal. But I recognized that even though she was two generations older than I, she was in tune with the sociopolitical views of my generation. The few friends that I was now brave enough to introduce to her raved about how cool she was. They loved her and wished their own mothers were as open-minded and hip. *God, if they only knew*, I thought. But their admiration began to shake my ingrained disdain for my mother. On long horseback rides with some of Mom's friends, who were closer to my age than to hers, I saw her wisdom in a new light.

By the time I graduated from high school, the Albany County Family Planning Clinic was going strong. I had even referred friends to it. I supported Mom's efforts and was proud of her involvement. Until I came face-to-face with it.

I had been playing in the University Symphony for two years. My stand partner through those years was a married woman with two young children. She had played violin in high school and college, but years of marriage and childcare had interrupted her practice. She was nice. I viewed the fledgling wrinkles under her chin and around her eyes with youthful arrogance. She was a decent violinist, albeit I thought she played rather stiffly, as if her old fingers had lost their elasticity. In hindsight, of course, I suspect that she was in her early thirties. We didn't talk much about our personal lives. I didn't even know that she had a job. I simply assumed she went home to her husband and kids every night and had all day to clean house, cook meals, and practice the violin.

During the summer between high school and college, I'd been accepted into a work-study program across the state, in Evanston. I shared lodging with four other girls. Some of us had studied more than Abnormal Psychology during that magical eight weeks. My wild summer was filled with late nights of dancing and boozing and hanging out with eligible bachelors. I returned to Laramie in the fall with a suitor on my heels; I was in desperate need of birth control. I had no insurance and no expendable income, and yet I could not bear to walk into the Family Planning Clinic where *everyone* knew my mother. After agonizing and taking too many chances, I simply *had* to get a prescription. I called a random gynecologist listed in the yellow pages and made an appointment using a bogus name. Arriving for my appointment with small change saved from waitressing tips, I pulled open the door to find my *stand partner* from the orchestra sitting before the appointment book!

"Your name, please?" she asked, all innocence and friendliness.

I wanted to fall through the floor. In trying to avoid potential recognition at the Clinic, I had walked directly into this trap. Bless her heart, the woman's pupils didn't even change when I offered her my bogus name, which she checked off on the appointment book, giving me a warm smile as she did so. A professional to the core, the subject of my visit to the doctor's office and my bogus name never came up between us, although we continued to sit side-by-side for two more years.

A family that keeps secrets doesn't press for details

I frittered away a couple of years at college. But my heart was not in it. I had enrolled in the only course of study that required no math classes. Unfortunately, my music major was preparing me for a death sentence. I loved music and even more, I loved being part of the large, living, breathing organism that creates music— an orchestra. But I didn't have the talent or single-minded dedication to perform professionally and I never wanted to be a teacher, especially not a teacher of stringed instruments.

By this time what had begun as a summer romance in Evanston had blossomed into a serious relationship. I was living with the guy while he worked towards a PE degree. He was enrolled in ROTC—this at a time when I felt that real patriots should be protesting the Vietnam war, rather than polishing buttons on uniforms. But I put my misgivings behind me. No one is perfect, I told myself. He endured my hen scratching on the fiddle and faithfully attended concerts. He enjoyed the outdoors and horses—although he did nothing but fight with my horse, a situation which I only comprehended much later.

As student teaching loomed, I jumped ship. I'd discovered that the happy-go-lucky mailman, who lunched at my counter at the dive where I worked part-time, was making more money than I would with a degree and ten years of teaching behind me. And—the post office was hiring! I was prepared for a showdown with my mother. "What, you're *quitting* school?" is what I expected. Instead she surprised me with this:

"Well, Linda. Maybe you need a break. Just don't burn any bridges. At least you're quitting on your own terms and your grades are good. You can always change your mind later."

I've often wondered if her calm response wasn't a sign of how hard she was treading to keep ahead of outright depression over her stagnated marriage and the disappointments that life hands out as the years pile up.

So off I went, with my new black, metal, lunch box, to work in an office full of men while my boyfriend finished school. As his graduation and commission into the Air Force approached, we decided to make it official. An officer must have a wife, not a live-in girlfriend. We celebrated Bob's first assignment to Mountain Home, Idaho, which was one of the three locations we'd asked for and one that was most dreaded by other Air Force families. For us, Idaho was close to home and similar in climate and terrain to where we'd grown up. We knew the area would feel familiar even if the base was nowhere near the mountains, as we'd been warned.

By the time I left Laramie, Glenn's health was fragile. Joan lived in California with her husband. Glenda was married and had a small child. The plumbing shop was floundering along, still providing free plumbing services to my mother, but barely solvent.

Mom seemed to have shrunk physically, although her personality was still larger than life and a circle of young admirers still swirled around her, offering companionship and, perhaps, easing the empty nest syndrome. I give her credit for never complaining about her brood abandoning her. Before I left town, I helped Mom pare down her herd of horses to lessen her physical labor. I worried about her getting hurt on some of the younger, less reliable mounts. Mom's riding skills were, like her rancher's persona, only skin deep. Not having grown up on the back of a horse, she lacked that intuitive connection to muscle and bone under the saddle. As she aged, her reflexes were slower and her joints stiffer, and surely her bones more fragile. Like an overprotective parent, I envisioned her lying in the middle of a field with a broken back.

Though it was hard to part with them, we had found homes for all but three horses. To ease the loss, we managed to sell a couple of the older horses that we'd loved and nurtured for so long to friends who pastured them at the ranch. It was almost like not letting them go. And it ensured that more able bodies would be regularly visiting the ranch and offering help with physical things like fence repairs and moving hay and grain around.

Then, I loaded up my own favorite horse—the one I was most anxious to remove from temptation because he'd already pitched my mother once, leaving her sore and gimpy—and headed for my new life in Idaho.

Mom's first visit to my house on the Air Force base was interesting. She had never been an advocate of the military. The

Wyoming

very sight of a uniform made her uneasy. She claimed it was because of her early childhood during the war. I'm sure she found all the neat little ticky-tacky officers' quarters Stepfordish. To be honest, I did too. But at least I had my horse. Each morning, after Bob left, I'd jog across the manicured golf course that, struggled to be green in Idaho's high desert, and jump aboard my horse for a quick bareback gallop through the sagebrush, under the tooth-jarring roar of F111s buzzing to and fro.

During Mom's visit, she and I escaped the incessant flight path to explore southern Idaho. I astonished her with a trip to the Bruneau Sand Dunes where we pretended we were Egyptians. We did the standard Sun Valley – Stanley loop. She was completely unimpressed with Sun Valley but predictably entranced by the Sawtooth Mountains and Redfish Lake. In Boise, we explored department stores and swank restaurants. Then it was back to the regimented life of the base which she gleefully left behind on her way to California to visit Joan and her family which now included two little boys. Joan's husband was working for a large bank. They lived on a small gentleman's farm outside Fresno, where they kept several horses, an assortment of cats, dogs, geese, ducks, and chickens.

By the following year, I had breaking news. This time I called Mom from my new location in Boise.

"Hey, Mom. How are ya?"

"I'm okay." She launched into her typical descriptions of what she'd eaten for the last five meals and who she'd ridden with. She always had a brilliant assortment of young people to talk about. When she came up for air, she asked: "So, what's up with you?"

I hadn't realized I'd been holding my breath till I exhaled a huge volume of stale air over the receiver. "Well, I've got some news for you," I began, tentatively. *Oh shit, she's gonna think I'm prego.*

"Yes?" she asked cautiously.

"Well ... ahh. Bob and I, er, ... I left Bob."

"Where'd you leave him." She was serious.

"We're getting a divorce."

"Ohhh." The impact dawned. "What happened?"

This was a perfectly normal question—one I had anticipated. But one that I had no sensible answer for, and therefore it was a question that annoyed me. I sighed.

"Did he get physical with you?" Mom interjected over my silence. Bob was a big man with a nasty, playground-induced scar on his forehead which made him look menacing.

"No, Mom. He didn't get physical. Although I did worry the last night I was in the house." I conveniently avoided revealing why I'd been worried on that last night, the night when he'd accused me of having an affair with a guy who stabled his horses next to mine.

"Well, what happened, Linda? I didn't even know you two were fighting."

"We weren't fighting. I mean, we really never even argued ... until that last night."

"Well, then ... ?"

"I just wasn't *happy*. It's hard to explain. I don't belong here. I'm not officer's wife material." I knew she'd get that, and she did. "And, Mom, you know he wants a passel of kids. He kept dragging me into town to look at houses that we could buy; a house so we could start a family, ya know? And God. I just don't want that."

"Shouldn't you have considered that *before* you agreed to marry the man?"

"I did, Ma. But everyone told me, 'Ah, don't worry. You'll want kids when the time is right.' Well, apparently the time is right ... for him at least. But it's not right for me. I really don't think it'll ever be right for me. I just don't want kids."

"That's too bad, Linda. Really it is. You know, I loved being a mother. I wouldn't have traded that experience for anything. But you have to do what's right for you. And if you really don't want kids, by God, you shouldn't have 'em just because someone else wants you to or because it's expected of you."

I was relieved that she seemed to understand my position.

"So where are you now?" she asked. "Do you need anything?"

"I'm in Boise. A friend helped me find a place and move some things. It's no palace, but until I can get a job, it'll have to do. I've tried to get back on at the Post Office. If that comes through, I'll be okay. My friend at the stables is taking care of Thunder for me."

One of the good things about a family that keeps secrets is that they don't press you too hard for details. It was easy for me to gloss over the friend business. Mom didn't ask who this friend was or who it was that helped me move, and I surely didn't offer any incriminating evidence.

A death in the family

And so I began a new life in Boise. A few months after my divorce I learned that Joan and her boys had followed her husband Jim to Ecuador, where he was in charge of opening a new office. They invited Mom for a visit. "Come on down," Joan urged. "There's plenty of room in our house, we even have a cook and a nanny. It is beautiful here."

Mom hesitated. Glenn's health was declining rapidly. He was in and out of the hospital with cascading organ failures. But Joan encouraged Mom to take a break. She knew Mother was stressed over caring for him. Besides, she'd never cared for Mom's new family. He was just a plumber; our family were *professionals*: academicians, chemists, lawyers, bankers. In visits to the ranch, she'd been rude and dismissive to Glenn and to Glenda. She was also concerned that Jim's employer would send them back to the states before she could lure Mom down there. She sweetened the deal.

"Mom, we've set up a trip to the Galapagos Islands. We have the tickets already, including one for you. It's the chance of a lifetime. The Galapagos are changing, they are one of the last pristine natural wonders of the world and they won't stay that way for much longer."

Mom agonized. She'd always dreamed of seeing that natural laboratory of evolution. But how could she leave Glenn now? He'd just been released after ten days in the cardiac unit of the hospital. But bless him, Glenn told her to go. He pushed and encouraged her, and convinced her he'd be fine under Glenda's and daughter-in-law, Vivian's, care. Mom agonized some more, questioning Glenda and Vivian, probing to make sure they felt comfortable about her leaving.

"You know, once I get to Quito, it'll be nearly impossible to reach me if you need to. And from the Galapagos there's no communication at all," she warned.

They both consoled her. They knew how much she wanted to take this trip. They recognized how faithfully she had tended Glenn during his recent spate of health crises. And, perhaps, they were in denial about the possibility of anything happening that they couldn't handle.

Meanwhile, my marriage over, I had moved to a glum little mobile home in Boise. The phone rang late one night. I answered it with an uneasy feeling.

"Hello, Linda?" It was Vivian, Glenn's daughter-in-law. She never called me. Her voice sounded hollow.

"Yeah ... Hi, how are you, Vivian?"

"Ahh ... not so good, Linda. I have some difficult news for you."

My stomach knotted. *Had Mom's plane gone down? Or had the tour boat sunk? Glenn?*

"What's the matter, Vivian?"

"Well, it's Glenn. I'm afraid he passed away earlier this morning."

"Oh, *God, no* ..."

"Yeah, Linda, I'm afraid it's true. He went quietly ... just slipped away in his sleep."

"Oh, no! Damn it. Does Yry know?" As soon as the curse words were out of my mouth I wanted to reel them back in. *My God. How callous and crude is that?*

"Ya. I'm sorry we didn't call you earlier, but we spent the whole day trying to reach Yry. It wasn't easy, believe me. And Linda, here's the thing, she can't get home. She's out there somewhere in the middle of the Pacific Ocean, and there's no way to arrange to get her back to the mainland and onto a flight back to the states any time soon."

"Ch-rist!"

"Linda, I know this sounds awkward." Vivian's voice was wobbly and tentative. "Your mom ... she wants us to go ahead with the funeral. She wants us to take charge and arrange it however we see fit."

"Vivian, I'm so sorry. This must be so difficult for you. You're so good to shoulder all this. How are Glenda and Bob holding up?" All of the Tracys had hearts of putty and were subject to copious tears and deep grieving.

"They're okay." Vivian answered vaguely. It was clear there was more on her mind. "But, Linda ... Yry wants you to be here and to act on her behalf. Can you ... get away?"

Hollowness swallowed my gut. "Of course I can get away. I'll arrange time off from work and get a flight from Boise tomorrow. But, gosh, Vivian, I don't know what to do. I just have no idea ... "

"Don't worry about the details. We'll just be glad to have you here with us. I've already called the funeral home. We set a tentative date for Wednesday, if that's okay with you. Tomorrow Bob and Glenda and I will go down and pick out a casket and do all of that. We just need you to be here for the ceremony ... to greet the guests."

"Oh God, Viv. I'm so sorry this all happened like this. I'm so sorry you have to bear the brunt of it all. Mom really trusts you, and I know she's relieved that you are in control. I'm sure Bob and Glenda aren't much help ..."

"Ya know, it's surprising. Bob's a mess, it's true, but Glenda is holding up better than you'd expect. Now you get some rest, and let me know when you'll be getting to town. I'll make sure we've got someone ready to pick you up at the airport."

"You are a rock, Viv. We're all so lucky to have you. Now, *you* must get some rest. You must be reeling from everything you've been through. I'll call you as soon as I have some information.

I put the phone back on its cradle. My ear was sweaty. The dumpy trailer was dead still, except for the menacing oil furnace that crackled by the door. "*God damn him!*" Inexplicably, I was angry. "The fucker up and *died!* Why in the hell did he have to die *now*, of all the times to die!" I was shocked by my own reaction.

My boyfriend, sitting on the couch, had heard the entire conversation. He knew a bit of the backstory about my mom's trip and my stepdad's imperiled health. He rose and came to me, wrapping his arms gently around me.

"You ok?" he asked quietly. "What can I do to help?"

"I'm fine. It's Mother I'm worried about. I can't imagine what this must be like for her. There's not a damned thing she can do. It took them all day just to get ahold of her. She can't make it back. She wants me to represent her, of all the insane things I've ever heard of. Hell, I've never even been to a funeral before. Geez, two firsts. No, three. First dead body, first funeral, and first commercial airline flight, all in one fell swoop!"

He released my squirming body. "You need to be alone, or do'ya want me to stay? I'll book a flight for you tomorrow and take you to the airport and take care of the dogs for you," he offered.

His gentle support touched me, and I began to relax. We retired to the bedroom to cuddle. Don was a single-engine pilot, and we had frequently flown together in his little Cessna. He loved airplanes. To alleviate my flight anxieties (which I really didn't have) he commenced walking me through every step of commercial flight procedure, from finding my seat to buckling up and the thump of the wheels retracting after lift-off. I let him natter on, listening with half my mind. The other half of my mind wondering if he thought I was a helpless nincompoop.

Wyoming

Late the following day I was in Laramie, absorbing the tsunami of Tracy tears. Viv was right. Glenda was holding up better than her brother. Her eyes were red and puffy, but she was in control. Her brother, however, appeared shell-shocked. It was as if his own mortality had suddenly reared up in front of him. His eyes were swollen and wet and his lips quivered.

I tried to reach deep inside myself to find some sort of appropriate emotional response. I felt inhuman. I was a fraud. For the life of me I could conjure no tears. The arrangements had all been made. The funeral was scheduled for the next day. I wondered what I would do. I'd have to remember people's names. I'd have to say something meaningful to my mom's friends and to an even larger audience of townspeople who'd known the Tracys for even longer than I had.

The service and the reception passed before my eyes like a movie reel. I was there, on stage—but I was really in the screening room, watching the film. I shook hands, hugged strangers, thanked people for their concern, consoled people, and fumbled to explain my mother's absence to folks who had never been outside of Albany County and who probably thought my mother was a reckless gold-digger who'd married Mr. Tracy only for his money.

As the years passed after our move to the ranch, Mom had slowly shifted more paintings and personal treasures from the basement to the main floor. Perhaps she was desensitizing Glenn to clutter. Or else his weakened health muffled his disapproval. After he died, the migration began in earnest; once again, every flat surface disappeared under stacks of papers, knickknacks, and trinkets. The walls disappeared behind a mélange of pictures: old oil paintings in ornate frames; Mother's own attempts at landscape painting; exquisite pen and ink drawings done years ago by one of her German cousins; pages ripped from calendars; and glossy posters that came tucked into solicitations for environmental issues. Mom sewed new living room curtains with a vivid print of African animals. The fabric was heavy, lined, and padded to prevent heat exchange. The cats left their basement prison and took over the sunny spots and the soft couch cushions from which they had been banned.

Yry, with more time on her hands now, blossomed anew. I'm not sure how she accumulated the contingent of young acolytes who flocked to her home individually and in pairs. She seemed to have a ready supply of energetic and intellectually brilliant people to ride with, to dine with, and to solve world problems with. During the Carter administration she jumped at the opportunity to demonstrate the power of solar energy. Using federal tax incentives, she retrofitted the electric heat system to work with photovoltaic panels attached to the roof.

And she traveled more. She continued her yearly visits to Joan and me, combining them with some other adventure: a trip to the Grand Canyon, to the Pacific Rain Forest, Glacier National Park, Yosemite, Yellowstone. At last she had the time and the money to explore every cranny of the western United States.

At the age of 71, she flew to Kenya for a two-week horseback photo safari. She returned with amazing photographs of elephants, wildebeests, Thompson's gazelles, lions, giraffes, and all sorts of exotic birds and small mammals. She described feeling guilty about riding the scrawny little horses that looked undernourished.

"Those poor horses were even smaller than my horses," she reported. "It sure made mounting easy. But once seated, it felt like the saddle would slide right over the withers of the poor skinny little beasts. The long-legged European men looked like they could just as easily add their own legs to the horses' four ... and maybe they should have. But those little animals were surefooted and always willing to go."

Collapse

A few weeks after Mom returned from Africa, she became ill. She'd been fastidious about using only treated water, "But those little African cooks," she observed, "they drink their water straight from the river. I don't think they fully comprehend how dangerous untreated water is for us westerners. I watched those young men in their outdoor kitchens. They worked hard preparing delicious meals for us, but I'm convinced they used untreated water to wash the dishes."

Mom refused to go to the doctor. She was sure she'd picked up an intestinal bug in Africa and that she just needed to flush her system with fluids and tough it out. Several days passed. She became so weak; she asked the neighbors to feed the horses. The nausea persisted, she ached—especially her back. Then the ache became a stabbing pain. Her heart was racing. *What in hell is going on? I wonder if I should call a doctor.* She was weighing her options and trying to force down more water when she began to feel lightheaded. A sheen of sweat dampened her temples and forehead. *My God. Is it my heart? Am I having a ...?* Midway to the phone, a knifing pain cut through her lower back. She dropped to her knees, gasping, fingers clenching the carpet, she crawled the rest of the way to the phone and stabbed the pre-programmed number for her daughter-in-law, Vivian.

"Hello?"

"Viv, oh, God ... Viv, help ..."

"Yry? What's the matter?"

"I'm ... oh, God, it hurts ... help me ..."

"Are you at home?"

"Ummmyaa"

"I'll be there as soon as I can. Hang on, Yry"

Twenty minutes later, Viv rang the doorbell. She waited a beat, then searched for the hidden key. She found Yry nearly unconscious, beside the phone which lay on the floor beside her, humming its off-the-hook tone.

Viv reached for the phone to call the ambulance, but my mom came to. "No damned ambulance ... take me in your car."

"Yry, I'm not sure I can get you to the car. Let me at least pull the car up to the door."

With the car positioned as close as possible to the front entrance, Viv muscled Mom upright and half carried her to the door and down the steps where she folded her into the car.

After twenty-four hours of emergency care at the hospital, Mom's condition stabilized. The good news was that her heart was fine. The bad news was bad. The doctor stood at her bedside and explained the situation.

"Mrs. Tracy, have you ever had problems with water retention or kidney infections?"

"No, never. I've never even been in a hospital except to have my two kids."

"Well, the x-rays revealed an interesting dilemma. Your left kidney is the size of a walnut. It is likely that this kidney has never functioned. This would indicate a congenital defect. Apparently your one functioning kidney has been doing the work of two."

"Well, it doesn't seem to have stopped me," Mom replied belligerently.

"No. Not till now. Your one kidney has served you well. However, what brought you in here was a kidney infection. The infection was interfering with that lone kidney's ability to flush toxins from your system. It's a wonder that the infection reached such an advanced stage. We've been able to stabilize you, and the IV drips are circulating fluids for you, taking pressure off that kidney while we treat the infection. But you must know ... that hard working kidney of yours has taken a hit." The doctor's hand gently touched her shoulder. "It will be a while before it is functioning at peak performance ... It may never regain the ability to keep your system flushed."

"What are you telling me?"

"Mrs. Tracy, you need to make some arrangements and lifestyle changes. You are now in Stage IV of Chronic Kidney Disease. If you're lucky, that brave kidney may filter for you for ten months, or a year. But soon, you will slide into the next stage,

End Stage Chronic Kidney Disease from which there is no turning back. You will then need dialysis. Full-time dialysis. This means that you will need to live near a dialysis center. Dialysis must be performed three times a week. The procedure takes between two to four hours. In between treatments, you may experience the effects of slow toxin buildup: lethargy, poor appetite, weakness, and even memory loss."

"What about a kidney transplant?"

"Unfortunately, at your age, transplants are not recommended."

"Well, I'll just have to come here for the treatments," Yry replied churlishly.

"No. We're set up for emergency treatments here. But we do not have chronic care. We can get you stabilized, but only a kidney center has adequate facilities for ongoing treatment.

She looked at him mistrustfully, "Where are these ... kidney centers?"

"The closest one is in Fort Collins."

"Well, that's impossible," she retorted." Driving to Ft. Collins three times a week? Isn't there a better option?"

"Actually, Mrs. Tracy, you'll need to live closer to the center. Your blood levels need to be closely monitored. Driving that road during the winter months will be more than you can handle. On the days that you are due for a treatment, you will not be feeling chipper."

Impatient with the doctor's grim prognosis, Mom abruptly changed the subject. "Well, how long are you planning on keeping me cooped up in here? The food is disgusting. I can't eat that crap. And I need to get home to take care of my animals."

Patiently the doctor tried to explain, "It'll depend upon your blood levels. Once we have your BUN and Creatinine numbers stabilized, you can go home. We'll set you up on some meds that will help keep your numbers in balance and you'll have to alter your diet and drink plenty of fluids."

Grinding her jaw, my mom nodded dismissively.

"Do you have any more questions, Mrs. Tracy?"

"None that you can answer."

Of course, as soon as Mom was released from the hospital, she began her own investigation into renal failure. After a cursory look at the information provided by Prevention Magazine, the National Kidney Foundation, the Mayo Clinic, and the American Medical Association, Mom dug deeper, exploring European treatments and holistic approaches to kidney health.

Bent on willing her kidney to health, Mom worked to regain her strength and devised her own health routines. She adjusted her vitamin and mineral regime to be more renal friendly. She discovered that it was important to restrict phosphorus and potassium in her diet, so she carefully monitored how much she ate of some of her favorite foods like cheese, potatoes, avocados, bananas, and spinach. And she kept a Jim Beam jug of water by her side to force fluids. She had read that half a gallon of water per day was best for kidney health and, although she felt like her eyeballs were floating and her belly sloshing, she guzzled water all day to fulfill that goal. By spring she was feeling chipper and ready for adventure.

We worked out a plan to meet at Glacier National Park. I would fly in and she would drive from Laramie. Then we'd head over to the Puget Sound and the Olympic Rainforest and travel down the Washington and Oregon coasts together in her car. In Portland I'd catch a flight back to Boise and Mom would continue alone to southern California to visit Joan.

We were excited about seeing Glacier, a first for both of us. I envisioned long hikes, cute cabins, and lots of photography. I was shocked to see Mom's condition. This was the first time I'd seen her since before her kidney infection. She had shrunk more, I was certain. But most alarming was her unsteady gait. Her big toe and ankle were tightly swollen and shone an angry purple color. She claimed it was gout and guzzled more water and choked down concentrated, unsweetened cranberry juice as if that were an elixir from the spirits.

"Mom, when was the last time you saw the doctor?" I asked her.

"For what?"

"Well, for anything. For follow-up on that kidney affair, for your sore foot? Something's not right here." I said.

"Oh those goddamned doctors. They don't know what they're talking about. They just wanna get people in there and start slicing and dicing."

"Yeah, but ... if you only have one kidney left, maybe you ought to take special care of it."

"I *am* taking special care of it, you nitwit. Why do you think I'm drinking this God awful cranberry juice? For the flavor?" She waved the dark purple jar of juice at me. "Believe me, I'm taking better care of my precious kidney than all those doctors combined. They tried to scare me with their dire predictions. But I'm feeling just fine. And that, my friend, is without their ridiculous medications that just made me feel sicker, anyway."

I was highly skeptical, but I was no match for her. I zipped my trap as best I could. But it frightened me to watch her hobble around with her sore foot. And all those hikes I'd envisioned? They evaporated in her pain and lack of stamina. I don't know what I expected. Good lord. The woman was 72 years old. She still had all her original parts, including her own teeth. Despite the issue with her feet and the perilous kidney situation, she was in better shape than many other people her age.

Mom resumed most of her usual activities. She continued to ride horses; she continued to visit Joan and me, driving the long distances between Laramie and Boise, then between Boise and Fresno or Palm Desert or wherever Jim's bank moved them. She always traveled heavy, her car filled with Jim Beam jugs filled with artesian water for her kidney. One year she arrived with an exchange student from Germany. The poor girl's feet had barely adjusted to solid ground after her 18-hour flight across the ocean, followed by the jimpy-jumpy puke bucket from Denver to Laramie. Early the next morning, Mom wedged Ursula into what remained of the passenger seat, which she shared with Mom's ailing 18-year-old Siamese cat. Ten hours later I unfolded Ursula and helped her wobble to the bathroom, while Mom fussed over the skeletal cat.

Thus it went for five more years. I continued my work at the Post Office. I dated a few men, opting for older fellows who already had kids, never allowing anything to get particularly serious. Then one year, I actually reeled a guy in. We met at a friend's house. He had a quirky sense of humor and quiet self-assurance. He was self-employed, loved what he did, and had time off during the week which meshed with my weekdays off. He skied with me every chance he got, much to my dismay, since truthfully he was a lousy skier. Later we joked that he chased me till I caught him.

One afternoon, just as ski season was wrapping up, I came rip-roaring up to his house in a raspberry red sports car that I was test driving. I was curious to see if a six-foot, three-incher could fit inside this little red rocket. He could, and I bought it. A few weeks later we took it out for its maiden road trip to the Oregon coast. We returned from the trip with our hormones in an uproar.

That fall, I brought Erich to Laramie to show him where I'd grown up and introduce him to Yry. They got along famously, as I knew they would. She loved his sense of humor and his complete denial of socially-engendered norms. His purple vest over a bright red shirt delighted Mom's hunger for the exotic.

Of course we had to go for a ride! We saddled up three horses. This was Erich's first horse experience, but his gentle nature made him a natural with animals. He paid keen attention to all my instructions and, with great gravity, hauled himself into the saddle atop the oldest horse on the place. Fudge was the second horse Mom had ever bought. He was the little foal who'd endeared himself to us by proffering his rump for scratches at the Talbot's pasture during our visits with Joan's little colt. Now, in his thirties,

Fudge had left behind his schoolboy pranks and exhibited model behavior. Erich's long legs made old Fudge look more donkey than horse. We rode to the very back of Mom's property. Meanwhile, a huge, dark front had built up behind our backs, and when we turned toward home menacing clouds raced toward us.

"Typical Laramie weather," I chortled. In minutes the storm blasted us with the ferocity of a cat-3 hurricane, pelting us with tiny ball-bearings of ice which accumulated in the nooks and crannies of our skimpy summer clothes and piled up in the lee of the sage brush. The poor horses had no choice but to face into the storm in order to get to the barn. We tucked our heads under upraised arms and trusted the four feet below to get us safely home. It was a miserable ride. Mom and I were both impressed by Erich's giggles and unflappable humor about the situation. No whining coming from that guy. He was into the experience!

This was one of my better visits home. With Erich as buffer, Mom and I got along better than usual. Face-to-face visits had never ceased being difficult and strained. We could talk briefly on the phone without touching off any earthquakes, and I wrote frequent chatty letters. But the more time we spent in the same room, the quicker my fuse burned. Mom's habit of ranting and preaching drove me crazy. It wasn't even that we disagreed. It was that she harped endlessly about world affairs and politics without saying anything new. Some nasty little switch would flip in my head and suddenly I'd be baiting her, arguing just for the sake of controversy. I'd say things I didn't even believe, just to prod her in a new direction or to shut her up. But Erich had a knack for interjecting some crazy non-sequitur that interrupted the flow of our inflammatory word wrangling. We'd all three end up laughing instead of dodging daggers.

But I was worried. Mom didn't look good. Had I continued to grow or was she continuing to shrink? She seemed so diminished from the tower of energy that she had been just ten years earlier. She struggled with everything: gates, saddles, horses who pushed their noses out of reach, jam jars, the can opener, the clasp of a necklace. Ever energy-conscious, Mom pegged her thermostat in the low 60s. She layered clothing like an artist layers paint onto a canvass. She sewed thick, padded linings into old terry cloth and corduroy bathrobe. She wore these like a cardinal's cassock over her long johns, her feet encased in down booties. And we were on the cusp of September—winter hadn't even begun yet.

It took several hours in the morning to get her up, dressed, fed, toileted, and ready to tackle the day. Then after lunch, she'd collapse on the sofa for a nap. And shortly after dinner, my night-owl mother trundled off to bed where she amused herself with nature programs on the VCR.

Erich and I returned to Boise, he high on horses, me lost in worry. I knew Mom shouldn't be out there all by herself. But she refused to discuss moving into town. She was lucky to have good tenants living in the run-down ranch house beside her house. More often than not, they fed and cared for her horses as well as their own.

Then in November old Fudge got sick. The vet came out and said Fudge was just too old. He had pneumonia and he would never recover. Dr. Allen gave him a sedative to ease his suffering, then left. Mom went up to the house, grabbed her sleeping bag and hauled it out to the corral, where Fudge lay struggling for each breath.

She settled down by the old sorrel's head, petting him, talking to him, grieving over a loss that represented so much. How many children had this horse babysat? How many panicky adults had he eased? How many cocky wanna-be cowboys had Fudge put in their place with his stubborn, I'll-have-it-my-way-quirks? He'd been patient and careful when those traits were most important. He'd been impudent and cagey with people who approached him with the wrong attitude. He'd grudgingly performed in amateur rodeos; he'd faithfully plodded through the chaos of parades. He'd coped with new-to-the-ranch horses, asserting quiet authority without the meanness exhibited by many pasture lords. He'd comforted weanlings through the shocking loss of their mother's milk. Fudge was like a history book of Mom's Laramie life. He'd moved up in the world right along with her when she bought the new property. He'd endured countless riding lessons and recklessly-planned outings to the back country. While her kids had abandoned her, this horse had remained—a staunch beacon to remind her how far she had come. She'd lost Fudge's father—her other favorite horse—years ago. Now his loss loomed—too much to bear.

It was a cold, blustery night. Mom stayed with Fudge, dozing off, perhaps even hallucinating at times, then waking sharply to hear his groaning breaths until they subsided around 4 AM. She trudged back to the house—defeated, exhausted, half-frozen, and feeling lonelier than at any other time in her life. She roused herself from a stupefied half-slumber around mid-morning the next day to call her tenants next door and ask them to feed the horses for her. Then she asked if they knew someone who could dig a hole for Fudge's burial. Fudge was the first and only horse to be buried on the property. It was a measure of distinction for him, a parting shot of grace bestowed upon his memory by a woman who felt his loss more acutely than she'd felt any other.

Later that day, she called to let Erich and me know about Fudge's death. Fudge had been Erich's first and only mount. He felt a special affinity for the old horse, and being the soft-hearted man he was, he grieved along with my mother. I was less worried about the horse than I was about her. She did not sound good. Her voice was low and thin. She was sniffling a lot. I suspected this sniffling was not the tearful variety. In all those difficult years of being a single mother with a passel of problems and disappointments, I'd only seen my mother in tears twice. Each outburst had come on quickly and dissipated just as quickly. No, this version of sniffling hinted at an impending cold.

When I called a few days later, my suspicions were confirmed. Mom was hacking and grabbing for air through congested lungs. We didn't talk long. She said she was going back to bed—an unusual daytime retreat for her. I called the following Sunday. Mom answered—sort of. The best she could do was to croak. It was a brief and one-sided conversation.

A wedding and a housewarming

Mom was sick for a long time. Her voice returned, but the cough persisted, and her energy was gone. She said her chest hurt from all the coughing. Her sentences were truncated by shallow gulps of air. The holidays came and went. She sent some half-hearted gifts, which I could tell had been wrapped and packaged by Vivian. The tenants were taking care of the horses full-time now. Mom barely had the energy to walk from the kitchen to the bedroom.

That spring, in 1990, Erich and I made the bold decision to build a house and get married, in that order. The wedding was small. We decided to tie the knot at our property, which consisted of a paved street and sidewalk with stakes marking the perimeter of our dirt. Mom was still too weak to travel. I told her she needed to get better so she could come to our housewarming and wedding reception which we hoped would occur in August.

We weren't able to move into the house until September, so the big party was scheduled for October. There was no way Mom could drive that distance. Generous, as always, Glenda volunteered to drive Yry from Laramie to Boise. The party was a great affair; Mom wore a stunning western style skirt and vest with cowboy boots, an outfit she had assembled for her friend Ursula's mountain top wedding a year or two earlier. She rallied for the big party, but she and Glenda couldn't stay long, as Glenda had to get back to work. I learned later that Mom slept most of the way home.

Back in Laramie, Mom didn't recover from the excitement of the journey and the party. She continued to be lethargic and unable to feed or ride the horses. Viv called each morning, asking what

Mom needed. She drove out to the ranch every other day to check in and keep Mom's pantry stocked. Vivian and I exchanged several worried phone conversations. Mom was just not getting better. Viv managed to haul her into town one day to visit a doctor, much against Mother's wishes. The doctor diagnosed bacterial bronchitis. He sent her home with a couple of medications and warned that the condition could flare into pneumonia if she didn't take proper care.

Meanwhile, I began to dread Sunday afternoons. The phone developed an ominous ring. If I wasn't home when the call came, I'd find the message machine blinking and a terse, dispirited comment from my mother. Each week I bolstered my positive thoughts and brightly answered the phone.

"Hi Mom. How're ya doing this week?"

"Ach, I'm just so tired."

"You still have the cold?" She insisted that she had only a cold, nothing more.

"It's not so bad, I don't think. I just don't have any energy."

"What did you have for dinner last night?" When all else failed I'd fall back on the standard prompt. Mom could usually give me a bean-by-bean description of each meal for the previous week. But even that topic was growing thin.

"I boiled an egg and ate a baked potato with butter."

"Is that all? That's not enough to keep a kitten alive."

"It's all I felt like," she answered grumpily.

She spent most of the day in bed—actually, on top of her bed. After Glenn died, Mom had abandoned the fuss of bed-making. She'd zipped together the two old sleeping bags we used back when we were a camping family. She lined them with a sheet, placed them on top of the bedspread and laid out her entertainments in a U-shape around the sleeping bags. Her TV hunkered at the foot of the king-sized bed. Her VCR sat on a cardboard platform on the bed with a stack of tapes nearby. Books, magazines, and mail competed with a Walkman for space on the bed. On the nightstand sat a remote control, a radio-alarm clock, and a single-cup hot plate to keep her coffee warm. The cats snuggled against her for warmth in the cold bedroom. Mom's life had been reduced to her bed. This was impossible.

Occasionally one of Mom's young friends came out for a visit. But without a set routine of riding dates, school, work, and families siphoned their attention from Mom.

The Sunday conversations continued, stilted and frustrating. Weeks went by with no discernible change in her condition. Finally, one Sunday in March, I blew a fuse. The conversation began like so many others had.

"Hi Mom, are you feeling any better?"

"Not really."

"Are you still coughing? You don't sound too bad."

"Not coughing. Just no energy. Tired all the time." Her responses had become succinct. In my mind, I could see the long phone cord stretching dangerously across the kitchen floor into the dining room. She'd be nursing a cold cup of coffee, the table buried under stacks of partially opened junk mail, dirty dishes, crossword puzzles, reading glasses, and Jack and the Beanstalk cacti.

"Have you been out to see the horses?"

"No."

"Don't you miss them?"

"No."

This was as stimulating as interviewing a slug. "Isn't it getting a bit warmer now?"

"Dunno."

"What did you have for dinner this evening?"

"A banana."

"A banana and what else?"

"Just a banana."

"Mom, a banana is a snack. It's not dinner."

"It's dinner enough for me."

Wyoming

"Mom, have you taken all the medicine the doc gave you for the bronchitis?"

"Baah, that damned medicine made my head woozy. I quit taking it weeks ago."

"Well ... did you call the doctor and tell him that the medicine made you woozy?" The short tether of the phone cord afforded little space for pacing.

"No, I didn't call the damned doctor to tell him his stupid medicine made me sicker than I was before...I read the side effects of that stuff ... It's right there in black and white ... He should know better, but these doctors don't read ... They just hand out pills and take kickbacks ... I don't want that crap in my system ... I feel badly enough as it is." Her sentences clipped between gulps of air.

"Mother. You have to work with the doctor. Doctors are not magicians. They cannot look inside your body and predict how a particular drug will react with your chemistry." I was staring at crocus buds poking through the cold crust of ground outside the bedroom window.

"Yadayada. These damned doctors ... don't know what they're doing. They've gotta pill for everything. Ya tell 'em ... this pill upsets your stomach ... and they add *another* pill ... to settle your stomach. You tell em them the second pill ... gave you a headache and they hand you a third pill ... to cure the headache ..."

"Mother!" I interrupted rudely. "Doctors are not magicians! Every person's chemistry is different. They have many different drugs to choose from. That is because one drug may work beautifully for nine of ten people. The tenth person, like you, needs a different drug. They can't know what's going on—how what they've prescribed is working in your body, unless you *talk to them*!" My voice had risen and my self-control was outside with the crocuses.

"Doctors are not ... the saints you think they are. They don't study ... nutrition. They don't use ... common sense. They reach for expensive drugs—drugs that *drug companies pay them to prescribe!*" This was the most words she'd strung together at one time since last summer.

I expelled a lungful of bottled-up air and exploded. "Your damned vitamins and minerals and enzymes and God-only-knows-what are not helping you now! You're too weak to even provide your body with proper nutrition. You've been diagnosed with a serious condition that will only grow worse. It's time for you to wake up and smell the roses!" I was furious, but Mom interrupted my rant.

"I don't need … any more … goddamned drugs. I just need … to rest … and take care of myself!" Heat, starting in a tight knot in my stomach had risen up my chest, through my throat and inflamed my face.

"Well *fine* then! Since you're such a medical expert and you know more than everyone else, you just take care of yourself! Don't be calling *me* up and telling me how tired you are. Don't be calling to complain that you can't catch your breath! If you refuse medical care, you can bloody well *die* out there all by your goddamned self. And quit putting Vivian through the torture of having to come out there and see you waste away, robbing her time and her energy when she needs it to take care of Bob, who's none too well, himself! This has been going on for nearly six months, and I'm bloody tired of you calling to tell me what an effort it is to walk from the bedroom to the kitchen, for God's sake. If you refuse the help that is available, you deny yourself the right to complain, the right for any sympathy from any of us!"

I waited for a beat, expecting her to box my ears across the 700 miles between us. The heavy silence on the other end of the line stunned me. I slammed the receiver down and turned to find Erich standing in the doorway, slack-jawed and pale.

"Oh my God!" I wailed, throwing my fists toward my eyes. He rushed to me and enfolded me in his long arms, pulling me in tight against his chest. Though we'd been together for over two years, Erich had never seen me cry. Tears sprouted, as a black tent of guilt and horror folded over me. "Oh my God, what have I done? How could I have been so cruel, so mean, so insensitive!"

Erich sat me down on the end of the bed and sat himself beside me. Taking both my hands in his, he spoke quietly.

"I know how you must feel, Linda. But I think she needed to hear that from you," he said gently. "She's the only person I know who's as stubborn as you are."

"What should I do now?"

He was silent.

He didn't even hear my question, I thought. He'd never heard me ask for advice before. *It probably didn't even register.* My brain was spinning like a sloppy fan belt. But Erich's pause was not lack of attention. He was a thoughtful man, inherently interested in finding the roots of a problem and solving it from the inside out.

"Well ... maybe you should give Viv a call. Explain to her what happened. She can either call your Mom or maybe go out and visit with her."

"That's a good idea," I replied, my mind grabbing for a solution like a drowning cat swiping at a twig. "Do you think I should call Mom back?"

"I don't know, maybe so ... after you've talked with Viv. You may figure out what you need to do just by hashing things out with her." He held me by the shoulders and looked into my soul. "Someone like your mother needs an electric prod to jolt them out of entrenched thinking. Don't be so hard on yourself. You are the only person strong enough to stand up to her. You did the right thing."

"Maybe you're right. I feel like an absolute piece of shit, though." I sighed heavily. "I've gotta go for a walk to settle myself down. Then I'll call Viv."

"You want company?" he asked.

"No. I won't be gone long."

I returned 15 minutes later and drug myself to the phone. Vivian answered on the first ring.

"Linda. I just got off the phone with your Mom."

"Aah, mmm. Did she tell you what I shit I am?"

"No—she said you said some things she didn't want to hear. She asked me to call the doctor in the morning and set up a visit as soon as possible."

"*Really*? Was she upset?"

"Yeah, I think she was. But of course she's upset. This is very hard for her. First, she's so sick, so weak and lethargic. It's hard for her to think straight. And, geez, Linda, she just doesn't know how to be sick. She has no life experience with illness. I think she's scared ... really scared."

"Well, I think she should be scared. For God's sake. You know this all started with Fudge. What on earth was she thinking, staying out all night in the middle of winter with a dying horse?"

There was a pause on the other end. Then Vivian gently said, "She wasn't thinking, Linda. She was feeling. She loved that horse so much. You know, I've thought quite a bit about this. Maybe, in some deep, dark place inside, she was making up for not being here when Glenn died. They had such a special relationship, you know...?"

This stood me on my head. Grieving for Glenn while she watched Fudge die? She and Glenn had a special relationship? Well, I didn't quite see it the same way Vivian did. But there was no need for me to burst her illusions.

Pneumonia

Yry did return to the doctor and was once again hospitalized. This time it was for pneumonia. What began as a bad cold had conquered her immune system and marched on to bacterial bronchitis and then crowned as pneumonia, the geriatric serial killer. Again, her condition was arrested just before it claimed victory. At first she was diagnosed with congestive heart failure. But as the diuretics and decongestants took over, it became apparent that her heart was merely the silent victim of heavy, congested lungs which failed to properly oxygenate her blood and had been squeezing the living daylights out of the ol' pump.

Now, a prisoner of the pharma-medical complex, Mom was living her nightmare, the victim of a full array of pokes and prods. Blood tests revealed that her kidney was on the ragged edge. She wasn't in full renal failure yet, but that reality was imminent. As soon as her lungs cleared, a team of doctors converged to map the future. Specific dates were set for an array of tests at the Poudre Valley Hospital in Fort Collins, where she would be prepped for hemodialysis.

The flurry of medical attention and dire warnings finally cracked her shell of skepticism. Mom was shocked. Shocked and scared. She called me. I could hear something different in her voice—a reluctance, awe, and utter disbelief that this could be happening.

"Linda, they're sending me to Ft. Collins," she said.

"I'm sorry, Mom. But I guess they know what they're doing. If Laramie Memorial is turning you over to another hospital, they must be admitting the limit of their own capabilities."

"They're telling me I can't live at home anymore. They say I have to move to Ft. Collins." My heart hit my gut as the full weight of her words landed.

"Why is that, Mom?"

"There's no kidney center here. I'll have to go in three times a week. They don't think I can make that drive all by myself."

"Well, for sure, during the winter, that would be a horrible idea."

"Linda, I need your help ..."

"Yeah, sure, Mom. What can I do?" This was the first time my mother had ever asked me for help.

"Can you come down here? Can you take me to Ft. Collins?"

Sweet syringa scent wafted through the open bedroom window as I curled the phone cord in my hand. "Yeah, I'll arrange emergency leave. When do you need to be there?"

"They've scheduled an appointment for me at Poudre Valley on April 5th. I have to come in for preliminary stuff a day or two early."

"I'll work it out, Mom. I'll try to be there on the first."

I was surprised by the compassion I received when I asked for an indefinite absence from work. I requested a month off, but explained that I wasn't sure how things were going to work out. Luckily, this was before labor relations disintegrated at the Postal Service. And in my favor, I had over a month's worth of annual leave saved up. I had used no sick leave during my fifteen years of employment, so I was in good standing.

I loaded my car with clothes, books, cassette tapes, and a new acquisition—a Tandy laptop. I was worried about how to pass the inevitable weary stretches of time waiting with Mother for things to happen. I envisioned sterile waiting areas and stuffy hospital rooms. How in the world would I manage to keep her entertained, her mind off the evils of modern medicine, her fears allayed? Ever since I was a kid, she'd told wild stories about her childhood and about various ancestors. But I'd never paid attention—had always thought she was exaggerating. The things she recounted couldn't possibly have happened, or could they? Now I was old enough to realize that I knew nothing of my family background. I had shadowy outlines of family stories, but nothing that I could recount with any authority. I decided that the most productive way to pass idle hours with Mom would be to interview her, to get her talking again about all those stories and to take notes so that, for once, I'd get the details right. My handwriting is so atrocious that I knew I couldn't keep up with her rambling in long hand. The laptop was Erich's solution. I was a novice with computers, and laptops had debuted only very recently. Erich was my Sacagawea into the digital age.

I rocketed the red race car 700 miles from Boise to Laramie with the fuzz-buster blinking and my eyes on the rearview mirror. The only way to endure that drive was with music blaring and power poles blurring. Driving half the speed of sound blunted the urge to fret about the future. But no amount of speed could obliterate the fact that I was headed for a crossroad. The gauze of a childhood memory invaded my mind. I was probably about eight; Joan would have been seventeen or eighteen, already in college. Mom had gone to a meeting or something; Joan and I were alone in the house. She, of course, was in charge—the stand-in parent. As a kid, I'd often thought it would be cool to have a babysitter. My friends' home-alone experiences sounded like fun; they either manipulated a naïve babysitter or they played games with the more adept sitters. But when Mother was gone, Joan was in charge. She was not a babysitter. No money changed hands at the end of her duty. Joan perceived herself to be a parental figure. She thought her wisdom could compensate for what she perceived as Mother's parental irresponsibility. Her guidance would be my eternal salvation and, by God, I should appreciate that.

But I did not appreciate Joan's wisdom. I hated being told what to do. Joan put no motivational psychology between her commands and her expectations of me. I reacted to Joan's dictatorship with all the passion of youth, completely absent of guerrilla wisdom. I could no more defend myself from her verbally than I could physically, but that didn't stop my will to fight Goliath.

So, that night we'd gotten into another of our knock-down fights. It was ludicrous, really. Joan was so much older, bigger, and stronger than I—I was beyond reason when I began punching her. Time after time, she'd grab me around the waist and toss me to the floor like a calf at the end of the lariat. Then all she had to do was straddle me and laugh while my legs and arms flailed wildly and ineffectually like an upside-down stinkbug. Sometimes, to add insult to injury, she'd tickle me, which at that point, was anything but funny. On that particular night, our verbal argument escalated. Who knows how it began, but like the time she tried to force me to look at a photograph of my father, this night branded my soul.

"You will never have a life of your own," she spat at me, bubbles of saliva gathering in the corners of her mouth. "You're the youngest so you'll have to stay here and take care of our mother!"

As I vibrated down I84, her words echoed despite the rock and roll blaring from the radio. Although I'd tried to run from it, her prophecy had rung true. Mother had stayed to care for her parents. Now it was up to me to care for her. *No! I have my own life. I have a home, a job, a husband.* But destiny was on my tail as I bumped across the cattle guard and rounded the corner to Mom's house just after the sun set on April first.

Climbing the steps to the front door, my heart thudded so high in my chest I thought I might choke on it. Before I could stab my finger on the doorbell, the dog had erupted inside to warn of an intruder. Inside, Mom yelled at the dog who yapped back, oblivious to her commands. The inner door opened and then the outer door. I stepped across the threshold into the dark mudroom and into a clutching embrace. We stood like that, the screen door still ajar against the back of my leg, the dog yapping from the living room. My mother heaved in my arms. As she at last stepped back, her voice was thin and uncharacteristically whiney.

"Why is this happening to me? I don't deserve this. I always took such good care of my body. This isn't fair."

My mother was crying. Her tears gave me strength. From somewhere, a modicum of wisdom guided my words. While my brain screamed, *No, you didn't Mother! You ignored all the advice! You self-medicated! You ...* the words that emerged from my mouth came from somewhere else—from Erich? From Boise? From the universe?

"No, Mom. It's *not* fair. I'm really sorry."

Again, she was in my arms, no longer sobbing, but just holding me—holding me like a lifeline. After the longest embrace we'd ever exchanged, Mom stepped back and pulled me into the living room where the dog danced nervously about my ankles, not yet sure whether I was friend or foe.

The smell of my mother's house assaulted my nostrils. I had noticed this smell after each of her visits to my home in Boise. It was an acrid smell, not unclean, but pungent, earthy, emanating, I was sure, from one of her health store concoctions. Here, in her home, the vitamin smell was primary, but there was also an underlying scent of neglected cat boxes. The heavy draperies were pulled shut against the windows, and like last fall when Erich and I had visited, the dining room table groaned under the weight of overgrown pots of cacti that fingered across piles of catalogs, books, mail, and saucers filled with pins, paperclips, or rocks. Dirty dishes were scattered about the house, like Hansel and Gretel's crumbs.

We talked for a long time that evening. She shared that she had recently reviewed her legal affairs.

"I made out a living trust. You and I are both named as trustees. And you have durable power-of-attorney ... just in case you need to take care of business ..."

Here it was again—the discussion of her hereafter. I had to fight the instinct to close my ears, to bolt. She explained how the living trust worked; that if she became incapacitated, it gave me authority to act in her behalf. The trust would seamlessly stipulate how her assets were to be handled after her death. A shiver crawled up my spine.

As we talked into the long hours of night, I noticed her fidgeting and itching at herself. Mom had always suffered from dry skin. She insisted that lotion was pointless. "Dry skin results from dietary deficiencies," she proclaimed. But her constant itching, scratching and rubbing was wearing on my nerves. Initially, I assumed the fidgeting was nervous energy. But then I realized that her back hurt her. We talked on. She nattered about the tenants; about Bob and Vivian; about Glenda and her children; about her cavalcade of young friends, each with their own Peyton Place dramas. One subject we covered fell through the cracks, catching only a thin filament of memory. This detail—about gold that she'd stashed in the house—would erupt later in an agony of embarrassment.

It was Sunday evening. Mom had an appointment with a renal specialist in Fort Collins on Wednesday. She wanted to go for a ride tomorrow. Given her wobbly condition, I had my doubts. But, I'd seen lesser miracles, like a man with a prosthetic leg and a grin as large as Texas sitting astride a horse. We would see how she felt in the morning. At last we turned in.

The next morning Mom was very slow to get up. She walked bent over, her hands clutching her lower back. I fixed us breakfast, and while we ate I broached a subject that had kept me tossing and turning throughout the night.

"Mom, before we go for that ride, there's something I'd like us to do together."

"Mmmm? What's that?"

"I think we need to go have a talk with your attorney. I'd like his advice on these issues that you've given me responsibility for."

"I don't think that's necessary. It's just a precaution … something he recommended, actually."

"Yes, but Mom, I have no experience with anything like this. And living as far away as I do, I'm a bit concerned. I'd just like to talk to him … discuss options, procedures, stuff like that. Do you think he'd meet with us today?"

"Call him and find out. His number is on the pad over there." She was bored by the subject.

While she was in the bathroom, I called Mr. P___, the attorney. I explained that Mom would be going in for surgery later in the week and that I was worried about the fact that she'd made me the executor of her estate.

"It's what she wanted," he replied.

"It may be what she wanted. I'm not sure what she was thinking, but I am not up to it. I have to be honest with you, Mr. P___. My sister will absolutely not accept my authority. She will fight and question every single move I make. Why don't we just put her in charge from the get go?"

"No. That won't work." He replied. "Yry expressly did *not* want Joan in control."

"Really? She must be afraid that I won't stand up for what's mine. I've always said that her money means nothing to me."

"I suspect you're right about that, Linda."

"Well ... obviously she trusts *you*, Mr. P___. If I could persuade her to put you in charge, would that be an acceptable protocol?"

"Only if that's what Yry wants."

"Well, I'm very worried. I think her health is on a slippery slope. We need to be in Fort Collins on Wednesday. I need to get this resolved before we leave. Would you be able to meet with us sometime today?"

Mr. P___ was kind enough to adjust his schedule so we could meet at noon. I had a couple of hours to persuade my mother that this was the right thing to do.

Mom was not happy about the trip to town. Ever since we'd moved out to the ranch she'd harangued us all about squandering gasoline with unplanned and frivolous trips to town, so I bolstered my position by pointing out that Vivian was supposed to take her husband, Bob, to the doctor and wouldn't have time to shop and deliver for us. We needed milk for Mom's coffee and some lettuce and avocadoes. She grudgingly approved. It was a struggle getting her dressed and out the door. I was astonished by how weak she was. It seemed like she was measurably weaker than even the night before. I drove my car right up to the door and had to help Mom negotiate the stairs from the front door to the ground. Then I practically folded her like a fan to wedge her into the front seat of my little sports car. She grunted over the discomfort in her back.

There are advantages to small towns. I found a parking place directly in front of the lawyer's office. The receptionist saw me struggling to unload Mom from the passenger seat and sent Mr. P___ out to help. We maneuvered Mom into his meeting room—a serious looking space, lined with an army of color-coded legal books, large, dark brown chairs surrounding a long, gleaming table.

After exchanging pleasantries, Mr. P___ and I got down to business. I asked a few leading questions and emphasized my concerns about being unable to quickly respond to tenant issues from so far away. Mr. P___ agreed that making sure rent money was collected and attending to maintenance issues would be difficult for me. I asked him if we could put him in charge. He admitted that this might be a logical solution. I looked over at Mom who had nearly disappeared in the big leather chair, her head canted at an angle. She almost appeared to be dozing.

"What do you think of making Mr. P___ the executor, at least temporarily?" I asked her. My fingers were crossed under the table.

"Yeah," she muttered, almost disinterestedly. "I guess, if that's what you think is best..."

Surprised at how easily she acquiesced, I raised an eyebrow at Mr. P___. While his secretary scurried to amend the paperwork, he brought Mom a cup of coffee and began to chitchat with her about his own daughter, who was attending college in Washington State. After the papers had been signed and notarized, relief washed over me like a narcotic. I was still in shock that we had been able to change Mother's mind. I had expected a battle royal, but she was exhausted and wanted only to return home to her bed. She was itching ferociously. I could see, from the look on the secretary's face as we steered Mom through the office and out to the car, that I was not the only one shocked by her condition.

When we got back to the ranch, the neighbors were just coming home. I gratefully accepted their help getting Mom out of the car and back into the house where she headed straight for her bedroom. She'd forgotten all about riding. Thank God!

While Mom dozed, I went out to putter around the corrals, checking on the grain, the hay, the tack. Things had changed during the years I'd been gone, but not much. I couldn't resist bridling the mare that I had given to my mom before I left town. Lady was the second horse I had trained, and I was proud of how well she responded to a light touch on the reins. I had also appreciated her red sorrel color and strong Quarter Horse confirmation which was so much more acceptable than our silly white and palomino parade horses. The white hairs that peppered her muzzle and eyebrows startled me. In my mind she was still a nubile eight-year old. I did the math in my head three times before I could accept the fact that my little Lady was 25 years old. Still, it felt great to hop onto her bare back and head out across the sage, eyes roving to locate the ubiquitous gopher holes.

I returned to the house a couple of hours later, expecting Mom to be up and fussing over my disappearing act. But she was still in the bedroom. This made me uneasy. I knocked on her door. A bleary sound responded.

"Mom? Are you okay?"

After an indecipherable response, I slowly opened the door, "Mom, I'm coming in." She was in her nest, with a book-on-tape grinding in her cassette player. She wasn't asleep but she wasn't alert either.

"There's still time for the ride, if you want," I said to her gently.

"Oh, goddamn it to hell," she muttered. "My back hurts too much."

"What did you do to your back, Mom?"

"I have no idea. I don't remember lifting anything or twisting. I don't remember hurting it at all. It must be all this lying around that's doing it to me."

"Maybe I can massage it?"

She rolled over and I tried massaging her lower back, but she squirmed like a bead of mercury. On top of the aching back, her skin was on fire. There were no marks, no sign of a rash; her skin was dry, but no more so than it had always been.

Mom hadn't eaten since breakfast, so I suggested supper, but she wasn't interested.

"Help me get to the bathroom," she demanded.

This was the first of many more such trips. She absolutely wasn't strong enough to go 15 feet from her bed to the bathroom on her own. I'd get her settled in bed, then I'd return to the living room to read. Thirty minutes later I'd hear her moaning or thrashing, so I'd return to her bedroom to help her into another position or to the bathroom again. Around 7 PM, I placed a soft-boiled egg cup, a peeled banana, and a few walnuts on a tray and brought this into the bedroom for her. In between scratching, fidgeting, and moaning she ate about half of what I'd brought her. Then it was back to the bathroom. She thought the pain was caused by constipation, so she'd stay hunkered over the commode waiting for something to move. But nothing moved aside from her fidgeting hands.

Night from hell

It was around 10 PM when I heard a yelp and a simultaneous thump from the bedroom. I rushed in to find Mom on the floor beside the bed. She'd tried to get up on her own. By now my own back was aching. The Postal mantra whirled through my mind, *lift with your legs, not with your back.* This was particularly difficult to do when she needed help from the floor. Luckily, nothing was damaged aside from her pride, and at that point, I'm not sure she was really engaged with her pride.

"Mom, why didn't you call me?" I asked. "I was just there in the living room."

"I don' know ... damn it to hell anyway."

I got her to the bathroom and waited at the door until she was finished, then helped her back to bed again. "Mom, we need to rig up a call bell so when you need to get up you can ring for me and I'll hear it even if I'm in the kitchen or the bathroom or something."

I found a small brass bell in one of her display cases. It was probably something her father had brought home from the orient 70 years ago. I attached a ribbon to the bell and to her wrist so if the bell fell or got lost in the bed clothes she'd be able to locate it. We made a game out of the bell, which she seemed enchanted with for the first hour or so. But sometime around midnight, she became so befuddled that she forgot to use the bell. I strained to hear her thrashing and fussing. At one point, I tiptoed into the bedroom, unsure if I'd heard the vague shiver of the bell or if I'd nodded off on the couch and dreamed about the bell.

I caught her in an ungainly posture, not prone, not upright, at the edge of her bed. Her nightgown was hiked up and she looked at me with red-rimmed, bleary eyes filled with wonder and fear.

"I ... I ... oh, God ... I think ... I messed myself."

"Well, let me help you get to the bathroom and we'll take care of that."

I have no idea where my composure came from. My stomach was lurching. Not only had she wet herself, but she'd also leaked diarrhea which was smeared across the sheets and trickled down the back of one of her shockingly emaciated legs. I would need to clean her up; me, who as a reluctant teenage babysitter had only changed a handful of diapers; me, who'd had no children's poops or pukes to attend to. I wrapped her arms around my neck and locked my arms under her armpits.

"On the count of three, stand up."

We slow danced to bathroom, which, like the rest of the house, was as cold as a Popsicle chest. I turned on a small heater in the corner and started running the icy-cold hot water tap, waiting for the water to heat. Mom sat perched on the edge of the commode like a baby bird clutching the edge of the nest. Her startled blue eyes locked on mine for a moment, then dropped. Recalling my brief stint as a nurse's aide after high school, I washed my mom's body, marveling at how little of it was left. She looked like a patient on a geriatric ward, not like the mother who had spat in the eye of propriety, had spanked my bottom, and rinsed my wounds. Once robust breasts sagged like deflated balloons against the small swell of her tummy. Her buttocks hung like crinkled linen. I hoped my shock did not register. I had become the adult, my mother the child. While I carefully washed and dried her, one section at a time, she began fussing and rubbing her skin.

"I just can't stand this itching," she lamented. I rummaged around the bathroom cupboards till I found an old jar of Jergens that looked like it might have been Glenn's. I rubbed some of that on her arms and legs. But it did no good. She was right. This itching was coming from the inside out.

I poured her a glass of cold tap water and left her sitting on the lid of the commode while I changed the sheets on her bed and rummaged around for a clean nighty, all the while with my ears attuned to any unexpected movement from the bathroom. Again I maneuvered her back to bed and scooped up the soiled linens and dashed downstairs to put them in the washing machine. By the time I got back upstairs the ringing of her bell was unmistakable.

"What is it—what's a matter?" I asked breathlessly.

"Gotta go to the bathroom."

My teeth were grinding as I stared down at her in disbelief. Again, I helped her up, and we stumbled to the bathroom. She collapsed on the commode and sat there, comatose. Nothing happened. I waited. Nothing.

"False alarm?" I asked, grinning to lighten the mood.

"I feel like I have to go. I think that's why my back hurts. I'm constipated."

"After that diarrhea?"

"Huh? Leave me alone. I need some privacy for God's sake."

"Okay." I left the door ajar and went to collect the dirty dishes from her nightstand. I was headed for the kitchen when I realized she'd hiked herself off the pot and was standing in the doorway to the living room, where her cowboy boots were perched against the wall. There was my mother, in her nighty, canted against the doorway trying to jam one of her bare feet into one of her boots.

"Mother, what on earth are you doing?"

"Riding. I'm going ... Fudge ... I'm ... Natalie ..."

I had been exasperated, angry, exhausted. But now panic crept in on fairy's toes. "Mother. It's almost two in the morning. It's dark outside. The horses are out in the pasture, *you have no clothes on!* You can *not* go riding right now."

"I'm cold," she said. "My back hurts. I want to go to bed." It was like her brain had split into two tracks and they were sliding past each other without a wave or a whistle. I carefully removed her foot from the shaft of the heavy boot and steered her back to the bed. I tried to tuck her in and cozy her up, but she was thrashing and moaning, tossing and turning, itching, fidgeting, like a ground blizzard skittering across the road.

I stood beside her bed for a long time, contemplating. *What should I do? Should I try to lie in bed beside her? Pull a chair into the room to keep an eye on her?* My head throbbed with tension. My own back felt like I'd been bucking hay for two days. My sandpaper eyes rested on one of the big pillows on the other side of the bed. A big, unused pillow ... *I understand. I know now, how a person can snuff out the life of another human being. It would be so easy, really. The pillow is right there ... she's losing her mind along with her health.* All those childhood warnings to *me:* "Don't you ever put me in one of *those* places! I do not want to live if I can't live on my own terms. I'll go out in the pasture. I'll put a bullet in my head ..." These were the things she'd preached. *What lay in store for her now?* I wondered. *It is too late for her to put the bullet in her brain. Is this what I should do for her?*

Like drops of sap dripping from a cut limb, the hours crawled. I entered Mom's fugue state. I could hardly wait for the old grandfather clock to gong seven so I could call Vivian. I needed help. Mom wouldn't last another 24 hours—nor would I. Her appointment at Poudre Valley would have to be moved up a day.

Vivian, ever stalwart, agreed to call the hospital for me. She called back half an hour later to let me know she'd arranged for an early admittance. She asked if I could get Mom loaded into the car by myself.

"No way," I responded. "But I have the phone number of one of her riding friends. I'll ask if Natalie's husband can come out and help me load her up. Thanks so much for arranging things at the hospital for me." Vivian gave me the name and contact information of Mom's nephrologist and a few other contacts I might need.

By the time Natalie's husband, Dar, arrived, Mom was no longer coherent. I kept thinking how lucky I was to have gotten her in to see the attorney the day before. I don't think any of us had realized how close she was to the ragged edge of competency. It was all I could do to get her somewhat dressed and to pack a few things in a bag. Dar followed me into her dank and dark bedroom and together we wrestled Mom into a seated position. She didn't even recognize Dar, who was one of the young friends she had spoken so kindly of only 36 hours ago. He was a tall, slender young man, with a thinning hairline and a quiet demeanor. He kneeled beside Yry, gazing into her face like a lover. "Yry, I'm here to help you get to your appointment. I'm going to help you get up and walk to the car. Linda will drive you to the doctor's office, ok?" His gentle voice cracked my heart.

Mom looked up at him, uncomprehending. "Whaat ...? Ok ..." She looked like a child taking instruction from her father.

Dar positioned Mom's arms around the back of his neck and placed his long arms around her torso, just under her armpits. On the count of three, they both rose. I slipped under one arm and he held her on the other side. We walked her, like a life-sized Raggedy Ann, through the house. At the stairs Dar actually picked Mom up and carried her like a bride to the waiting car. She was mumbling, "Where are we? What are we doing? Are we going somewhere? Oh ... that hurts ... I want to go back to bed ..."

"I'll lock the house up, Linda. You just head on out. Good luck getting to Ft. Collins," he murmured.

I thanked him profusely, moved nearly to tears by his thoughtfulness, his strength, the simple fact that he would interrupt his busy morning to come all the way out here to help us. Mom had such a wonderful network of friends. She may have felt isolated and lonely during her earlier years in Laramie, but she had bridged that gap with a myriad of bright, engaging, and eager friends. And best of all, they were all younger than her, which I now realized was a tremendous advantage when you're getting on in years.

I worried about having to stop along the way for Mom to pee. It would take about an hour and a half. Luckily after a bit of fussing, she settled back into the seat and nodded off. As the white lines slipped away under the car, I remembered my first goosebump experience pulling a loaded horse trailer on this road. I'd just gotten my learner's permit and was eager to take on this responsibility along with the other ranch chores I'd been managing after Mom's marriage. We were hauling one of our mares to the Colorado State Veterinary School for a follow-up on the previous year's cancer treatments. Highway 287 is a two-lane state highway, famous at that time for the many young lives it claimed; eighteen-year-olds, eager to party on 3.2 beer, stormed the road on weekends and often came home in a coffin.

That morning we were approaching a slight but long, uphill grade. A semi hauling a double decker load of cattle was crawling up the hill ahead of us. I put on my turn signal and pulled into the oncoming lane, thinking I had plenty of time to pass the truck. I was right beside the cattle car when I realized I had miscalculated how long it would take to accelerate with the added weight of the trailer behind us. My foot jammed the accelerator to the floor, aided by every muscle in my body, as an approaching semi loomed larger and larger directly in front of us. I suspect the rig I was passing braked to let me in early, I swung in front of him in just a blink of time, the horse trailer washing dangerously in my wake. The road swam in front of me, my sweating hands still strangling the steering wheel as I waited for Mother to explode. But for the wind noise, you could have heard a pin drop in that cab. I slowly exhaled and heard Mom do the same.

"I am *so* sorry, Mom."

"Well, we're alive. The trailer's still there. The horse appears to still be standing," she was peering through the back window of the pickup. "I guess you learned something," she replied gently, without taking her eyes off the ribbon of road stretching up to the summit in front of us.

As we crested that same hill now, on the road to her rickety future, I looked over at my dozing mother and pondered how many times my actions might have scared her half to death and yet she carried on with a calm I'd failed to recognize.

The hospital

Presiding over a quiet, tree-filled residential area, Poudre Valley Memorial Hospital was easy to spot from the freeway. I drove directly to the emergency room, knowing I couldn't do what had to be done without help. After turning my mother over to the white coats, I parked the car and dashed back into the emergency area to facilitate the admissions process. Mom disappeared down a hallway as I plowed through a mountain of paperwork. She would be separated from her shabby clothes and endure a battery of tests before being wheeled up to a private room on the seventh floor. I checked out the hospital cafeteria and wandered around the lobby like a lost puppy until word reached the desk that Mom was comfortably settled in her room. The kidney specialist would make his rounds sometime between 3 and 5 PM. By the time I got to her room, Mom was sound asleep. It was surreal. After the grueling night we had just come through, neither of us getting more than half a wink of sleep at a time, now beneath bright white lights, gleaming chrome, and antiseptic smell, my mother slept like a stone, flat on her back—a position in which she was never comfortable. I marveled at the power of drugs or whatever it was that had calmed her itching and fidgeting.

With a few blessed hours to myself before having to stake out Mom's room waiting for the doctor, I checked in to a Motel 6 near the hospital. My head felt thick and the bed looked inviting, but I'm not a day sleeper. From my motel window, the remnants of old farm country stretched out between the freeway and residential areas, behind which the distant Rocky Mountains reached into the sky, tugging clouds down to milk moisture from them. Holes in the clouds shifted and shimmered, providing narrow alleys for golden streams of afternoon sunlight to dance across the landscape.

I opened the laptop and rested the tips of my fingers on the keyboard while my eyes stared vacantly at the brewing storm in the distance. This had to be a journaling moment. Where were my ideas? My epiphanies? My emotions? I tried every trick I knew to tease something erudite out of my brain. But free-writes, word association, lists, nothing worked. My heart was hollow.

The only thing that flickered through my willful brain was the dread of the inevitable confrontation with the sister I had worked so hard to erase from my psyche. The road ahead was narrowing. Even if my mother was in denial about her horizon, I sensed that she'd soon be riding off into her own sunset. Her departure would require Joan and me to breathe the same air, to look each other in the eye, put aside our hurts and misunderstandings, and deal with the detritus of the only thing we had in common. Memories played tag in my head. I thought about the chatty letters I'd written to Joan when I was in the seventh grade. Naturally, I'd written as if speaking. These were personal letters and, I thought, windows through which she could see who I was becoming. I told her, in '60s teenage slang, about my classes and teachers, and what popular music I was listening to, and about my new junior high friends.

When I opened my next letter from her, out dropped my own letter, marked up in red pencil to correct my spelling, punctuation, and grammar—always the teacher, the elder, the stand-in parent! My face was hot, as if I'd been slapped across the miles. I stormed downstairs to show Mom. Poor woman. Stuck between us again. She grabbed the offending letter, glanced at it, and shook her head. "That's Joan," she said. "Ever the perfectionist."

"Yeah, but Mom, it was a personal *letter*, not an essay. For God's sake, if she knew how much I loathe writing, if she knew how much effort it takes for me to write a legible sentence ... *God*! I was writing *slang*. Of course there are spelling errors. Does she think I'm gonna crack the dictionary just to write her a lousy letter?"

"Linda, I'm sorry. Sometimes Joan just doesn't think about what she's doing ..."

"Looks to me like she did quite a bit of thinking, to mark that letter all up more than my English teacher would, for Chrisake!"

"She thinks she's being helpful," Mom continued. She was using logic to make me feel better, but there was shrapnel in my heart. It would stay there ... forever. "Let me just keep this," Mom said, waving the folded letter in the air. "It really is outrageous, and I don't blame you a bit for being angry. Just try not to take her so seriously. It's not worth the energy to let her get to you like that."

From then on, my letters to Joan were short, terse, and written only when etiquette demanded a reply or a thank-you note. And I chuckled whenever some other recipient of my missives would comment on how much they enjoyed hearing from me and how well I wrote; how much it sounded like I was right there in the room with them. Many years later, I would stumble across that red hot letter again, tucked into a box of Mom's correspondence. But by then, the rift between Joan and me was so large that the sight of the letter didn't hurt, merely confirmed my conviction, "You can choose your friends. You're stuck with your relatives."

Then I remembered Joan's visit to Laramie a few years later. It was after Mom and Glenn married and we'd all moved out to the ranch. I hadn't seen my sister for several years. Again, adults had admonished me to drop my childish grievances. People counseled that as we each grew older and lived apart from each other, things would lighten up between us. I'd actually talked myself into believing this nonsense. Joan and her husband, Jim, arrived from California in the evening. It was summertime and I was wearing shorts and sandals. When we heard their feet crunching the gravel toward the front door, I bounced up to turn on the entryway light and to greet them. Smiling, anticipating a new, more mature relationship with my sister, I opened the screen door. She stood a step below me, so we were eye-to-eye. But apparently her gaze had begun at ground level because her greeting to me, within earshot of all those sitting expectantly inside, was, "My, how big your feet are!"

Behind her and one step lower, Jim exclaimed in surprise, "Why Joan! Whatever kind of greeting is that for your poor sister?" He laughed off her rebuke and strode past me into the living room.

"Hi, Mother. God, what a trip that was. I could sure use a beer."

Glenn and Glenda gaped at his temerity. As Mom got to her feet, I pivoted toward the living room, once again determined to be an adult. "Joan, Jim, this is Glenn." Looking at my stepfather I said, "Glenn, meet Joan and Jim. And this is Glenda," I said pulling my stepsister toward me like a prized possession. "Glenda, Joan and Jim."

"Good evening," Joan replied. "Where's the bathroom?"

Meanwhile, Jim had stepped around from behind Joan and was shaking hands with Glenn. I pointed Joan to the bathroom, wishing the floor would give way under her weight. Jim greeted Glenda, then embraced Mom in a son-in-law hug. Glenda's dark green eyes met mine, deep pools of incredulity and hurt. I raised my eyebrows and shrugged. As Glenda and I had gotten to know each other, I had been vague about my relationship with Joan. To be honest, I was embarrassed by my hatred of my sister. In less than a year, Glenda and I had forged a stronger relationship than I'd ever had with Joan. Okay, she was a few years younger than Joan, but there was no animosity between us. No competition, no comeuppance. I knew things she hadn't a clue about. But that was mutual. She could run a household. She could drive, and she shared her hopes and fears with me. She took me with her and introduced me to her friends.

Joan and Jim stayed for about two weeks that summer. They waltzed in and out of the house, always hell-bent for some important date with friends or a business meeting. Joan continued to virtually ignore Glenn and Glenda. And when Glenn's sister, E.D. visited from Colorado, Joan talked at her and her husband until she bored herself, then dropped them abruptly to go riding with Jim.

Joan wasn't finished humiliating me though. I don't remember the details, but Joan and I were in the corrals. She provided some uninvited advice that infuriated me, and I told her to go to hell. The next thing I knew she had me in a headlock, half submerged in the water trough. Spittle gathered in the corners of her mouth—a trait I had forgotten about—as she yelled, "You need a little discipline, you hooligan. You know what would have happened to *me* if I used such language to my elders? I'd get my mouth washed out with soap!" Her hand skimmed a wad of moss from inside the tank which she swiped across my face. I fought and yelled like a trapped tiger, but she was still too big and too strong. It was futile for me to fight my big sister. Why did I always do that?

A few days later she and Jim left. I felt a collective sigh of relief from every sentient being on the ranch. As I rearranged my feelings in her wake, I basked in the smug satisfaction that Joan had completely alienated herself from the Tracy family. Through our mutual disgust, Glenda and I drew that much closer.

I had to purge all these vile memories from my brain. They would just drag me down and undermine me when it came time to deal with Joan. I tossed and turned through the night.

I returned to the hospital, expecting to find my mom raising holy hell. But she was still groggy. She cocked an eye at me when I asked if she was thirsty. But after a few limp sips from a jointed straw, she sank back to the pillow and returned to her dream world. I hoped it was a good one, with healthy horses, verbose riding partners, and sweet sage in place of the closed, disinfectant smell of her room. Around 4:30, the hallway grew noisy.

"Aghgh," Mom grumbled, trying to find her voice. "What's all that racket?"

"I think dinner is about to arrive."

"Ohhh ... I get dinner here?"

"Of course. Are you hungry?" I asked.

"Yes!" she announced, with energy. "And I'm thirsty. I want some coffee."

"Not sure about the coffee, Mom, but you can have all the water you want. We just have to keep track of how much you drink."

"Blechhh! That water isn't worth drinking. Where's *my* water?"

I fought the urge to argue. "I'll see what I can do for you, Mother. But for now, you'll have to just pretend this is ranch water. Close your eyes, hold your nose, just like you used to tell me to do when I was supposed to drink whiskey for a sore throat. Remember that?"

I was pleased to see just a hint of a gleam in her eye. But the mood evaporated when her food tray arrived. She poked and pushed the food on the plate, wrinkling her nose in disdain. "This isn't *food*. This is *pap! Phhhw.*"

She was already nodding off before the tray was removed. A nurse arrived to take her vitals and to tell us that the doctor was on the floor and would be in to talk with us shortly. Elaborate whistling alerted us to an impending visitor. Dr. Greene bounced around the corner, his lips still whistle-puckered, his eyes engaged with the clipboard in his hands. He stopped beside Mom's bed and looked up at her from under a shock of thick, milk-chocolate-brown forelock.

Extending his hand to her, he said, "Good evening, Mrs. Tracy. My name is Dr. Pat Greene. I'm with the Fort Collins Nephrology Clinic. I understand you had a pretty unpleasant night, last night?"

"I don't understand what's goin' on," Mom admitted. "I'm so weak. I can't think straight. And my back's been hurting. And the water you people have here is undrinkable."

I watched Dr. Greene closely, expecting him to suppress a frown or a grin, but he maintained a perfect poker face. "Oh, I'm sorry, Mrs. Tracy. But I can see from the lab reports here that it is completely normal for you to be tired and lethargic at this point. And you know, that is why you're here—so we can get you back up on your feet again."

He turned to me now, and extended his hand. As I introduced myself, I sized him up, quite shocked at how young he looked. His luminous blue eyes held my own as he explained what to expect next. I was distracted, trying to do the math: a four-year degree at 22, plus what, seven years med school and internships and all of that? Thirties? My mom's specialist was younger than I?

"When Mrs. Tracy was admitted this morning, she was in a highly toxic state. You see, our kidneys function a bit like a sophisticated sewer system. Throughout our bodies, cells are continually regenerating and breaking down. As they die, the refuse, so to speak, is carried by the circulatory system to the kidneys which strain the garbage and send clean blood back to work."

"Oh," I replied. "I thought the kidneys were part of the digestive system. Shows you what I don't know."

"No, you are absolutely right," he said, nodding his head in a way that made his bangs flop over his eyes. Dr. Greene went on to educate me about the finer points of kidney function and dysfunction, explaining that Mom's difficulties with edema, itching, fatigue, and weakness were all classic symptoms of a toxin overload. Water retention put excess pressure on the heart and made it hard for her to breathe. Her blood pressure was also dangerously high. They'd stabilized her by implementing emergency peritoneal dialysis and inserting a tube to drain excess fluids from her lungs.

He turned back to my mom, but she had already dozed off. We walked into the hall together. "So, potassium, you said ..." Her cravings for potatoes and bananas, the soft-boiled egg I'd tried to feed her, all these things made her itching worse.

"Yes," he replied. "In addition to dialysis, our kidney patients must be careful about what they eat." He went on to explain the different types of dialysis and their respective advantages and disadvantages and what he'd be recommending for my mom.

"Tomorrow morning we will meet to review your mom's options. Dr. Simmons, will describe the surgical procedure in which the shunt is implanted for hemodialysis. We will explain the pros and cons of dialysis to your mother and make sure she understands the risks."

"What about a kidney transplant?"

"I'm afraid Mrs. Tracy would not be a good candidate for a transplant. For one thing, that procedure requires a protracted period under anesthesia, which is highly risky for elderly patients. Also, there's the issue of supply and demand. You can imagine that we have many individuals on the wait-list for kidneys; many of these patients are young mothers whose kidney function was compromised during pregnancy."

"I can see where you're going, Dr. Greene."

He smiled warmly. "I suggest you get some rest. We'll go over all the details in the morning. I think your mom will be a good deal more lucid by then."

"Thanks, Doctor. I was beginning to worry about dementia. By the way, would there be any problem if I brought water from home for Mom? She's pretty spoiled by her artesian well water..."

He grinned. "No problem at all. I'm used to patients complaining about the food. But I think this is the first complaint I've heard about the water."

After checking in with Mom one more time, I headed out for dinner and the solitude of my motel room. Stepping out of the massive hospital, the scent of spring lay heavy in the air. A rainstorm had drifted by, mingling the scent of flowering ornamental trees with the dusty agricultural smell of damp soil and distant sagebrush; it was a uniquely western urban perfume. In my room with my take-out food, I opened the window, trading sweet fresh air for the freeway drone. Remarkably, I slept like a baby that night.

The Queen of England makes an encore

The next morning, the Queen of England had replaced my Raggedy Ann mom. Propped up in bed, her dark hair made her skin look translucent against the hospital-white sheets. Without her over-painted eyebrows and lipstick, she looked more sophisticated. She was in no mood to beggar fools. It wasn't that she expected special treatment; it was that normal treatment was, for her, so outrageously abnormal. She'd lived alone for 14 years and in each of those years, she'd become more adamant about having things her way. She was beyond compromise. Wastefulness drove her mad—not simply wasting money, but the unnecessary waste of resources. Everything in a hospital is designed for disposal, from Kleenex to needles.

"Morning, Mom ..."

"When are you getting me out of this nuthouse? It's ridiculous. I wanted to save the carton of applesauce from breakfast for later. I must have dozed off and someone came along and took my applesauce away!"

"I'll get you another carton of applesauce, Mom ..."

"Good God, I used the toothpaste one time and that disappeared too! They brought me a whole new kit. ... And the water, egad. That's enough to make me puke. It's full of chlorine and God knows what."

"I'll bring some water from the ranch later today."

A nurse came in to check the pouch into which fluid drained from Mom's lungs. Oddly, Mom cooperated and spoke kindly with the woman who gently manipulated the clear plastic tube that stuck out from between Mom's ribs. Then she had Mom blow into a respiratory tube to exercise her lungs and chest muscles, explaining all the while how important it was to clear out the mucous and fluids from her lungs.

Meanwhile, an aide came in with a wheelchair. "Hi, Mrs. Tracy. How are you feeling this morning? Are you ready for a little hot rodding around the hallways?" The youngster smiled innocently; I waited for a volley from Mom, but her reply was civil.

"I should walk. I need the exercise."

As the nurse repacked the lung tube, the aide fluttered about, getting Mom into a robe and organizing the catheter, IVs, and assorted accoutrements that had become part of Mother's wardrobe. Wisely the aide asked me to push the wheelchair along, just in case. We made it to the end of the hall before Mom's strength flagged and she sank into the chair with a sigh.

We'd barely gotten her settled back in bed when a herd of white coats with clipboards showed up. Dr. Greene introduced Dr. Simmons, the surgeon; and Dr. Livingstone, the anesthesiologist; and Dr. Carter the cardiologist. They all hovered around Mom's bed like a flock of snowy egrets. Dr. Simmons began with a review of what he'd told me the night before. This time, though, Mom was alert. She asked about a transplant and got the same reply I'd gotten.

"Well, what if I just don't do anything? What if we just get the fluid off my lungs and I go back home."

"That is one of your options, Mrs. Tracy. Without dialysis, you might have ten days or two months. We can send you home with some medications that will ease the discomfort, but as the toxins build up, your vital organs will begin to shut down, one at a time. But this would give you the option of going home to your own bed.

"On the other hand, if you opt for hemodialysis, there are a number of uncertainties that you need to consider. First, is the danger inherent in general anesthesia. Dr. Livingstone and Dr. Carter will provide details about that. But, provided you waltz through the surgical procedure and we get you established on a three-per-week dialysis routine, you will still experience bad days. Typically, my patients tell me that the day before treatment is pretty much a lost day. They begin to feel pretty ragged around the edges."

Mom remained silent; her expression revealed nothing.

"Then there's the day of treatment: The treatment itself takes several hours. Toward the end of the day you may begin to recoup your energy, and your appetite will pick up. Then you'll have a day or two before you begin the slide back down again. You'll be riding a roller coaster."

Mom stared at him for a moment, as if she expected more information—or more encouraging information. "This ... hemodialysis will buy me a few more years, though. And I can build up my strength again so I can take care of my animals and go riding when the weather's nice?."

Is she dreaming? I wondered. Dr. Greene repeated the part about treatments three times per week and the need for her to live near a treatment center. Since Laramie had no kidney center it would be impossible for her to live so far away from the Fort Collins facility, especially given the nature of the road between Laramie and Ft. Collins.

"Can't I get the equipment set up at my house and hire someone to come in three times a week?" She was beginning to sound petulant. Dr. Greene agreed that if she were a Saudi princess, sitting atop an unlimited oil reserve, she might be able to do something like that. But Medicare would certainly not pay for it.

As Dr. Greene described the expected quality of her life on dialysis, I was anticipating her refusal. Mom had always been smug about having all her own pieces and parts. "I still have my tonsils, my adenoids, my appendix, my uterus, and my own teeth." She would pronounce. "I've only been in the hospital long enough to deliver two kids." She was also adamant about end-of-life issues, hammering home the notion that quality of life trumps quantity of life. Listening to Dr. Greene's prognosis, I saw little possibility of quality and not even all that much quantity of life with dialysis. It sounded to me a lot like spending the last few years of your life hammered with chemo treatments. I was already preparing myself for the next couple of months—the last months of my mother's life. And yet, she kept asking more questions about dialysis.

The surgeon showed her a diagram of how the shunt would be surgically implanted in her lower left arm. Once fully healed, this would become the site where hemodialysis needles would be inserted: one needle pulling blood out of the body to be filtered in the machine, and the other needle guiding the cleansed blood back into her body. Mom studied the image carefully. She seemed intrigued by the science behind it. But she balked at the idea of anesthesia. "Why can't you just give me a local numbing agent, like the dentist does?"

This time Dr. Livingston spoke up, "Working with major arteries and veins requires absolute immobilization. We can't risk reflexive movements like coughing, sneezing, or flinching." Peering over his wire-frame spectacles, he went on to explain the specific risks and statistics associated with general anesthesia, which are increasingly significant for the elderly or individuals with compromised organs. "Now, obviously, we wouldn't present this option to you, Mrs. Tracy, if we thought the risk too high. But, at the same time, all surgical procedures are accompanied by risk of infection, blood clots, or simply too much stress to the heart."

And now it was Dr. Carter's turn to assure Mom that although she'd been having a lot of problems with circulation and blood pressure, those difficulties were directly related to the inflammation in her lungs and the toxins in her system. The excess fluid in her lungs was a direct result of poor kidney function. Her heart was actually in fine shape and pumping admirably well considering the circumstances. He felt safe in recommending her for the procedure as soon as the fluid in her lungs had been removed.

Dr. Greene wrapped up the meeting by reiterating that the next step was in Mom's hands. If she opted for long-term dialysis, she would be kept at Poudre Valley for however many days needed until her lungs were clear again. Then the surgical procedure would be scheduled. She would have to remain in the hospital while that implant healed. As soon as the shunt was deemed ready, she would be released to the Northern Colorado Kidney Center for ongoing outpatient treatment. If, however, Mom decided to forgo long-term dialysis, her condition would be stabilized, and she would be sent home with a drug regime to make her final weeks and months as comfortable as possible.

My eyes shifted between Dr. Greene's face and Mom's. He presented the pinnacle of professionalism: the perfect balance between sympathy, gravity, and fact. Mom's face was inscrutable. I expected something. She was, after all, receiving her death sentence. If it were me, I wondered if I'd burst into tears, faint, or curse a blue streak. Dr. Greene shifted his clipboard and pen into his left hand and gently touched Mom's shoulder with his right hand. "We'll leave you now to mull all this over. I'll be back around dinner time and we can talk more, if you need to." The other three snowy egrets all nodded their heads in agreement with Dr. Greene.

"The decision is yours. We are here to help you make the transition, no matter what you decide," said Dr. Simmons. With that they turned their white-coated backs and squeezed through the door like water gushing through the narrows.

The room expanded. Silence roared. Mom stared at the wall behind me. I stared at Mom. Who would be the first to speak? The quiet spooked me.

"What are you thinking, Mom?"

"Well," there was a long pause and her eyes shifted to me. "Will you stay with me till I get through all this and get back on my feet?"

"Ahhh." *What in hell does she mean?* "Well, I think I've got a month, at least ..."

"Thank you, Linda. That helps a lot. Well, I guess I just have to reconcile getting cut on."

"Really, Mom? You're going to go ahead with the hemodialysis?"

"I don't see that I have much choice. I hoped to hell it wouldn't come to this."

I was floored. I tried to adjust my response to mask my shock at her decision. Never, in a million years, would I have anticipated that she would choose this draconian measure to elongate her life by just a few years. We talked for a while about things at home. Now that her mind had cleared, she was all business. There was a tenant issue I needed to check on and she wanted the phone so she could call the ranch tenants and talk to them about the horses, cats, and the dog that they were caring for in her absence. And of course, I was ordered to bring her water from the ranch! I jotted down a list of other items she wanted me to bring.

I fled the hospital and stepped into a gorgeous spring morning. Trees on the hospital grounds and nearby residential streets were bursting with pink and white blossoms. Willow trees glowed with iridescent yellow-green leaves. Immaculate, kelly-green lawns beckoned with the promise of picnics and backyard barbeques. A chorus of birds twittered and whistled with an ecstasy of plenty. *When did Fort*

Collins become so beautiful? As a kid, I had always hated our occasional trips to Fort Collins. Many of my classmates looked forward to shopping excursions here—a town that was perhaps half-again as large as Laramie. I remembered a dusty downtown with broad streets that accommodated pull-in parking on both sides—I always wondered if this was because the shit kickers didn't know how to parallel park. The low-slung storefronts hugged concrete sidewalks, their flat, too-large signs, sun-bleached and drab, their glass display windows dust-smudged.

Now downtown Fort Collins had blossomed into an oasis perched before a backdrop of still snowy Rocky Mountains. Traffic sauntered through two narrow lanes with a tree-lined island between them. The sidewalks had been widened to accommodate tidy trees that sheltered benches and flowerpots from the hot summer sun. *I guess I'll have plenty of time to explore this area,* I thought, as I headed back to the freeway.

As I retraced the drive with my nearly comatose mother just two days earlier, I replayed the picture Dr. Greene had painted about life on dialysis. For a young mother, awaiting a transplant, desperate to see her baby march off to first grade, to graduate, to get married, hemodialysis would be a bridge to life. But for a woman of 77, dialysis was nothing more than misery on a bridge to death.

On this trip, I saw the scenery between Fort Collins and Laramie differently. Iron-rich rock stacked into unexpected hoodoos that surveyed miles of juniper strewn, red soil. Raptors rode the currents, peering into the scrub brush in search of rodents and rabbits. The land undulated in shallow mesas and hills, cut by lazy creeks that would be dry by July. Psychedelic patches of pink and yellow prickly pear cacti screamed for attention. Beside the road, California poppies waved in the wash of passing semis, pickups, and SUVs. It was charming. It looked completely different from the dry, brown-grass, wasteland of my memory. During the next few weeks my frequent road trips through this area would emblazon the changing landscape in my mind—from the flat-as-a-pancake, dry prairie grass south of Laramie, rising in elevation to the red mesas and hoodoos, and then dropping down again into the fertile black and green farm land just north of Fort Collins. And always, the blue sky above, scattered with a moveable feast of clouds and storms that ambled about on a mercurial jet stream.

After running errands at the ranch and in town, I loaded up a crate of Jim Beam jugs filled with artesian water and chuckled over the ruckus these would cause in the rigidly controlled confines of the Poudre Valley Hospital.

We passed the next few days fighting boredom. At least I was fighting boredom. I have no idea what Mom was fighting. I'd perch beside her bed with the laptop balanced on my knees and probe her for the stories she used to love telling, the family stories that I could never keep straight in my head. She was tired and lethargic, her voice uncharacteristically flat, her speech truncated. She spoke like a wary criminal, unwilling to offer more detail than absolutely necessary.

Finally Mom's vitals improved, and her lungs cleared enough to schedule surgery. Although her energy and enthusiasm lagged, her heart trotted on like an endurance pony. The night before the operation, the surgeon and the anesthesiologist visited her room to repeat their caveats about risk and to explain the procedures leading up to the surgery and what to expect afterwards. As they talked, my mind played with the possibility that this time Mom would hear the futility that I heard, that she would get cold feet and decline the operation. I made mental notes about all the things that could go wrong during the two-hour operation. After the doctors' visits and after dinner, a long evening loomed.

She disliked the harsh fluorescent light above the headboard, so after the sun went down, the room took on a cave-like feeling. Sucking air for courage, I probed. "Mom ... are you absolutely sure you want to go ahead with this ... a ... dialysis?"

She didn't even skip a beat before answering, "Of course I'm sure. What choice do I have?"

Well, I thought, *you could just let nature take her course, as you always said you would.* But I clamped my mouth shut. This was not my decision. Instead I asked, "Are you nervous about tomorrow?"

"Not especially. It's not brain surgery."

Again, after all those years of eschewing doctors, hospitals, and surgeries, her calm demeanor surprised me. I settled in beside her bed once again, with the computer open and my fingers hovering. She watched my face, which was illuminated by the blue light of the screen. *God, I wish I had better interview skills. If I could just get her talking.* My head buzzed with questions, but I couldn't settle on the proper way to formulate them. Mom and I had talked about politics and religion, but we'd never shared the inner landscape of feelings. The mere mention of fear equated to capitulation. With the remote but unavoidable possibility of something going wrong on the operating table, had her world view changed? Sometimes the uncertainty of what comes next works on atheists and agnostics when death peeks around the corner.

She wasn't in a loquacious mood. It was as if illness had robbed her of the energy to breathe, to talk, to think. Her answers to my questions came in flat, succinct phrases, completely lacking her normal drama and inflection. I drew in another quiet raft of air and tried again.

"Soooo ... looking back at your life so far ... are there ... any things you might change if you could do it all over again?"

She was quiet—for a long time. I was beginning to think she hadn't heard my question or that she was drifting off to sleep. "Noooo ... I can't really think of anything I'd do differently. ... But ... ya know, there is one thing. I really loved being a mother." (She'd mentioned this once before and it surprised me then as it surprised me now.) "As a matter of fact," she continued, "at one time I dreamed of having seven children." *(What?)* "And seven husbands." *(She was kidding?!)* "Each, of a different nationality."

She had been gazing at the wall across the room as she spoke, as if probing the inner lining of her mind. Now she turned her face to me, and her eyes met mine with a twinkle.

I've been told that my face amplifies my emotions, so I'm sure it registered surprise in extra-bold font. Grinning, I exclaimed, "Mom! I really didn't think you could shock me. But you just did!" She chuckled. "Are you serious, Mom? I had no idea."

"I *am* serious, Linda. I did love you kids. And I always wanted to know more about different cultures. What better way, than to marry into one? Ya know, I began studying the Talmud when I met your fatheh. Of course, that didn't really go anywhere. And he really wasn't of another nationality. He was just a spoiled mama's boy." There was a pause between each sentence, as if she were reaching deep inside for air to push the words out.

My head was reeling. At this point, I didn't know about Mom's affair with the Chinese guy in New York. And she didn't bother to edify me by sharing that. It was something I'd learn much later, in going through her old diaries and correspondence. I sat there, in the now darkened hospital room, staring at my mother, my mouth open—speechless. She laughed at my shock and then we were both laughing—big, deep belly laughs that brought on a coughing fit for her.

The elephant in the room

From a Jim Beam jug, I refilled the measured pitcher of water from which the nurses were tracking Mom's input. From the pitcher, I refilled her glass and she guzzled her artesian water through a plastic straw, grinning like a mischievous child as she slurped. We laughed some more while I rebalanced. Why in hell didn't I seize this moment to ask more direct questions about Mom's love life? Or about my father, about whom I knew nothing more than that he was a jug-eared pariah. That would certainly have made the process of writing about her a lot easier. Perhaps I was too squeamish, too immature, or simply not ready to hear the gritty details. Or maybe I was too distracted by a different curiosity—how was she dealing with the great unknown?

"So ... in facing this upcoming surgery ... have you, uhm ... Have you rethought your ideas about religion? God? That stuff?"

"It's a little late for something like that, don'tcha think?" Her voice flattened out again, weariness creeping back into her delivery.

"I just wondered. I've heard that often things look different at times like this. Anything's possible, ya know."

A nurse strode into the room. "Time for vitals one more time before we settle in for the night," she announced with faux cheer.

After the nurse finished and before the aide invaded to help settle Mom for the night, I screwed up my courage to ask another question that had been rolling around my mind. "So, you're ready for the knife tomorrow morning, eh?"

"Yeah, I guess." Monosyllabic.

"I guess it's time for me to go on home ... or to my little home away from home at the Motel 6. So, ah ... by any chance ... have you, ah, let Joan know what's going on?" I spoke haltingly, sucking at my top lip.

Silence. Then, "No. Not really." Pause. "Of course, she knows I haven't been feeling well. She gave me pretty much the same lecture you did. But she's always rattling off about something. I ignore her most of the time."

"Does she know you're in the hospital?"

"No."

"Well, for God's sake." I was rattled. I wasn't sure what I expected. I wasn't sure what was expected of me. "Don't you think she should know?"

"Yeah. Prolly. Look, I just didn't feel like dealing with her," she confessed.

Wyoming

I thought about the deep, dark secret Mom'd never been able to tell Joan, though I was positive she'd figured it out on her own. I understood Mom's reluctance; she was the last person I wanted to talk to, as well. But she had to be told. What if Mom were to die on the operating table? She'd be rightfully livid if I were to call her out of the blue to tell her that her mother was dead.

Blowing air through loosely pursed lips, I said, "Uhm, how about if I call her tonight? I really think it's important for Joan to know."

"Yah, that would be good. Would you do that, Linda?" She looked at me searchingly.

"Yes. Of course I'll do that for you, Mom. But, uh, I don't have her phone number. Do you?"

"Yah. In the address book." She chinned to the pile of odds and ends she'd asked me to retrieve from the ranch.

"Okay, Mom. I'll call her tonight, and I'll be here bright and early in the morning. Hope you sleep well. Good night." I leaned over her bed and brushed her forehead with my lips.

A bank of pay phones leered at me as I passed through the hospital lobby. *May as well get it over with.* I wondered how to greet a sister I hadn't talked to for over 20 years. After that infamous visit to the ranch when she'd alienated the Tracys and tried to wash my mouth out with moss, Joan had resumed her letters and extravagant holiday gifts to me just as if nothing had happened.

The years passed. I struggled to reciprocate with gifts for Joan, Jim, and later their two kids—whom I'd never met. When I started college I had to find ways to cut a budget that was tighter than the cinch on a bronc. In addition, my new husband Bob did not exchange gifts with his siblings and felt it unfair that our budget be stretched to include gifts to my sister. I agonized over the letter in which I explained to Joan my hope that we could mutually agree on a new gift-giving tradition. I explained how challenging it was to select appropriate gifts for her and Jim because I'd never seen their home and was unfamiliar with their personal tastes. I hedged, that of course the kids were a whole different

My Life With an Enigma

ball game, and with guidance from Joan and Jim, it'd be fun to buy little gifts for the boys. But for us adults, I suggested we might get more from exchanging a holiday phone call. Before sending the letter, I asked Mom to read it.

"I follow your logic completely, Linda. I think your solution to the problem is wise and thoughtful. That said, I'm not sure how Joan will receive this. She's always loved gift giving, you know."

If my judgment hadn't been clouded by the ridiculous assumption that we'd both grown up and learned to operate with reason and respect, I wouldn't have been so shocked by Joan's response. She fired a letter back in which she castigated me for my lack of imagination; she accused me of being empty-headed—given that I was fussing over Christmas in August, and she suggested that perhaps I had bought stock in Ma Bell since I seemed so eager to subsidize their expensive phone connections. She revealed something else when she accused me of caring more for my foolish stepfamily, whom she supposed (correctly) I would still be exchanging gifts with. Her vitriol was so bitter that I couldn't decide if I was angry or scandalized. All the years during which I had tried not to say anything to her that could be misconstrued or that might result in a lecture about my morals, my values, or my intelligence, hung like a deflating hot-air balloon over my head. At this point, I realized there was really no way I could get along with this person. No matter how hard I tried, I would always be inept in her eyes.

This exchange of letters was the final straw in our sibling relationship. For the second time in my life, I showed Mom a letter from Joan. "I need to show you this, Mom. Not because I want you to intervene or to take sides, I simply want to show you why I can no longer communicate with my sister."

Standing in the dining room of the ranch house with late summer sun streaming through the windows, Mom read the letter slowly. Several minutes passed as she collected her thoughts. I expected her to commiserate, then try to talk me into softening my position. She expelled a sigh and looked from the page in her hands to my eyes.

"I can't tell you what you should do. You ... we don't deserve this kind of attitude. Joan's behavior toward the Tracys has been a huge disappointment to me. This letter is a disappointment to me. But ... she's my child. I cannot change who she is; I love her and will continue to love her, despite herself."

"I understand that, Mom. Really, I do. But at this point, I have to honor myself. When I'm in Joan's presence, I become a person that I don't like or respect. She brings out the worst in me. I'm not saying it's her fault, it's simply the way things are. I won't be writing to her again. I just can't participate in a relationship with someone who has no respect for me."

Mom never second-guessed my decision or tried to talk me out of it. I never spoke badly about Joan in Mom's presence, and I tried hard not to speak badly about her to other people either; however, I did share the part about my "lack of imagination" with a very close friend. For forty years we've traded sarcastic giggles over that tag line.

Now, my hand resting on the handle of a pay phone, I shivered in the morgueish hospital lobby. I punched the string of numbers I'd copied from Mom's address book. As the dial tone connected and rang across the states, I rehearsed my first lines, wondering who would pick up, Joan, Jim, one of the kids—whom I'd never met?

"Hello?"

"Hello, Joan. Linda, here. Look, I'm sorry to disturb your evening, but there's something I think you should know."

Dead silence. Of course she wouldn't make this easy. "I'm calling from Poudre Valley Hospital. Mom's been here for about a week. She's scheduled for surgery tomorrow ..." More silence. *What the fuck. Had she hung up?* I decided to play her game and let the silence hang while I stared at the shiny number pad in the wall phone in front of me.

Despite the overly refrigerated hospital air, my hand clutching the phone felt clammy.

"So, dialysis, I suppose?" she asked at last.

"Um, yeah. It's not a complicated surgery and should only take about two hours. But, at her age and given her recent health issues, there are risks..."

"Well, of course." Her tone was dismissive. *God, I hate this woman.* All those years of trying to understand my sister and her need to be right—to be in control—vanished in the heat of the moment. I was through making excuses for her. I was past feeling sorry for her insufferably pompous academic discourse. I clamped my lips shut, waiting for her to say whatever.

"Do you need something from me?" she asked. Her detachment further inflamed me. I was on a runaway horse headed for a wall. Would we clear it?

"Not right now. I just thought you'd want to know."

"Yeah, of course. Thank you. Jim and I tried to get her to move down here with us, but she would have none of it. 'Can't leave Wyoming and the ranch,' you know." Her voice mimicked Mom's melodic emphasis of the state's name.

"The thing is, following the surgery, after she's recovered and they get her all set up with the dialysis regime, some changes are in store. She can't continue to live in Laramie and get treatment in Ft. Collins."

"Why can't she get the treatment in Laramie? You know these hospitals are very territorial."

Big, silent breath. "She can't get treatment in Laramie because there is no dialysis center there. Laramie Memorial has an emergency dialysis unit, but that's good only for acute cases."

"Do you have a plan?" she asked.

I sighed. Heavily. "Well, I'll have to investigate her options. I really haven't had time to do that and frankly, I wasn't sure it would be necessary. I sort of expected her to forego dialysis."

"Well, if she needs it to live, why would she forego it?"

"One just never knows. I've had my hands full just getting her down here and getting her condition stabilized. It was touch and go for a while. Do you want me to call you tomorrow after the surgery?"

"Yes. I would appreciate that."

"It's been a very long day. Good night, Joan."

"Good night, Linda. Thanks for calling."

Oil and water, I thought as I slammed the receiver into the cradle, gathered my things, and headed for the stairs.

Surgery

Freeway traffic noise rumbled to life just as the sun began to lift the lid off the night sky. It was another clear morning, the scent of freshly tilled soil perfuming the crisp air. After breakfast at the hospital cafeteria, I bypassed the elevators. I was feeling fat and stodgy from lack of activity. The seven flights of stairs got my blood circulating. Mom wasn't in the best of moods. She took the food and water restrictions as a personal affront. Nevertheless, I noted that she cooperated with the nurses and aides who hovered about prepping her for the upcoming surgery. They fawned over her, declaring that she was a model patient. I've since learned to suspect this is what patient care specialists say about all their patients, no matter how they behave.

Soon a gurney arrived to roll Mom through the maze of Stepford hallways. I walked with her as far as the service elevator which consumed her before I could really do or say much. She had already been given a sedative, so perhaps my missing terms of endearment didn't register.

I retreated to the waiting room in the surgical wing and tried to read, but the words wouldn't connect. I turned on the laptop, but grew angry at the blinking cursor. I wandered up and down the hall, gazing at the hospital's wall of pride—color head shots featuring the doctors and staff. Conversations with the doctors echoed in my head. Up to this point, I'd been a staunch supporter of the death with dignity movement. Now, I had to reconsidered what I thought about this loaded subject.

The trickiest issue concerning death with dignity involves individuals who are unable to call their own shots. Accident victims, people with diminished brain function, coma victims, these are the people who must depend upon the judgment of a friend, family member, or chosen proxy to make this final and momentous decision for them. Had I been in charge of my mother's decision for this procedure, I would clearly have made the wrong choice. Everything I thought I knew about my mother's personal beliefs was upside down. Her frequent admonishments to never put her in a "home" volleyed with her other remarks about going into the hills with a gun rather than lingering in a hospital bed. As I kid, these comments terrified me. Now I was equally terrified because she'd flip-flopped. It was clear that she'd have to move out of her house. Where would she go but some sort of home? I felt like I'd been thrown into a shark tank with my hands and feet cuffed together.

And then there was her notion that she'd be up and riding her horses. The woman couldn't even walk to the bathroom. Her muscle mass was gone. Even if her former stamina returned, I seriously doubted that my mother would do what it takes to rebuild lost muscle. That's a daunting proposition for a thirty-year-old athlete; but for a woman in her 70s who'd never believed it necessary to go to a gym or to do calisthenics it would be impossible.

How long could we count on friends and neighbors to take care of Mom's menagerie, I wondered. It all came down to the fact that she envisioned returning to the ranch; and that was simply not possible. Eventually, I recognized that she was in denial. Yry, woman of steel, was living inside a bubble of her own fabrication. She had not heard the same things I heard coming from the doctors' mouths. Once I recognized this reality, I began to hope that something would go wrong on the operating table: a tiny slip of the scalpel, a miscalculation in the anesthesia, her heart simply stopping ... *My God, Linda. Are you really wishing your mother dead?* Yes, I was. Full bore pacing now, I argued with myself:

Don't think like that! You'll jinx her.

But she won't be happy when she realizes what she's signed up for.

But it's her decision, not yours. It's her life ...

Or her death. Death would be better.

No it wouldn't, what a beast you are!

I'm not a beast, I'm a realist.

You're a beast, plain and simple. Dear God. This is why people believe in God. In times like this it'd be real handy to be able to pray, to absolve myself, to ...

Oh for Christ's sake. Shut up. You're being silly and melodramatic. This is a minor procedure. She'll come out of it just fine and you'd better be ready to help her.

The door to the surgery swung to life. Dr. Simmons approached with his funny foot-flopping gait and a smile cracking his face open. He was still decked in blue scrubs which accentuated his sparkly eyes.

"She came through easy-peasy. She'll be in recovery for another hour or so, then they'll bring her back to her room."

"Really?" I wished I could share Dr. Simmons' enthusiasm. *I wonder if he can read my disappointment ... certainly not the typical response he gets to a successful operation,* I thought. "Thanks, Doc. Good job." I tried to fake the appropriate response to cover my disappointment. Things would have been so much easier if he'd come out shaking his head.

The next few days were chaotic. Mom came out of the anesthesia confused and impatient. The morning after the operation, the night nurse caught me as I passed the nurse's station and filled me in about Mom's adventures during his shift. He'd checked on her around 4 AM and found her hanging off the end of the bed, the IV tree tipping over the bed at a 40-degree angle and her IV hoses strung tight as a lariat with a calf on the end.

"She was incoherent and fought me like a wild stallion. I had to call in the troops to get her back in bed and settled down. I'm afraid we had to restrain her because she just kept trying to get back out of bed."

Way to go, Mom, I thought. "Didn't some buzzers go off to alert you or something?"

"Nope. She never uses her call button. We don't have the monitoring equipment here that they have on ICU."

The staff was on a 12-hour rotation. Though I was immensely impressed by their devotion and level of care, I couldn't help but wonder if sometimes, during the wee hours of the morning, they nodded off. *What would have happened if he hadn't had to go in and check on her meds?*

I took Mom's breakfast tray from the aide who was distributing them up and down the hall. "Morning, Mom. I hear you had quite a night," I said as I placed the tray on her table and pulled it toward her.

She was groggy. "Ugh." Her eye's slit open for a beat, then closed again. Her chin dropped and she resumed her sleep-puffing. It wasn't a snore, but an exhalation through loose lips.

"Breakfast is here, Mom. Let me pour you some coffee. They at least have good coffee here, don'tcha think?"

It took the new shift nurse poking and prodding for vitals to get Mom to prop her eyes open. She behaved like a teenager with a hellacious hangover. She sipped gingerly at the coffee. The nurse began chatting amiably.

"I hear you gave Randy quite a rodeo last night."

"Hunh? Oh. That man? That fat man? I had to fight with 'im."

"Why were you fighting with him, Mrs. Tracy?"

"Escape. We were tryin' to get outa here."

"Who was trying to get out, Mrs. Tracy?"

"We all were. It was our chance to escape."

"Escape?"

"Yeah. Damn it. Didn't work. Dunno when we'll get another chance."

The nurse and I exchanged looks. I was appalled. The nurse seemed unconcerned—amused even.

"Mom," I just had to figure this out. "Who was trying to get out?"

"The people. All us prisoners here."

"Mom, you're not a prisoner. You're a patient. Remember, you had surgery yesterday?"

"Hunh?"

"Here, try some of this toast and peanut butter, Mom." I handed her a slice of bread which she looked at as if it was contaminated. "How about some applesauce?" I opened the carton and dipped the spoon in. She opened her mouth like a baby bird. "Are you hurting anywhere?"

"I'm sore," she reported.

"Where are you sore?"

"My arms." She rubbed her shoulders and armpits.

"That's probably from all the excitement last night," I suggested.

She ate a bit more then began to nod off again. I caught up with the nurse later. I was beginning to wonder if a disaster was looming. One hears of hospitals that abuse and neglect older patients. I thought about fat Randy. He seemed very nice and very diligent. But I was confused. The nurse smiled and assured me that people on narcotics often hallucinate.

"We've had some pretty dramatic scenarios around here. The more vivid the imagination to start with, the wilder the plot lines are when they're medicated. Your mom was on morphine last night. Some people just don't do well with morphine. Obviously Mrs. Tracy is one of those people. We'll be switching her over to Darvocet today. If she's still having problems, we have other options. We'll just keep working at it till we get the right combination for her."

Mom's escapades made her the talk of the ward. Each aide, nurse, or specialist who visited that day commented on her wild night. Because of the bed rails on the side of the bed, she'd had to escape off the foot end of the bed. When Randy found her, she was hanging onto the footboard for dear life, with her ass hanging out of her gown. Had he found her a moment later the IV would likely have ripped out of her arm.

I kept trying to tell her that she'd had a really vivid dream. I didn't want to use the word hallucination for fear she'd just get stubborn about it. But each time I walked into her room she'd launch into the story again, as if for the first time. Clearly she believed that a bunch of people had been running down the hall trying to escape, and she'd tried desperately to catch up with them but got stuck. She was very frustrated.

As the day wore on and the effects of the morphine lifted, she began to hear her story as the rest of us did. She understood there was something fishy, but it had been so real to her. She wavered for weeks afterwards, knowing it had been a dream, then thinking, no, it had been *real!*

For several days after the operation, Mom was fully immersed in recovery. She had to continue with respiratory therapy, plus she had a vigorous routine of physical and occupational therapy, both of which she pooh-poohed. Of the physical therapy, she said, "They act like it's some sort of big deal for me to raise and lower my arms. Puph! And occupational therapy? Are they gonna come out to the ranch and help me open gates and throw hay over the fence? *That's* my occupation. But no, they're worried about whether I can tie my shoes and brush my teeth."

Her Gatling-gun speech pattern had returned. Apparently she was making good progress despite her rumblings. She was still incredibly weak and unable to fend for herself when a social worker nailed me in the hall one afternoon.

"Do you have someplace arranged for your mom?"

"Ummm, what do you mean?" I asked.

"Well, Poudre Valley will be releasing her in a few days. Do you have home health care set up or a reservation at a rehab facility?"

"Good lord. They're releasing her? She's nowhere near ready to be on her own." I was thinking, *Rehab facility? What is that?*

The social worker led me to her office where she outlined my options and loaded me with glossy brochures and phone numbers. I would learn later that "rehab facility" is a euphemism for nursing home. She encouraged me to also research the next step, which if things went well, would be an assisted living facility. I was enrolled in a crash course on the American elder-care system, which in the early 1990s involved few options, most of which were grim.

I spent an entire day scouring Ft. Collins rehab/nursing facilities. These were the epitome of everything Mom had railed against. They looked remarkably similar. Upon entrance, my nostrils clamped against the ureic smell of stale diapers and gummy wastes. There was always a hall, braced with handrails on either side and cluttered with diagonally parked wheelchairs, their occupants in varying degrees of sleeping-with-their-eyes-open. Bird-like hands shot out unexpectedly, reaching for passers-by. Faint cries of "help me" prevailed. Somewhere a TV nattered with mindless daytime game shows or soaps. Hunkered in a hub of similar hallways, a beleaguered staff of nurses, aides, and administrators fluttered, regularly interrupted by the petulant demands of their more assertive patients. Occasional shrieks, whoops, and moans escaped from resident rooms. Invariably as I attempted to leave these places, their security locks defied me, and I'd end up setting off an escape alarm. The more with-it residents lurked, eager to chuckle and show me the secret password.

Toward the end of that day, I had narrowed the choices down to two of the less Dickensian looking places. The next day I would investigate assisted living facilities. Mom would get dumped into a nursing home at least initially. There was simply no way to work around this. Even if I moved to Laramie or Fort Collins, I could not care for her on my own. She needed full nursing care. In a perfect world she could graduate to assisted living if she did well with her rehab and followed orders. But an upgrade to assisted living was meaningless motivation for her.

That was the first night that I didn't go visit Mom at the hospital. How could I have faced her after what I'd seen of her future? What on earth could I have said to buoy her spirits? Instead, I went downtown and stared in boutique windows, inhaled tantalizing aromas of yuppie food, walked past groups of people happily passing the evening over wine, beer, and sinful looking appetizers. Then I ordered a meal to go, retrieved my parked car, and returned to the Motel 6 where I poured myself a rum with coke and devoured my dinner despite a flip-flopping tummy.

After a fitful night I steeled myself to break the news to Mom. She wasn't in her room. I wandered down to the physical therapy room and found her working out with a walker. It wasn't going well. Mom's mind was four steps ahead of her physical ability. She kept shoving the walker at the same time she was trying to move forward.

The therapist patiently repeated, "Slow down, Mrs. Tracy. Use three counts. First push, then right leg, then left leg. Step into the walker before you push it again."

I watched from the doorway. Mom was civil, polite even, to the therapist. Her behavior to the hospital staff amazed me. I expected her to explode at their condescending manners. They simplified every task, breaking things down into steps as one might for an infant. Mom was as patient with the employees as they were with her. This was, perhaps, what was lacking between us.

When Mom saw me, she brightened. My heart sank, anticipating the coming confrontations. She had a few more exercises to do, then she shuffled along beside me to her room.

"So." She announced. "They're booting me outa here."

"Yeah."

"I can't go home yet, so why in hell are they booting me out?" She was understandably querulous.

"I know, Mom. It pisses me off, too. It's not as if the hospital isn't getting paid while you're here, for God's sake. But I guess it's a matter of beds. They apparently have more patients than beds in this place."

"Well, what in hell do they expect me to do? I'm working as hard as I can to get stronger."

"Yeeeah. Well, in this case, there is only one option."

"Which is?"

"A rehab facility. I spent yesterday checking out the possibilities. I found one that might work till you're up and ready to be on your own again."

"Well, how long will that be? I need to get back to the ranch. I need to take care of things. I'm worried about the cats, especially Shamoo. He is so shy. He must be starved for love by now."

"I'll go back to Laramie tomorrow. I'll check on everybody, and I'll get you some more water."

We were back at her room. She sighed. I helped her into bed. She still had things attached to her, ports for this and that hung off her like Christmas ornaments. After getting her settled, I went to find the social worker to report my progress. Assisted living facilities were the agenda today.

I had seen a few of the assisted living places yesterday while checking out the nursing homes. Some facilities ran both ends so a patient could transition from one level to the next. What I'd seen so far was bewilderingly dismal. It was bad enough that Mom would have to sacrifice her home for communal living, something she'd never been cut out for. But being stuck in an outpost 60 miles from her support system was the ultimate blow. One of my primary goals was to find some place that would allow Mom to have her cats. Cats are an odd substitute for horses, but the comfort of her furry companions would fill the void a little bit.

I shook a lot of hands that day. Administrators were eager to lure my mother and her money into their lairs—those that had space available, at least. I was sinking deeper and deeper into depression when, on the last visit of the day, I found the perfect place. Well, at least from my perspective it was perfect. I felt the vibe as soon as I pulled open the big glass door that opened into an airy great room with peaked atrium that ushered warm light through a multi-faceted skylight. This was one of those expensive conglomerates that offered three distinct levels of care with gradations in between. Some people lived in stand-alone cottages or duplexes that surrounded the two main buildings. Tall shade trees and lovely manicured lawns with well-tended flower beds contributed to a campus feel. One building housed the nursing and Alzheimer's facility. Across the parking lot sat the assisted living building which was designed like an apartment house. Individual units varied in size from one-room studios to two-bedroom suites. All the units had kitchens, and the bathrooms oozed with grab-bars, non-skid surfaces, wheel-chair accommodations, and emergency pull-chain buzzers. Residents had access to three meals a day in a lovely dining room with linen tablecloths and napkins, or they could fix their own meals in their rooms. There was an exercise room and even a small warm-water swimming pool. The place smelled innocently clean—like freshly cut wood, not sterile—like it had been scoured by harsh sanitizers. During the week a bus circulated around Fort Collins ushering residents to doctor's appointments, social gatherings, or shopping excursions. The walls were tastefully decorated with muted wallpaper and soft mauve paint. Soft gray carpeting felt rich underfoot.

Best of all was the fact that this facility currently had an available bed in the nursing home and there was a studio apartment that would be available in a couple of weeks. This was the jackpot. Janelle, the director, invited me to bring Mom in for

Wyoming

dinner and assured me that we could reserve her room if we got a deposit in soon. This led to my next scramble. How to pay for all of this? Would we have to liquidate assets? Sell the ranch? An ever-deepening vortex loomed.

Early the next morning, I was on the road again. This time, as the early morning sun painted highlights on the whizzing scenery, numbers raced through my head. I've never been good with numbers so the process of computing my remaining leave days and the coming expenses for Mom kept my brain whirring for the entire drive.

While in Laramie, I checked in with Vivian and Glenda, updating them on everything that had happened. Then I consulted with Mr. P___, who thankfully now controlled her finances. After we had gone over the books and financial options, I felt better about Mom's future needs. I had been worried that she wouldn't be able to afford the nice place. I also worried that at some point we'd have to liquidate all her assets so Medicaid would pay the bills. But for now, at least, things would work out.

Next I went out to the ranch and made a list of things with which to furnish Mom's Ft. Collins apartment. I called a couple of Mom's young friends to round up muscle and trucks to move the bed, dresser, a few chairs, and other items. I also called my husband, Erich, to fill him in. He had been a prince throughout this ordeal. He never pressured me for more information than I could give. When I was particularly distraught, he had clever ways of framing the comedic aspect of the situation. There's nothing healthier than a good laugh to relieve stress, and Erich's gift was making people laugh. I always felt better after talking with him.

On the way back to Ft. Collins I began second-guessing my decisions. I was a cad for not offering Mom the choice of coming to live with us in Boise. Erich and I had already talked through that possibility. Erich was willing, but I was not so sure. We'd have to forfeit our master bedroom with Jacuzzi tub because it was the only bedroom on the main floor. We'd be crammed into the much smaller upstairs bedroom and den. Besides, I wondered how much better off Mom would be in Boise. Sure, she'd have us. Erich would be good to her, better than I would be; I knew I'd get angry and frustrated by the sacrifices. But she would be completely reliant upon the two of us. Rather than being 60 miles from her support network, she'd be 700 miles from them. She would still have to forfeit her horses, her ranch, her dog, her cats. Good lord, how would we introduce more pets to our two geriatric cats and one geriatric dog? No. It would not be a pretty picture if Mom came to live with us in Boise.

We had been married for less than a year. It was the first spring in our new house, and I was depressed to be missing the changes in our yard as last fall's plantings came to life. Erich described the little changes that he observed, the buds on the ash trees, the rhododendrons with flower buds the size of turkey eggs, the quail that dashed across the street with a string of fluffy babies in tow. I was so ready to be home. I was actually grateful to have used nearly all my available leave from work. Without the excuse of having to get back to work, I wasn't sure how I'd extract myself from Colorado. My selfish nature was leaking out all over the place. Guilt hung over me like a judge's robe.

As agonizingly slow as the last three weeks had been, my final week of annual leave sped by, the days compressed with details of Mom's release from the hospital; admittance to the nursing home; preparing a floor plan so that her volunteer helpers could place the selected furniture items in her assisted living space as soon as it became available; explaining the upcoming moves to Mom, then explaining them again—and again, because she simply couldn't wrap her head around why she couldn't go home.

Moving her into the nursing home went better than expected. I think she viewed this as an extension of the hospital, an interim step before the next—which it was. But the next step was the bitter pill that Mom couldn't quite swallow. I was disappointed when I walked Mom through the front door of the assisted living reception area. She squinted at the sun streaming through the atrium and asked for her sunglasses. Her room wasn't ready yet, but Janelle showed us where it was and showed us a model of one like it. Mom grunted.

"You can have Shamoo here with you, too, Mom." I needed some small indication of acceptance on her part.

"Yeah, but what about Penny and Lucy?" she demanded petulantly. She was worried about the remaining cat and the dog.

"Well, Vivian is going to take Penny. You know Viv will give her a good home. She's a cat lover just like you. And Viv's daughter, Cindy will take Lucy. Cindy can drive here from her home in Boulder and bring Lucy to visit with you."

"Who's going to take care of my horses?"

"The ranch tenants will get a break on their rent. They're happy to take care of the ranch while you're gone. They have to care for their own horses anyway, so it's not a big deal for them. They offered to look after things before I even offered them a discount."

Mom didn't respond. She stared at the wall in front of her, lips pursed. I explained all this over and over again. I marked the day on her calendar when the guys would come from Laramie with her furniture and personal things. I explained that everything was already packed up and ready to go: dishes, clothes, pictures, books, nature program tapes. I had tried to think of every possible thing that would make her feel more at home.

"I'm sure there'll be things you want that I've forgotten, but you can ask your friends, Sue, or Viv, or Glenda to bring them to you. Everyone is looking forward to being able to come visit you now that you're out of the hospital," I assured her. "And if you need to buy something, just call Mr. P___; he'll make sure you get whatever you need." She sat mutely.

I was able to sit through one of Mom's dialysis treatments before I went home. It seemed interminably long. I couldn't imagine her sitting still for three hours, three times a week. I was still mystified that she had made this lifestyle choice. It was so contrary to everything she had ever worked towards. Did she still believe that she would return to her life on the ranch someday, as if nothing had happened? Was she that deeply in denial about her condition? Had the doctors confused her by dumping too much medicalese on her when they discussed her options?

At last, it was time for me to return to my life in Boise, my job, my husband, my beautiful new home. I felt like I was escaping from a Kafka film. Then that thought made me feel guilty because it was my poor mother who had endured and would continue to endure the nightmare. I was confident I'd found the best possible place for Mom to live. It would be a while before it dawned on me that my choices had been based upon my own aesthetic, not hers. I love new, clean, bright spaces. Mom, on the other hand, liked clutter, strong colors, heavy drapes, dungeonesque environments.

Along with photos of our blooming yard, Erich had sent me the soundtrack to the movie, The Mission, which I looped throughout the long drive home. It's a wonder I didn't blow a speaker. I couldn't wait to sleep in my own bed, to feel Erich spooned behind me, the cat nestled into my belly and the dog draped over our feet. I continued to question my decision about leaving Mom in Colorado. A better person would have insisted that she come to Boise with me. But in my heart I knew how resentful and mean I'd have been in that situation.

It was May third; Erich was tinkering in the garage as I pulled up to our house. Never had his arms felt so good. Our house was gorgeous. The rhodies had burst into bloom—big, fat, provocative purple flowers, with tall, fragrant, golden azaleas interspersed between them. Inside, Erich had filled the Jacuzzi and placed floating candles in the water. Our favorite classical piece, Schubert's Trout Quintet, danced through the air. I was even looking forward to marching off to work the next morning at 6:30. Routine to the rescue.

Back in *Wyoming*

I called Mom two or three times a week. Each time I expected her spitfire conversation. But she remained lethargic, uncommunicative, unhappy. I'd ask about the food, (formerly a guaranteed conversation starter), what her neighbors were like, if she had everything she needed in her apartment. Her responses were vague. One topic that she returned to each time: "I want to be home. I want to be in Wyoming. I don't belong here." The only word that sparkled was "Wyoming."

Each time, I commiserated. "I'm sorry, Mom. I wish you could be there, too."

In early July, Joan went to Colorado. She called me to share how badly Mom looked. She reported that Mom had lost weight and was depressed and listless. All she could talk about was Wyoming. Two days later my sister called again to say that she would be moving Mom to Cheyenne. She had found a place that would take her, but she couldn't have the cat. There was a dialysis center in Cheyenne and the facility had a van that would take her to her appointments.

I was stunned by all of this. I could have sworn that I investigated Cheyenne, and in April there was no dialysis facility there. But she'd pulled one out of her hat. Interesting. Forty some miles of an even more treacherous winter road would still separate her from home. But, as Joan pointed out, she would at last be in Wyoming. Of course, this move meant she'd have a whole new set of physicians and care givers, none of whom I knew. But if it would add some bit of color to her life, so be it. I fought the urge to feel like I'd failed her by not setting her up there in April before I left.

Joan spent one week with Mom, making arrangements and getting her things moved. After Joan left, I began getting phone calls from the director of this new facility. Why me, not Joan? At first the calls from the director seemed like simple things; I thought a bit of confusion was normal till Mom had time to settle in. But she didn't seem to be settling. Mom would miss dinner. Or she'd miss a doctor's appointment. Then she missed a dialysis treatment. The director was more churlish with each call. If Mom couldn't take care of herself, this facility had no fall back. We'd have to find her a nursing home in Cheyenne. The calls escalated. It felt like I was fielding calls from the principal for my misbehaving first-grader. Mom missed another dialysis treatment. The grounds keeper found her wandering around at the edge of the property. The director was sure Mom was exhibiting symptoms of Alzheimer's, and quite clearly this facility could not and would not deal with Alzheimer's patients. When I asked Mom why she'd missed her appointment, she claimed she'd gone out to the parking lot and the van wasn't there, so she'd tried to walk to the clinic.

I looked at my calendar and saw that I had a long weekend coming up the second week of August. I explained to the director that I would come to Cheyenne so we could work out whatever solution was needed. Two days later I came home to find a message from the director: "Call me as soon as you can." My throat hit my gut.

Mom had failed to come downstairs for dinner. The staff realized they hadn't seen her all day. There was no answer on her door when they knocked, so they forced entry and found her lying dead on her couch. It was August 8th. Mom had lived in Wyoming for exactly one month. She had endured dialysis for three months.

The coroner listed her death as heart failure. We did not ask for an autopsy. There was no point. But I wondered about that diagnosis. How could her supposedly robust heart have stopped *now* after all it already had been through? The more I thought about this, the more convinced I became that Mom had willed this upon herself. This woman, who had fought authority, fought social expectations, fought for women's rights, could not have simply slipped away. All those *Prevention* magazines plus her study of vitamins, minerals, and enzymes had given her a hint of how supplements and pharmaceuticals alike can interact and offset each other. I understand that missing her dialysis treatments scrambled her brain. But perhaps she was doing some of that on purpose? Perhaps she was taking some pills and not others. She had always presumed to know more than doctors did and she had never followed doctor's orders, but instead made things up as she went.

Here is my theory: Mom got herself back to Wyoming. But she finally realized that living independently on the ranch would never happen. Once, while still in Colorado, some of her younger friends had gathered her up and driven her to Laramie for a day's excursion. They had saddled one of her horses and leveraged her aboard. She rode around the yard for maybe five minutes, her friends walking alongside, like parents on either side of a carnival pony. That day's excursion had left no doubt in the minds of her friends that she would never return to the ranch. Perhaps the truth finally registered for her as well.

So, she worked on Joan, convincing her that she'd be better off in Cheyenne. Once across the border into "*Wyoming*," Mom took back her life. She sure as hell wasn't going to die in Colorado. But back in her beloved home state, she could give up the fight. She would do it on her own terms. She would fail to take this pill and take too many of that pill, gambling that she could jigger a toxic reaction. This would be her answer to the laws against Hemlock.

After fielding the call from the director, I had to call Joan. She accepted the news without comment or apparent surprise. We agreed that I would head straight for Cheyenne the next day to empty the apartment and close out the account. Then I would meet Joan at the ranch. My boss granted me as long as I needed to take care of things. Erich was on the phone all evening clearing his calendar.

After an ominously quiet ten-hour drive the next day, we pulled up to Manorwood Senior Center. It had the standard half circle driveway to accommodate loading and unloading of mobility-challenged elders. I finally met the director who had grown so cold over the phone. Now her claws were retracted.

"Linda, I'm so sorry about the loss of your mom. We think she went peacefully. The aide who found her reported that she was lying on the couch with a book in her tape player. She just drifted away."

I nodded.

"Here, hon, you go on up, look around. When you're ready, I'll have some papers for you to sign."

I clenched my jaw at the "hon" and took the key that dangled from her outstretched finger. I was learning to pick my battles and this woman's inappropriate familiarity was unworthy. As Erich and I walked across the lobby, I glanced around at the dreary wing-backed chairs that lined a wall of dark floor-to-ceiling draperies. The carpet was standard heavy duty, well used, motel grade stuff. A few dusty artificial plants stared from Elizabethan looking tables. The place looked tired, so different from the bright atmosphere of the place in Fort Collins. As the elevator door closed on the scene, I reminded myself that at least Mom didn't have to squint against the sunlight in that lobby.

Erich stood two paces behind me as I opened the door to Mom's room. Brightly colored end caps of syringes and tubes scattered about the light brown carpeted floor spoke of futile resuscitation. *(Thank God! Didn't we have a no resuscitation order?)* The couch was wedged into a fake bay window. The coffee table had been thrust aside; books, magazines, and cassette tapes dribbled onto the floor. One of Mom's china coffee cups lay haphazardly askew on its saucer. Some miracle had kept it from flying off the table with the other things. Mom's Walkman lay in a jumble near the couch. I clicked the player open to peek at the cassette hidden within. It was a personal recording I'd made for her years ago—a letter I had dictated to my recorder explaining my frustrating go rounds with a cantankerous elderly neighbor while he installed my sprinkler system. The cassette was probably six years old, yet she still played the thing—to hear my voice, I guess. The other cassettes were mostly books on tape: *The Big Sky, The Virginian, Riders of the Purple Sage.* I sank to the edge of the couch. *So this is how it was for her in her last days, moments. She died alone. Strangers came and poked and prodded her shell because no one was here to run them off.*

Erich touched me gently on the shoulder. "What can I do for you?"

His touch roused me back to the present. "Ahh," my eyes skimmed the contents of the room. "We'll need some trash bags and maybe some boxes. Could you ask *that woman* if there is someplace nearby we could take these few furniture items as a donation or something? I don't see any point in hauling them back to Laramie and then dealing with them all over again." He knew which woman I was referring to.

"Are you gonna be okay till I get back?"

"Oh ... yah, sure." There was much to do and precious little time. I was supposed to swing by the Schrader Funeral Home, which was handling the cremation, to pick up whatever personal items came in with her. The whole thing about cremation creeped me out, but she had been adamant about that. I also didn't understand why I couldn't just pick up her personal items when I picked *her* up. But, I supposed the personal items were a lure to get me in the door for more paperwork.

While Erich was running his errands, I began stacking things in piles—the first of many piles to come. I thumbed through the papers and things that had been stacked on the coffee table. Each item seemed important in some vague way, yet simultaneously irrelevant. *This is really it*, I thought. *No more Mom.* The fate which Joan had laid at my feet oh so many years ago had played out to its conclusion. *I am an orphan.* That sounded utterly ridiculous and I snorted at my own drama, but it was true. I did feel like an orphan and this seemed especially poignant when I thought of those many times as a child that I had worried so about being left in Joan's clutches.

Joan was the hurdle on the horizon. I hadn't seen her since her infamous visit when I was in junior high. Oh God, I just wanted this part to be over. Erich knew that Joan and I didn't get along. I'd tried not to taint his impression, so when the subject came up, I said we just rubbed each other the wrong way. Erich could defang a rattlesnake while its rattles were still buzzing. I figured his presence would neutralize the tension between us.

By the time we had Mom's personal items sorted, had squared the account with *that woman*, and found the cremation place, we were both shot. Before leaving Schrader's, I called out to the ranch, hoping Joan was there. When she picked up, I explained that we'd just finished in Cheyenne and would be heading over the hill to Laramie after grabbing a bite to eat. We were too tired to do anything more tonight, so we'd check into a motel and meet her at the ranch in the morning. She was fine with that. I was surprised to learn that she was staying at the ranch overnight. *Too tight to pay for a motel room?*

After a leisurely breakfast next morning, it was time to confront destiny. My heart fluttered as we passed the familiar and not-so-familiar sites on the four-mile drive from town. Looking at the once cinder-covered turf between the railroad tracks and the county road, I remembered galloping bareback beside the Amtrak trains, imagining the gape-mouthed awe of those dudes watching me from the observation car. Of course, in my limited mind, all the passengers on a train must be east coast dudes. I have no idea why it never occurred to me that there might be some old crippled cowboy on his way to the next rodeo, who'd be smirking at my inflated ego. The old coal-train residue that had once coated every surface within half a mile of the tracks was so thick between the rails and the road that it felt like galloping through sand. Now, there was hardly a visible trace of the black soot.

We passed the three-tower radio station that had been a hallmark of Laramie, its transmission reaching far across the Wyoming and Colorado plain. The station still stood, but it looked forlorn. It still marked the familiar bump where pavement dissolved to gravel. Dirt and dust billowed behind the car as we rattled across the washboard. I expected gophers to dash across the road, but we saw none. Another mile and a half brought us to the turn off to Mom's place; a thatch of cottonwoods and a six-foot storm fence moated the buildings. The house and barn were invisible during the summer months, but now mid-August had already brought a touch of gold to the leaves, reminders that soon the house would rise up again amongst a puzzle of bare limbs.

We bumped over the cattle guard and absorbed the remaining mile to Mom's property line where another cattle guard welcomed me home. The strange silence of no noisy geese or barking dogs heralded the big changes that were already in motion.

This time it was me crunching across the gravel yard and coming up the steps in anticipation of seeing my sister. But no one greeted me. Erich, right behind me, placed a hand on my shoulder.

"Hellooo," I said as I stepped through the entryway.

"Yeah, in here." Joan's voice led me to the kitchen where she was perched on a chair in front of the open frig.

I walked in, Erich still one step behind me. I was formulating my introductory greeting as Joan announced, "My husband and oldest son are out in the barn inventorying the tack and feed. You can start in on your old bedroom."

Erich's hand fell off my shoulder; my words stuck in my throat. *My husband? He has a name, doesn't he? My oldest son? Isn't he Jim's son too?* Determined not to overreact, I grabbed Erich's hand and drew him up beside me as I said, "Hello Joan, nice to see you. I'd like to introduce you to my husband, Erich Korte."

"Hello Erich Korte. We've got a shit load of work to do here. This fridge is a science project. You would not believe the stuff I'm finding in here. Best you two get at it. I don't have much time and I don't suppose you do either."

Erich's hand had tightened around mine. This was the first time I'd ever known him to be speechless.

"Umm. Let's see. I assume you have a plan?" I asked, trying to mask sarcasm.

"Well, first is to get this damned kitchen in some semblance of order so the whole house doesn't rot. Then, we need to scour the place for anything of immediate value. Obviously, we aren't going to be able to deal with the entire property right now. When's her body going to be ready?"

"They said I could come by tomorrow afternoon."

"I've set up an appointment with the attorney. He'll read the will at one this afternoon at his office."

"Well, what exactly do you expect me to do back there in my bedroom?"

"I suggest you find anything that would be of value to you."

"Shouldn't we wait until the will is read before we do anything?"

"This dump needs a thorough cleaning at least. We can gather up dirty dishes and wash them and put them away. You can bring in whatever you brought from Cheyenne and put it where it belongs."

"Fine." I replied and turned on my heel. Back in my childhood bedroom, Erich slid the door closed behind us and slammed a fist into a palm. "My husband? My son? When will her body be ready?" His face was red and his blue eyes bugged behind his trademark round, red-rimmed glasses.

I sat on the bed and rubbed my face.

"I have never been treated so rudely in my life," Erich exclaimed. "And the advertising business is full of bastards. No wonder you don't get along."

"Yeah." I shook my head. "I thought maybe things would be better. I always hope, ya know? Everyone always says things will get better between us. But everyone is wrong."

"My husband. My son!" he repeated in disbelief. "Your sister is a piece of work."

So, we hid out in my old bedroom. Some things had changed, but much was the same. The curtains and matching bedspread were the ones Mom and I had sewn when we all moved out to the ranch. I'd been thrilled to pick out my own fabric and color for the walls. The western themed print I'd picked at 14 looked banal to me now. The green, hand-painted wooden flip top desk that Mom had let me use stood where I had left it, as did the dresser and dressing table with a three-way mirror which had so thrilled me at the time. A cheesy print of galloping horses chased by an angry gray sky still hung on the wall beside the bed, trying to buck its way out of a warped kit frame. The changes to the room weren't apparent, till I opened the sliding closet door. There, Mom had begun her honey-combing routine. Her penchant for storing and stacking was reminiscent of the ongoing labor of a paper wasp, always expanding its safety net. I began sorting through things. Some of them were my own detritus, those things kids leave in their wake: too important at the time to toss, but not important enough to take into a new adultish life. Most of those items came with a story that Erich gleefully pried out of me. He was an enthusiastic romantic who attached great wonder to the life that formed me before we were one.

At noon we emerged, and I returned to the kitchen where Joan had advanced her assault from the fridge to the pantry cupboards. "We're going to break for lunch. I'll meet you at P___'s office."

"Whatever," Joan replied. "Jim brought some things. We'll fix sandwiches."

"See you at one." I gratefully turned my back on her.

The shit hits the fan

When Erich and I got to the attorney's office, we were escorted into the same dark, formal, room where Mom had changed the executorship of her estate just a few months earlier. Joan and Jim had already arrived with their son Jamie, whom Jim introduced to us. Erich and I slid around the table to the far, unoccupied side and sat in the plush leather chairs. Mr. P___ was smooth and professional. He revealed nothing about our last meeting. After the usual greetings, condolences and preamble, P___ read the will from start to finish. Mom had been specific, right down to the cremation of her body and the order to gather friends together at her ranch, bring out all the booze and food available, and throw a great big party. She was adamant that no one was to wear black and that there would be no tears, only laughter. *Yup, I thought. That's my Mom.* None of this was news to either Joan or me. She had been as liberal about voicing these commands as she had been about threatening to go off into the hills to shoot herself if she got sick.

The room absorbed Mr. P___'s words. After he finished, he reverently laid the papers down in front of him and looked first to Joan and then to me. "Are there any questions?"

"Yes!" Joan burst out. "Would you read that part about my sons again?"

Mr. P___ read the legalese and then interpreted it in English. "What this means, is that each of your sons will receive one eighth of the cash value of your mother's estate. But their inheritance will be held in two separate trust funds which they may not access until they are 31 years old." I glanced surreptitiously at Joan's face, the lines of which were drawn in a mask of fury. But Mr. P___ blithely continued: "You, Joan, will be a co-signee on these accounts, with Jim as your backup. You may not withdraw funds except for educational purposes."

"So, do I understand that Linda will receive half of the estate and I will receive one quarter of the estate?" Joan's brow furrowed.

"You will receive one quarter for yourself, personally. But you will receive the other quarter on behalf of your children." Mr. P___ explained steadily.

I worried for the enamel on Joan's molars. But I dropped my head, as if hearing a death sentence. Joan's anger was palpable, but she said nothing more.

"So," Mr. P___ continued, "Do you both agree to the accounting of your mother's assets that is included here?"

"Yeah. I guess," Joan said. "I'd like a copy of that list to study later on."

"That can be arranged." There was a pause. I could hear an old-fashioned pendulum clock ticking from one of the vast bookshelves that surrounded us. "So ... there are no other assets that either of you are aware of?" His words were slow, carefully enunciated, and pointed, as he glanced at each of us.

I began squirming uncomfortably in my chair. I wanted Joan to raise the issue. But strangely she was silent. I waited. Mr. P___ looked at each of us thoughtfully; his eyes bored into my soul. I couldn't stand the indecision any longer. "Ummm...Well...What about the...gold that she hid in the house, Joan? Do you know where she hid it?" I asked tentatively.

Now, all eyes were riveted on me, as if God had just spoken. What in the world? I wondered. My brain was spinning like tires on ice. *I wonder if she thought we could just keep that between us? Or maybe she didn't know that I knew about it?*

"What gold?" Joan exclaimed.

My eyes downcast, I sat very still, trying to interpret this new twist. I was sure Mom had told Joan about the gold. She used to mention it when she came for visits, distributing bounty from her jewelry box. Mom learned the lessons of war and failed states well. She never fully trusted banks, presuming them to be only as good as the government that controls them. "When an economy fails," she always warned, "gold and jewels will buy what bits of paper can't." Since I knew Mom was disbursing her valuables to Joan as well as to me, I assumed she was also telling Joan about the gold so it could be retrieved after she died. And of course, in my immature aversion to talking about her eventual death and her estate, I had always closed my ears when she talked to me about the hidden gold. Too much information!

"Linda?" Mr. P___ asked me.

"What the *hell* are you talking about?" Joan demanded. She was frustrated to begin with and now I had apparently dropped napalm.

Did Mom tell only me? I wondered. Or is she trying to play coy about the gold so it doesn't become part of the estate and so she doesn't have to share it with her precious sons?

It was one of those classic moments in life when you wish the floor would open and let you slide unobtrusively into the void. If Joan was unaware of the gold, she would be furious to have been left out of this information. Damned good thing she didn't know who was originally to be the executor of the estate! But if she did know about the gold and was trying to circumvent the estate rules, she would be furious with me for having blown the whole thing wide open. I was doomed to swirl in the wrath of her fury either way. Her disapproval washed over me in hot waves across the long shiny table. Me, the stupid little ninny of a sister. The slow one, who didn't learn to count to one hundred till second grade. The last in her class to learn the alphabet. (Hell, I still don't know my alphabet.)

"Well ..." I wanted to stall, to gather my wits that had run to the far corners of the pasture. "Umm ... well, she used to talk about this stash of gold that she'd hidden in the house somewhere ...?"

"Go on, Linda." Mr. P___ spoke calmly. He sensed deep conflict. Perhaps he'd even anticipated this.

"Yeah, well, you know how she was always afraid of the banks failing and whatnot? So she had this stash of gold in reserve, just in case ... ya know?" I glanced at Erich who was wrestling to keep a grin off his face.

"So, did she also tell you where this stash is?" Joan questioned sarcastically, her chin propped on braced elbows, one hand fisted into the other.

"Well, yeah. But, I never paid attention. I wasn't interested in...you know ... her money."

Wyoming

Joan's hands collapsed onto the table with a thump. "Jeezus. Holy Mother of God!" Her eyes singed me.

Jim and Erich had both shrunk into their leather chairs, watching the family drama unfold. Jamie watched with curiosity.

A tiny smile tugged at Mr. P___'s professional mien. "Well, I suspect something will jog your memory as you begin going through her possessions, Linda. If and when you find valuables that are not included on the list, just let me know. We can add, as needed. Do either of you have any more questions?"

After the meeting in town, we all returned to the ranch house. I was prepared for a berating from hell, but Joan controlled her rage admirably. I really couldn't blame her for thinking I was a fool in this case, and I knew that I'd be turning over every groove in my head, trying to recall what Mom had said about the gold. The thing was, she hadn't just mentioned it once, cavalierly. She had repeated this information to me on several occasions. She really wanted me to know there was gold in the house and where it was. *What a freakin' idiot I am!*

Rather than rehashing the meeting, I was relieved that conversation focused on the immediate future. We sat in the living room and shared our respective time constraints and decided to schedule Mom's memorial party for Saturday so that we could all be home by Sunday night. The subject of Mom's obituary surfaced. On the drive across Idaho, I'd worked on a draft. There were some things I felt strongly about including. I handed my draft to Joan. Her first response, "Well, this is way too long. They'll never print it."

"What do you mean they won't print it?"

"It's too long! They charge by the word and we can't possibly afford to print something this expansive."

"I don't think the *Laramie Daily Boomerang* restricts the length of the obituaries they print. It's not like there isn't space enough in the paper. And I'd be surprised if they charge by the word. I'll check on that." Surprisingly, she didn't really have any corrections. Perhaps she thought it a waste of her precious time to edit what she considered would be ultimately cut by three-fourths.

We turned our attention to the party. There was plenty of liquor in the house; all we needed was mixers and beer. "Your husband and I will get the beer and some trays of finger food from the grocery store while you go to Cheyenne and pick her up." Joan said. "My husband and son need to keep cleaning this dump, make it presentable."

What does she have against using people's names? I wondered.

"If the paper doesn't get the obit published till tomorrow, that won't leave much notice for the party," I offered.

"Well, we need to call people," she answered, matter-of-factly.

"I have her address book here," I said. "That will be a good place to start."

It took an hour or two to put together a list of names and phone numbers. We took turns calling Mom's friends. Many of them offered to help spread the word, forming an organic phone bank. People called friends who called other friends. Word fanned out across Albany County.

Around four in the afternoon, I escaped to the car for the hour-long drive to Cheyenne. It was a relief to be by myself, although I felt for poor Erich, being stuck with Joan on the booze and grocery run. Maybe Erich would be able to crack Joan's crustaceous front.

The Schrader Funeral Home squatted on a corner lot, looking like a small-town courthouse with its monochromatic sandstone blocks and colonial pillars. A formal sign beside the double doors invited visitors to ring the bell during off hours. The door being locked, I assumed I was there during off hours. I recognized Mr. Schrader as he ambled toward the glass door in his pressed white shirt, blue striped tie, and dark blue blazer. He'd been kind and not too fawning when I'd come in earlier to sign the paperwork. As I stepped into the spacious reception lobby, I instinctively sniffed the air for the smell of burning flesh, but the only scent I picked up was the mothbally smell of formal linens. A new set of papers releasing the remains to me awaited a signature. Because Mom wanted to be scattered to the Wyoming wind, I had opted out of any fancy container for her ashes. After I signed the appropriate papers, Mr. Schrader brought forth, from a closed cabinet behind his desk, a plain white cardboard box. It resembled a party-sized, to-go container. He gently slid it across his desk toward my chair. I thanked him, reached across the desk to shake his hand, then grabbed Mom in both of my hands to swoop her off to the car. I was startled by how heavy she was. *Ashes ... aren't they usually light?* Mom, in her box, was not light. A vision of the box collapsing in my arms halfway to the car, ashes smothering me as they floated skyward made me cradle the box more protectively. At the car I hesitated. *Front seat? Back seat? Cargo area?* I didn't want Mom backseat driving, so I scooted some stuff off the front seat and placed her there. *This time we don't have to argue about the seatbelt, Mom.*

It felt very weird having Mom sitting there beside me and yet not. Her presence pricked at me, not unkindly, just insistently. She felt so there that I had to keep glancing at the box to remind myself that she was, in fact, not there. As a child I'd grappled with night fears about flames creeping up the wall of darkness beside my bed. Fire freaked me out so badly that I had been smoking for six months before I finally mastered the art of striking a match. The very thought of cremation made my skin tingle. But there was Mom, sitting beside me, all nice and quiet. I had no choice but to deal with her ashy remains. *Why would a dead body consumed all at once by flames seem more gory than a body filled with preservatives and stashed in a box for slow decomposition and bugs gnawing at it for years?* The more I thought about it, the more I understood and respected Mom's wishes. It made sense. The body was just a shell. There were no nerve endings, no brain waves to register terror. It was a matter of shucking an old wardrobe. Anyone concerned about leaving a delicate footprint would opt for dust over big holes in the ground.

"Well, Ma, you're just gonna have to deal with my music this time around. I know you never liked rock and roll, but damn it, that's what I need right now." I slid a cassette into the tape player. "Let me introduce you to U2, Mom. I ski to this stuff. Cool, eh?" I watched the rearview mirror jingle to the bass beat. *Poor Mom. She would hate this!* But I needed something hard and strong to wipe my mind clean. I need strength, courage, power.

Celebrating Yry

I never feel confident in social gatherings. Aside from the normal terrors about what's growing between my teeth and possible mismatched socks and earrings, I have namenesia. I have tried all the tricks: repeat the person's name when you're introduced, use said name in a sentence, use mnemonic riddles or associations ... Frankly, trying to come up with a riddle—*then remember said riddle?*—only serves to remove me from the moment so not only have I forgotten the person's name but I have also ignored their conversation and now know absolutely nothing about said person. I have abruptly reversed directions in the grocery store while trying to pull someone's name out of the recesses of my mind. Erich shared namenesia with me and we often laughed that someday during an introduction, one or the other of us would be so frantically spinning the empty rolodex that we'd lose each other's name. "Oh, yeah, so nice to see you again, Alice. Let me introduce you to ... er ... uh, this guy that I live with."

As we rattled around the house trying to stay out of each other's way and making sure there were no undiscovered surprises lurking in the bathroom, living room, or kitchen, I turned the pages of Mom's address book in my mind and tried to engrave those names in my short term memory. The first to arrive were the steps: Glenda and Vivian and their kids. Glenda, try as she might, couldn't keep the tears from leaking from the thick fringe of eyelashes that swept her green eyes. I threw my arms around her and whispered, "It's okay now. She's in a better place. She's looking down on us and laughing her ass off." Glenda responded to my coaxing with a brave smile as she surreptitiously wiped the dampness from her cheeks. Next, a big hug for Vivian. "You were her rock, these last years," I said. "I hope you know how much we appreciated what you did for her. And Mom loved you, Viv."

Then Leah Talbot appeared like evening mist encircling the mountains. One of Mom's oldest and dearest friends and mentors, she wrapped me in a warm embrace. I couldn't remember the last time I'd seen her, but I was pretty sure I was still just a kid. Now it felt good to hold her, woman to woman. Something wordless passed between us before, over Leah's shoulder, I saw another dear friend waiting for the love. People poured into the house. They rolled in as if we'd announced free Mega Buck lottery tickets. Before long the house was abuzz. I needn't have worried about people's names because they all took responsibility for introducing themselves.

In the 40 years she'd lived in this community, Yry had developed a wide array of friendships. If they didn't already know each other, Mom's friends new *of* each other through endless tall tales Mom had shared. And the same was true for me. I'd heard her talk of many of her newer young friends but had never met them. And of course, they'd all heard about Joan and me. As elbow room shrank and the noise level approached rock concert level, I stepped back to savor the moment. Folks tended to huddle in pods of three or four, but the pods shifted and morphed like sand dunes and frequent bursts would rise above the din: "Oh, you're *Susan* (or Jennifer, or Dave)! I've heard *so* much about you, I'm so glad to finally meet you ..."

Mom's friends had embraced her command. They wore bright colors. They laughed and joked. They connected dots and shared stories. Glenda and Vivian manned the refreshments, Joan mingled freely, her voice occasionally erupting in a delighted guffaw. Then I noticed Jim.

He'd planted himself in the entryway and was greeting people as they came to the door. He was the most demurely dressed person in the group. *Maybe his business suit is his second skin*, I thought. But what really got my attention was the formal greeting that he stiffly served each newcomer: "Hello, I'm Jim, Joan's husband. I'm so sorry we have to meet under such tragic circumstances." Most of the guests looked at him a bit sideways, unaccustomed to such formality and certainly not expecting such a dark greeting. I watched as people shook hands politely with Jim, then moved past him into the living room and joined the frolic that ensued. I smiled and shook my head. *He means well, the dear man.*

Releasing Yry

Eventually the crowd thinned down to the very core of Mom's dearest friends. Joan and I had already spoken for the one or two patterns each that we wanted to save of Mom's many sets of china and glassware. We offered the remainder to friends and, of course, to Glenda and Vivian. Each person we offered a gift to was humbled and touched to be offered something tangible to remember Yry. A few tears emerged as these stragglers quietly boxed their prizes and headed home.

One last task remained. For this, Joan and I would have to interact and to do so with equanimity. On this point, Mom's instructions were unequivocal: her ashes were to be released to the land she so loved, the land she called her own, though who ever really owns the earth we inhabit? Dawning brilliant blue, the day had followed the typical weather pattern for this high elevation valley. As the sun crept across the sky towards the mountains in the west, a few puffy clouds appeared, gradually propagating into shape-shifting communities that dappled the sky as the air above swirled in swiftly changing temperatures. By late afternoon the sky was like a holey blanket, swelling cumulous clouds swirling, and sun slanting through peek holes.

Wyoming

We saddled the last two horses remaining from Mom's once robust herd. I took Lady, who had formerly been my horse, but because of her reliability and good disposition, I'd left her for Mom to use. I didn't know much about the other horse; it was one of the few who'd not been hand-raised by one of us. We both looked at the box that was Mother, now sitting patiently beside the barn door. Joan bent over it, cautiously opening the top flaps. I stood on the other side of the box, peering down. Inside the cardboard box, a heavy semi-opaque plastic bag held what was left of Yry. Joan glanced up at me as she began to separate the bag from the box. I nodded and walked over to Lady, mounted, and stood waiting for Joan to hand the bag to me. Since I was aboard a horse I knew intimately, this was completely logical and natural. For once, we were on the same page without even having to discuss it. Talking quietly to Lady as she approached, Joan reached up with both hands to transfer Mom to my arms. Then she led her mount to the gate, which she closed behind me before mounting the bay gelding. We were ready for anything, since we knew so little about this horse and it had not been ridden for quite some time. But the animal, aside from a slight side-step-prance, responded to Joan's signals without argument. I'd forgotten how Joan's well padded, five-foot ten-inch frame dwarfed the smallish horses Mom preferred.

We left the corrals under a typical Laramie God-sky, conjuring Albert Bierstadt, and headed for a low bluff that overlooked the houses and buildings, not far from the little pond through which my friends and I swam our horses on hot summer days. Three barrels stood nearby, relics of my old high school rodeo days. Upon seeing them, Lady's ears pricked forward and I recalled one of Mom's friends telling me how much she enjoyed running Lady around those barrels. "Man, I just let her go. She knows every move, every step. I have to hang on tight when she banks around the turns!" I smiled at the memory and spoke softly to Lady. The nervous energy from Joan's mount had transferred itself to Lady and she now danced under the saddle, too. We stopped before we got to the three barrels, and turned to look at Mom's ranch: the two houses, the huge old barn with the faint "Paul" lettering, and the smaller sheds and corrals fingering outward toward the pastures. Joan's connection to this place couldn't have been as intense as my own because she'd moved away from home before we moved out here. But my adolescence had passed here. I knew every creak of every rickety board in the old barn. I remembered flirting with the neighbor's husband when I was 14. I was both arrogant and naïve at the time, knowing I was a better horseman than he was, sensing something in his looks and conversation that felt different from talking to schoolboys, eager to test the budding feminine mystique which I was just beginning to recognize as a tool of power.

Miraculously, the ubiquitous Wyoming wind was a mere whisper on this afternoon. *Well done, Mom.* I cradled her moldable form between the saddle horn and my unused womb. After a few moment's pause, Joan and I exchanged glances again. "What do you think?" I asked. "Is this far enough?"

"It's as good a place as any, I suppose," she replied.

"Should we get off or what? You wanna say anything?" I was ready to follow her lead, for once.

"It would be fitting, I think, if we held the bag between us and let the breeze take her."

"Sounds good to me." I tucked the end of my reins under my thigh and pulled Mom forth, examining the makeup of the bag. Two heavy duty staples clamped a fold in the top. I gently pulled them apart, then carefully hoisted the bag into the palm of my right hand. Joan had pulled the gelding close to my right side.

"Nope, that's not gonna work," I said, realizing I needed a third hand. We each circled our horses around again to get them settled. Again, I snugged the reins under my right thigh, and this time I grasped Mom by the loose top end with my left hand. My right hand supported the bottom of the bag.

"Wait, which way is the wind blowing?" Joan asked.

"Ah, yeah, we better do this in the opposite direction."

So we circled around again, this time facing away from the ranch buildings. With my right hand clutching the bottom side of the bag and my left arm crossed over my body stabilizing the awkward bag from the top, I leaned far to my right, offering the free bottom end to Joan. "On the count of three, I'll let go of the top and we just tip it, okay?"

She nodded.

"One, two," her hand was on the plastic, "three!" I let the top of the bag go and grabbed my reins to steady the horse. The bag flopped down and opened just as an errant cross breeze reached up from God knows where and whirled the ashes directly into Joan's face as her horse shied at the sound of the bag. She let loose of the bag and reined her horse in, spitting and coughing. I watched, transfixed, as the larger pieces of ash caught the breeze and floated toward the barn. The sky was *magnificent*. Low clouds scudded across the prairie, illuminated by slanted rays of sun, some of which streamed through a hole in the sky. I swear that a ray of sun ended at the top of Mom's barn.

Oh man, I suppose I'll never hear the end of this, I thought, assuming Joan would blame me for mismanaging the bag.

She surprised me though, with a wry chuckle. "That's just like her. She had to get one last lick in!"

I didn't quite know how to respond, so I just sat and waited for her to pull herself together.

"Well," Joan said, "Now, at last, she's a *real westerner*." Her voice was a mixture of melancholy and gruffness. Her hand reached under her sunglasses, to remove a fleck of ash? Or a tear? I will never know.

Epilogue

Joan and I agreed that we'd have to finish going through the property next spring. Joan needed to prepare for school which was starting in a few days. My annual leave was dried up. Erich and I would leave in the morning. Joan said she'd see to having the utilities shut off and the locks changed before she left. I thought having the locks changed was overkill, but I guess she was worried about someone else finding the gold before we did. I would discover much later that Joan did not leave when she said she was going to. Instead, she stayed an extra five days, filling a dumpster with stuff as she searched the house in vain for that damned missing gold.

Afterword

As I was poring over the minutiae of Mother's life, the following missive fell out of a stack of notes scribbled on envelopes and the backs of junk mail. There was no salutation and no date. It was scribbled in shaky longhand. It is sad that this explanation was some thirty years too late. And I find it interesting that even this near deathbed confession contains details that differ from the story she had told me so many years earlier.

> Here I am and I don't know how long I shall be around. My heart is weak and my kidneys are bad quite suddenly really. but it (jarred) me—I won't live forever and perhaps not for very long.
>
> So it's time I tell my secret. Maybe I should have told it long ago—I would have liked to but I was afraid. You see, fifty years ago the world was a very different place, really quite victorian still. Girls lived with their parents until they got married and their main objective was marriage and a family. That was how I was brought up. My mother did not try to push me out and my father did want me to be prepared to take care of myself but he didn't push either.
>
> So here I was in my twenties full of all those old dreams of the love of my life that hadn't materialized yet when I came out west for the first time.

Here I met someone who liberated me from my shyness and I fell head over heels like a kid of 16. That's how it happened and he thought he was sterile. Evidently he was almost so as he'd never had any children.

I considered an abortion, a highly dangerous thing at that time; done only in back rooms secretly. Besides that it wasn't for me. I wanted the child of my love to be born.

So I came back home to my family but I did not tell them at that time. Instead I went to W. Virginia where I had a good friend. I stayed there and had my baby with the intention of putting her up for adoption. However, on the day she was born and the night thereafter I changed my mind. I left her in somebody's care and came home again. I was not trained to hold a decent job and would have had to farm her out if I got any job I could handle so I told my Mother and she was great. She did not throw me out of the house. This happened to girls who got pregnant out of wedlock in those days.

Then we told my Father. who took it in good stead also. After all they had money to support us. Actually I think Mother was glad to have me back home.

We fabricated a story about "him" being a foreign correspondent killed in the war and I went and brought my baby home where she had a family to live with.

In those days there were no such people as single mothers and unwedded mothers were ostracized. That was why I never told you my dear, when you were little because I was afraid you would blab it to your friends as children often do.

And when you were grown I was still afraid to tell you or mess up your (coming) marriage. And later I could never get you alone without kids and husband. The few times I had you alone you didn't give me an opening. I was still afraid of hurting you. That is why I work for Family Planning so that young girls can have knowledge to protect themselves. At my time there was no such thing. Mostly knowledge was kept from kids, sex was not discussed in any way. My Mother having been brought up as a Catholic was especially so. I found out about sex through books that I ordered secretly and I and my friend Ellen poured over them.

I should say something about your father who is certainly dead by now for he was years older than I. At the time he was in a dysfunctional marriage. He had a wife who ran away from him until she heard that he had another interest. I suppose she was after the money. He was a rancher. I left the country so they could work it out.

When they did he married another woman. So that was that. I was not happy but I had you to love and care for and my family to give me the chance.

Yry 1917

Yry parade ready at the town house – 1960

Parade ready – 1961

Linda pet parade ready - 1961

Yry & Linda at the town house - 1965

Cheers! New Year's Eve - 1965

Glenn & Yry Las Vegas honeymoon – 1967

Acknowledgements

The completion of this book has progressed at a glacially slow pace and in fits and starts. Along the way I've benefited enormously from the encouragement of my mother's friends and of mine. Equally critical to the process have been the advice, prodding, and feedback of a host of people who never knew my mother, but who were introduced to her through blog posts leading up to the book, or from Wordspinners, my writers' group.

I owe particular thanks to Ursula Denison for her friendship with Yry and with me, and especially for her translation of old, handwritten, German letters that were beyond my meager skills to interpret. I can't think of Yry's difficult final year without gratitude to Don Prehoda for his guidance and professionalism. I wish I could thank each of Yry's many wonderful Laramie friends, who were there for her in many ways and many times when her children could not be there for her. I've been lucky for the support and love of the entire Tracy family, who gathered me and my mother into their fold, and particularly to Glenda Hornig, who has been more sister than step.

Professor Devan Cook provided inspiration and writing guidance in the early stages of the project. I received valuable feedback from early readers, Diana Durland, Brian Kindall, and Dia Osborne. Unexpected lift came from faithful blog and Twitter fellows who kept asking for more as I posted early chapters in serialized form: AuntyUta, Craig Pindell, Jane Chesebrough, Lisa Brunetti, Otto von Münchow, Keith Wilson, Gerard Oosterman, Catherine Sommer, Bryan Hemming, Renee Johnson, to name just a few.

Special thanks to my editor Ken Rogers, poet, teacher, writer, and filmmaker extraordinaire. And I'm eternally grateful for my eagle-eyed proofreader, Diana Durland. The beautiful cover is the work of Chris Joyal of Eyespot Creative-Graphic Design.

Sources:

Cosgrove, Ben. "The World of Tomorrow: Scenes From the 1939 New York World's Fair." 2014. *Time-Life* 2019
https://time.com/3879706/1939-new-york-worlds-fair-photos/

Palmer, R. R., and Joel Colton. *A History of the Modern World.* 5th ed. Borzoi: Alfred A. Knopf, Inc. 1978.

Swipe – Worthy; Inspiration for Marketers & Copywriters. 2019. Mike Schauer. Newspaper Institute of America. 2019
https://swiped.co/file/getstarted-writing-ad/

Wikipedia. 2019. IND's World's Fair Line. 2019
https://en.wikipedia.org/wiki/IND_World%27s_Fair_Line

Yry & Linda in Boise - 1982

www.ingramcontent.com/pod-product-compliance
Lightning Source LLC
Chambersburg PA
CBHW071234290426
44108CB00013B/1412